Essentials of Writing

Essentials of Writing

William E. Messenger
University of British Columbia

Peter A. Taylor
University of British Columbia

Prentice-Hall Canada Inc., Scarborough, Ontario

Canadian Cataloguing in Publication Data

Messenger, William E., 1931-
    Essentials of writing

Includes index.
ISBN 0-13-287939-5

1. English language - Rhetoric.   2. English
language - Rhetoric - Problems, exercises, etc.
I. Taylor, Peter A. (Peter Alan), 1936-
II. Title.

PE1408.M48 1988   808'.042   C88-093668-1

Prentice-Hall, Inc., Englewood Cliffs, New Jersey
Prentice-Hall International, Inc., London
Prentice-Hall of Australia, Pty., Ltd., Sydney
Prentice-Hall of India Pvt., Ltd., New Delhi
Prentice-Hall of Japan, Inc., Tokyo
Prentice-Hall of Southeast Asia (Pte.) Ltd., Singapore
Editora Prentice-Hall do Brasil Ltda., Rio de Janeiro
Prentice-Hall Hispanoamericana, S.A., Mexico

ISBN 0-13-287939-5

Production Editor: Katherine Mototsune
Cover Illustration and Design: Deborah-Anne Bailey
Composition: Darlene Simpson
Manufacturing Buyers: Matt Lumsdon/Sharon Houston

    2   3   4   5   AGF   93 92 91

Printed and bound in U.S.A. by Arcata Graphics

Table of Contents

Chapter 3 — *Step 3*: Organizing Your Material: Planning Development and Constructing an Outline   **41**

Chapter 4 — *Step 4*: Developing Your Material: Writing the First Draft 62

Chapter 7 — Revising Sentences   115

Chapter 10 — *The Last Step*: Preparing and Proofreading Your Final Draft   189

Chapter 12 — Writing a Research Paper   212

Chapter 13 — Writing Examinations and In-Class Essays   255

Preface

You can think of writing either as a **process** or as a **product**, the finished piece of writing. If, like most students, you think of "writing" as the finished product, we hope this book will help you think the other way. We think that by changing the way you go about writing, you can produce work that is more satisfying both to you as a writer and to your reader. And though you will of course still be aiming to turn out a good *product,* your increased satisfaction will arise partly from a greater appreciation of the *process* by which you get there.

Using this Book

First browse through the book to see what kind of material it contains. Especially, have a look at the following features:

- the table of contents
- the index
- the glossary of terms
- the simplified outline of the writing process on the inside front cover
- the list of marking symbols on the inside back cover
- the separate chapters on argument, on the research paper, and on writing essay examinations and in-class essays
- the special exercises on idioms and on sentence-combining

Your instructor will probably determine the order in which you study the material. The chapters generally follow the steps in the process of writing. But since this process is recursive, continually doubling back on itself, the order is flexible. But do read the **Introduction** first. And before you hand in any written assignments, go carefully through Chapter 10, so that you will know about the appropriate **manuscript conventions** and about **proofreading** — for example how to check for such things as spelling errors.

And chances are you will want to work closely with Chapters 6 through 9, which focus on **revising** and which you can use as a **handbook** while you are also working on material in other chapters.

Projects

Most of the chapters include writing projects of various scope and complexity. Some are simple exercises designed to help you master certain small principles. Others ask for short pieces of writing — perhaps a paragraph or two that will give you practice using a certain technique. Still others are major writing assignments that let you apply all the principles and techniques you've learned about.

* * *

Acknowledgments

In addition to cherishing a long-term general gratitude to our colleagues, students, editors, and other friends, we are specifically grateful to the following reviewers of the manuscript for their support and their helpful comments and suggestions: Barry Cameron, University of New Brunswick; Cecilia Lanz, Southern Alberta Institute of Technology; Victor A. Neufeldt, University of Victoria; and Sheila C. Trant, Centennial College. For permission to quote from published material, we are grateful to the following:

Excerpt from BASIN AND RANGE by John McPhee. Copyright © 1980, 1981 by John McPhee. Originally appeared in THE NEW YORKER. Reprinted by permission of Farrar, Straus and Giroux, Inc.

Excerpt from "Rattlesnakes: All They Ask Is a Little Respect," by Malcolm Stark, which appeared in *Canadian Geographic*, June/July 1986. Reprinted by permission of The Royal Canadian Geographical Society.

Excerpt from *Canada and the Canadians*, by George Woodcock. Reprinted by permission of the author.

INTRODUCTION
The Elements of Writing and the Process of Writing

THE WRITING CONTEXT

You talk differently at different times, depending on who your listeners are and what the circumstances are. Similarly, whenever you write, you write on a specific **occasion** with its own particular circumstances. That is, you write about a specific topic, to identifiable readers, with a specific purpose in mind, and using language that you choose for that occasion.

Think of these elements as making up **the writing context.** Here is a diagram of it:

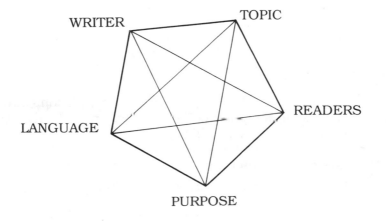

Each element of the writing context is related to all the others. Everything connects with everything else. Understanding how these elements act and interact will help you decide how to proceed through the process of writing.

Writer   You are the writer. Different topics, purposes, and readers will affect the way you present yourself on different occasions. You can't present all of yourself all of the time. On any particular occasion, decide what you want to emphasize.

Readers   Specify your readers as clearly as you can. If you don't know them personally, try to visualize them as they read and react to your writing. Try to imagine yourself as they might see you.

Purpose   Every piece of writing has a purpose — sometimes more than one. Here are some possibilities:

- to argue about a controversial issue
- to describe something you find interesting
- to inform your readers about something that will interest them
- to amuse your readers
- to express yourself on something you feel strongly about

Topic   Your topic is what you are writing about. Different topics make different demands on you as the writer and on your readers. Some examples:

> Quebec in World War I
> Cooking in a Microwave Oven
> Cable TV in the Maritimes
> My Favourite Vacation Spot
> Women on the Farm in the 1950's
> The Day My Father Burned the Barn Down
> A Recreation Program for Seniors
> Financing an NHL Franchise

Language English is a good deal more than a dictionary's list of words. The resources of language also include such things as the ways words can be put together and the emotional responses certain words and phrases evoke in different readers.

Using Questions

To help you think about these elements, frame questions about each of them in relation to the others. The way you answer such questions can help you prepare to write, because the more you know about a given occasion — a particular writing context — the more control you have. Here are a few examples of the kinds of questions you can ask:

Writer-Topic: What do I know, think, and feel about my topic? Did I choose it?

Writer-Readers:	What do I know, think, and feel about my readers? Did I choose them?
Writer-Purpose:	What is my overall or primary purpose?
Topic-Readers:	What do my readers think about the topic?
Topic-Purpose:	Which came first, topic or purpose? Does one determine the other?
Readers-Purpose:	For what purpose will my readers read what I write? Do they at all determine my purpose?
Readers-Language:	In what ways will I have to watch my language for these readers? What style do they expect?
Readers-Writer:	What do my readers think or feel about me? How do I want them to feel about me?
Readers-Topic:	What do my readers know about my topic?
Purpose-Language:	To what extent does my purpose determine or affect the language and style I can use?
Purpose-Writer:	How does my purpose affect the role I play on this occasion?

THE PROCESS OF WRITING

When you ask and answer such questions about the writing context, you are well along in the first step of the process of writing. Here is an outline of the six steps in that process. Think of them as making up three stages: **planning** (1-3), **drafting** (4), and **revising** (5 and 6).

Step 1: Determining Your Topic, Readers, and Purpose
  Establish and narrow your topic; define your readers and your purpose.

Step 2: Finding Material
  Find out what there is to say about your topic; generate material, discover data, think up ideas.

Step 3: Organizing Your Material
  Decide how to organize and develop your material; formulate a thesis and draw up an outline.

Step 4: Writing Your First Draft

Step 5: Revising
  In successive sweeps, carefully revise (sweep 1) the whole paper and its paragraphs, (sweep 2) the sentences, (sweep 3) the words and phrases, and (sweep 4) the punctuation.

Step 6: Preparing and Proofreading Your Final Draft

You can see that most of the work takes place during planning and revising. Inexperienced writers too often assume that writing the draft is the most important step; but within the larger process, it is only one of several steps, and often one of the smaller and easier ones.

Here is another way of illustrating the writing process:

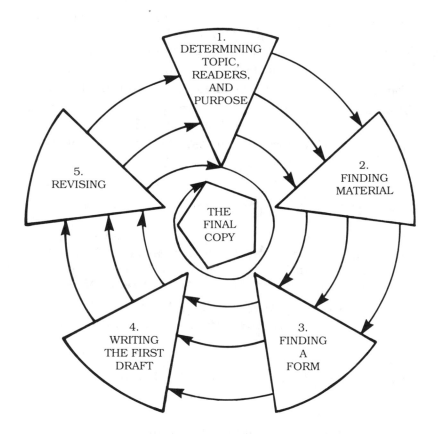

Showing it this way emphasizes that the process is recursive: whatever step you are engaged in at a given moment, you keep circling back to earlier steps. Often two or three steps are going on at the same time.

But the circle isn't closed; see it as a spiral rather than a circle. You're making progress while you're cycling and recycling your thinking; you're focussing your material and your ideas more and more; the spiral gets tighter and tighter, until eventually the process leads to its desired end: the finished product.

The Steps in Particular Contexts

You won't go through all the steps for everything you write. It depends on the occasion. For example, imagine yourself writing an examination for a history course. The question:

> Discuss the main causes of World War I.

There's your *topic*, already narrowed and focussed. Your *reader* is your instructor, and your *purpose* is to explain the major causes of the war by presenting evidence from your study, and thus to show that you know the material. The first step is all taken care of. Steps 2 and 3 (**finding** and **organizing material**) would amount simply to sorting out what you remember into an orderly form. After a few minutes of jotting ideas and sketching a rough outline, you would begin **writing your draft**. You would try to leave yourself time for some **revising**, but most of it will have to take place during the writing of the draft. But you would hope to have a few minutes at the end for **proofreading**.

But if you were assigned a term paper on the same topic, the proportions of time spent on various steps would be quite different. You would take time to plan much more carefully, and you would budget time for careful revising.

A SAMPLE CASE

Suppose you wanted to write a letter applying for a job. On this occasion as on all others, the process begins with thinking about the five basic elements of writing:

1. yourself as the *writer*
2. your *readers*: they want to hire the best applicant
3. your *topic*, namely yourself and your qualifications
4. your *purpose*, which is to persuade your readers to grant you an interview
5. your *language*: you want to find and arrange words so as to produce the desired effect

Here is the way one student, Tracy Wheeler, used the six steps of the process in applying for a job in a supermarket.

Step 1   Determining Topic, Readers, and Purpose

Before she sat down to write the actual letter answering the advertisement, Tracy asked herself questions. Here are some of them, and the answers she came up with:

Writer-Topic:

Question	*Answer*
What do I know, think, and feel about my topic?	Since my topic is myself and my qualifications for the job, I know it very well. I feel strongly about it, and I want to let my confidence show.
How much choice do I have in the topic?	Practically none, since I need a job. But that's okay, because I know my topic (me and my qualifications) better than anyone else.

Writer-Readers:

Can I choose my readers?	No, but I have to imagine them as clearly as I can.
What do I know, think, and feel about my readers?	Since the occasion has chosen them, I don't know much about them. (More than one might read my letter, even though I'm addressing it to the personnel manager, as it says in the ad.) How I feel about them: since they have the power to say yes or no to my application, it's scary, but I need to balance confidence and respect.
How do I want my readers to feel about me?	As positive as possible.

Writer-Purpose:

What is my overall purpose?	To persuade them to hire me. But my immediate purpose is to get an interview.
Do I have any secondary purposes?	To present myself strongly; to come across as the kind they'd like to have working for them. I should show a real interest. And I should emphasize what I know about the job.

Such detail may sound excessive at first, but you can see that Tracy came up with several specifics about the context to help her through the process of writing. In fact, the longer and more detailed your answers, the better. The more you write, the clearer the occasion will become in your mind — and on paper. And it is important to WRITE DOWN both the questions and the answers:

- Writing ideas down enables you to hang onto them. Even good ideas can drift away, or be driven out by later ones.
- Writing them down puts them on record so that you can check them again later.
- Writing them down forces your mind to work on them and involves your hand and your eyes. The physical act of writing ideas down spurs your thinking, generates even more ideas.

Answering such questions gave Tracy a good grasp of how she needed to see herself in relation to the occasion (applying for a job), her topic (her qualifications), her readers (the personnel manager), and even what kind of language and tone she should use (confident, but respectful).

Step 2   Finding Material

In order to focus her thinking about her qualifications for the job, Tracy began by listing what she could bring to it from her previous work experience: jobs in a convenience store, a laundry, a video-rental store, and a dance studio. She talked to a friend who worked for the company that placed the ad. She shopped at the market, watching to see how others handled the job she was applying for. She dug out an exercise she had done in a life-skills class in school: making a résumé—a conventional form that allows readers to get a quick idea of an applicant's qualifications. Her notes reminded her that a résumé should include the following:

- personal data (address, phone, date of birth)
- previous employment (in reverse chronological order)
- education (including specific dates)
- other interests and experience that can help an employer decide who is right for the job (hobbies? sports?)
- names of people willing to provide a recommendation (two or three will be enough; be sure to ask them first)

Here is the résumé Tracy wrote to enclose with her letter:

```
TRACY WHEELER                              1129 N. 18th Ave.
Telephone: 829-7974                        Winnipeg, Manitoba
```

<u>Personal Data</u>

```
Date of Birth:  July 17, 1968
Place of Birth: Verdin, Manitoba
Health:         Excellent
```

<u>Experience</u>

June 1987– Sept. 1987	Esso Convenience Shop, Brandon, Manitoba. Salesperson. Supervisor: Philip Malahov. Duties: cashiering, taking inventory, pricing and stocking merchandise
Sept. 1986– June 1987	Paloma Cleaners Ltd., Brandon, Manitoba. Presser. Supervisor: Katherine Dunstable. Duties: pressing, removing stains, making minor repairs, occasional cashiering.
July 1986– Sept. 1986	The Video Store, Winnipeg, Manitoba. Counter clerk. Supervisor: Thomas Raymond. Duties: cashiering on an electronic cash register, accounting, banking, selling merchandise, filing, taking telephone reservations.
Jan. 1986– March 1986	Prima Dance Centre, Brandon, Manitoba. Cashier. Supervisor: Panos Goudakis. Duties: cashiering, minor accounting, handling registration and telephone inquiries.

<u>Education</u>

Sept. 1983– June 1987	Churchill Secondary School, Brandon, Manitoba. Graduated academic program.
July 1986– Aug. 1986	Penrose Business College, Winnipeg, Manitoba. Certificates: typing, elementary accounting.

<u>References</u>

Philip Malahov Esso Convenience Shop 1757 Antelope Drive Brandon, Manitoba Tel. 217-1424	Rev. Karl Schultz Shilo United Church Shilo, Manitoba Tel. 428-6979	Thomas Raymond The Video Store 3472 Laurier St. Winnipeg, Manitoba Tel. 217-6564

Step 3   Organizing Material

Tracy decided to lay out the material for her letter this way:

> (My *thesis*, although I can't put it so bluntly in the letter, is something like "Since my qualifications are right for the job, and probably better than those of other applicants, you should hire me.")
>
> —Begin by introducing myself and indicating what position I'm applying for;
> —point to qualifications I want the reader to focus on;
> —show that I'm willing to do more tasks than cashiering;
> —end by noting where I can be reached to set up an interview.

She now had (a) lists of what she could include in her letter and (b) an informal outline, including a *thesis* (a statement expressing the main point of her letter), to keep her on track. She hoped she could get the thesis to come through as if it were the reader's own idea.

Step 4   Writing the First Draft: Developing the Material

Because she knew how important beginnings are, Tracy decided not to worry much about it yet, but just to get something down, and focus on her qualifications. She'd noticed that most of her previous work included handling cash and could be classed under the heading of "cashiering." She wouldn't have to provide the evidence in her letter, because it was already listed in the résumé (and listed *first* in three out of the four places). But because pricing and stocking had also been part of her work at the video store, she decided to point that out in this paragraph. In the next paragraph she decided to emphasize her flexibility, and she needed to specify what other kinds of things she would like to do — but in what order? She decided to try the order of most important to least: produce, then delicatessen, with bakery last. And she would end by making it easy for her reader to set up an interview. See the first draft of her letter on page 10.

Step 5   Revising

Tracy wanted to get the letter off soon, but she also wanted it to be effective, so she stifled her impatience, put the draft away until the next day, and promised herself to take as much time as she needed for revising it. She decided also to make several sweeps through it, not just one.

Personnel Manager
EatWell Markets
845 Scotia Street
Winnipeg, Manitoba

Dear Sir:

In answer to your ad in last week's <u>Gazette</u>, I want to
apply to work for EatWell as a part time cashier-stocker.

As you can see from the enclosed résumé, I have expereince
in retail grocery cashiering and taking inventory, as well
as pricing and stocking.

I can work on an electronic cash register. And I feel sure
that I can work in fresh produce, in the delicatessen, or
in the bakery.

I am prepared to begin training by November 1. If you want
to interview me, call me at 829-7974 any day before ten. I
can also come in to fill in an application.

Sincerely,

SWEEP 1

First she tackled the whole letter and its **paragraphs.**

She looked over her notes to see if the first draft brought everything in. Right away she noticed that the opening paragraph looked thin — a single sentence sitting by itself. And her notes reminded her that she had talked to her friend Doreen about working for EatWell. So she decided to flesh out the paragraph a bit:

> In answer to your ad in last week's <u>Gazette</u>, I want to apply for work as a part time cashier-stocker. A friend of mine, Doreen Arlesky, works at your North Lake store. She assures me that I would do well and enjoy the work. I am a student at Red River Community College.

Her notes also reminded her that she hadn't said anything about her person-to-person skills, qualities that would help make her an attractive applicant. She added a short paragraph just before the last one:

> I enjoy working with people and I can remain helpful and cheerful even under the pressure of lines and people's impatience.

Examining the individual paragraphs, one at a time, Tracy was bothered by the first sentence of the third paragraph. The part about the electronic cash register didn't seem to go with the rest of the paragraph, which was about the other kinds of jobs she thought she'd like to perform. She decided to tuck the idea into the previous paragraph where it now seemed to belong:

> As you can see from the enclosed résumé, I have expereince in retail grocery cashiering with an electronic cash register and taking inventory as well as pricing and stocking.

She also noticed that this change got rid of "work *on* an electronic cash register," a phrase that had made her sound more like a mechanic than a cashier.

SWEEP 2

Second, she gave her attention to individual **sentences**.

Tracy found more opportunities to make her sentences stronger and clearer. The last sentence of the new first paragraph seemed to dangle off the end. She realized that the reason she wanted to work part time was that she was a student. She combined the two sentences, and reshaped the opening phrase as a separate sentence:

> I am writing in response to your ad in last week's <u>Gazette</u>. As a student at Red River Community College, I want to apply for work as a part time cashier-stocker.

She also combined the two sentences about her friend:

> A friend of mine, Doreen Arlesky who works at your North Lake store, assures me that I would do well and that I would enjoy the work.

She liked the feel of the parallel *that*-clauses. And the whole paragraph was now much improved.

In the next paragraph, she found that moving the bit about the cash register had made the rest of that sentence hard to follow. She saw that it was another instance of parallel structure. To clarify it, she simply repeated the little word *in*:

> . . . I have expereince in retail grocery cashiering with an electronic cash register, in taking inventory, and in pricing and stocking.

Finally, she decided it would be better to revise the last sentence so that the letter would end with the information about how she could be reached, not with the weaker point about the application form:

> If you want me to come in for an interview or to fill in an application, call me at . . . .

SWEEP 3

Third, she focussed on individual **words and phrases**.

Starting at the very beginning, she was appalled to notice that she had assumed that her reader would be a man. She decided that it was equally likely that it would be a woman, and changed the salutation to

> Dear Sir or Madam:

In the first sentence, she noticed the little word *ad* and decided not to risk the slangy or informal abbreviation.

She had been bothered by the phrase *want to apply* in the first paragraph, but she hadn't stopped while drafting to find a better term. Now she paused, considered *wish,* and chose *would like* instead because it sounded more respectful than *want* and less stiff than *wish.* She made the same change in the last sentence, where, for the same reason, she also added *please* to *call.*

In the third paragraph, *I feel sure that* now bothered her. She had written it in the first place because she wanted to sound confident as well as respectful, but now it sounded forced. And questioning the phrase made her look carefully again at the whole one-sentence paragraph: it seemed to stick out. She had introduced it to show her willingness to be flexible, but now it felt forced, suggesting the opposite of confidence. She decided to drop it altogether.

In looking at the next-to-last paragraph (the one she had added earlier), she decided to add *other* to *people* in the final phrase because it helped clarify her point.

Finally, checking the last sentence again, she found that "come *in* for an *in*terview or to fill *in*" had an unpleasant jingle. A moment's thought — and the advice of a friend — convinced her that one would be just as likely, or even more likely, to fill *out* an application. Problem solved. But suddenly the word *ten* jumped at her: would her reader know she meant ten in the morning, before her first class? And checking her grammar handbook, she discovered that numerals are customary before *a.m.* and *p.m.* At the same time, she realized she meant *weekday,* and should say so.

SWEEP 4

Fourth, Tracy turned her attention to **punctuation**.

First she checked the salutation: yes, her handbook confirmed that in formal or business letters, the colon was preferable. Then, in the first paragraph, she saw that she had to supply a second comma to set off the parenthetical *who*-clause in the third sentence. And in the next-to-last paragraph, she inserted a comma after *people* because her handbook reminded her that a comma usually comes before an *and* at the beginning of a new clause.

Step 6   Preparing and Proofreading the Final Draft

Getting ready to type her final copy, Tracy checked her typing book for the form of such a letter. She chose to use the form without indentions because it seemed to her more businesslike. And in the complimentary close she decided to add *yours*; *Sincerely* alone was thought to be too informal.

When the letter was typed, but before taking it out of the typewriter, she went through it carefully one more time, looking for typographical errors and anything else she might spot. First she checked the address in the phone book — and was chagrined to discover that she had miscopied it, transposing the last two numbers. Then she began at the end of the letter and read backward, word by word. She found only one typo: *heopful* rather than *helpful.* Then she noticed a spelling error she had missed all the other times she'd gone through the drafts: she corrected *expereince* to *experience,* reminding herself that during those other sweeps she had not been looking explicitly at spelling. She checked her dictionary for the spelling of *part time* when it comes before a noun.

Adding the hyphen in *part-time* was easy, but the other three corrections all showed, even if only a little. She decided to retype — very carefully. The letter would be the reader's first indication of her attitude toward her work. She couldn't afford to appear sloppy.

Here is the letter as Tracy sent it off:

1129 N. 18th Ave.
Winnipeg, Manitoba

October 13, 1987

Personnel Manager
EatWell Markets
854 Scotia Street
Winnipeg, Manitoba

Dear Sir or Madam:

I am writing in response to your advertisement in last week's <u>Gazette</u>. As a student at Red River Community College, I would like to apply for work as a part-time cashier-stocker. A friend of mine, Doreen Arlesky, who works at your North Lake store, assures me that I would do well and that I would enjoy the work.

As you can see from the enclosed résumé, I have experience in retail grocery cashiering with an electronic cash register, in taking inventory, and in pricing and stocking.

I enjoy working with people, and I can remain helpful and cheerful even under the pressure of lines and other people's impatience.

I am prepared to begin training by November 1. If you would like me to come in for an interview or to fill out an application, please call me at 829-7974 any weekday before 10 a.m.

Sincerely yours,

Tracy Wheeler

Tracy Wheeler

Enclosure

Steps in the
Process of Writing

CHAPTER 1
Step 1
Determining Your Topic, Your Readers, and Your Purpose

THE IMPORTANCE OF PLANNING

You don't question how important **planning** is for much of what you do. You plan a trip to make the best use of your time and to avoid confusion and discomfort; and you can also plan so that you leave time to make discoveries along the way. You plan your academic program to get the most out of your courses and to make sure you meet the requirements. You probably plan even something as informal as a picnic.

Yet inexperienced writers often skimp on planning. They simply write out whatever comes to mind and then give the result a quick once-over to check spelling and maybe to change a word or two. Even if such writing is sometimes effective, it's chancy. Writing is largely a matter of making choices. Experienced writers stay in control so that they can choose among alternative ideas, techniques, styles, words, even punctuation. If you plan carefully, you'll be able to choose consciously. You'll work by design rather than by accident. If you make your choices consciously, you can make sure they are consistent and support one another.

> CAREFUL PLANNING PAYS

16

FINDING A TOPIC

Your instructors will probably assign most if not all of your topics. You may have to narrow them some, but usually your topic, together with your readers and your purpose, will be pretty much determined for you. But suppose that you are given an open assignment, for example in a writing course, or that you decide you want to try writing something of your own, for other than academic purposes. Don't panic ("What can *I* write about?") or complain ("I don't *know* enough about anything to write about it"). Experienced writers see topics everywhere. For example, there's one topic about which you know more than anyone else: *yourself.* Think about

> your interests and hobbies;
> your jobs, your experiences, your travels;
> your hopes and fears;
> your beliefs and biases;
> your friends, and their interests and experiences;
> your family, your pets;
> your room, your home, your farm;
> your town, your city;
> your school or college or university.

If you'd rather look outside yourself,

> *Look around:* chances are you'll see dozens of things that will suggest topics to write about.

> *Or read around:* in newspapers, magazines, books, even posters and billboards — what others are writing about.

> *Or listen around:* to radio, television, conversations — what people are talking about.

If you think, look, read, and listen with a piece of paper in front of you and a moving pen or pencil in your hand, you should soon have a long list of possible topics.

Project 1-a

Take a pen or pencil and a blank sheet of paper and spend *15 minutes* jotting down topics you could or might want to write about. Think about yourself and about people you know; look around you; think about what you have seen or heard or read about in the last day or two. Let your mind wander; give free association full play. Time yourself exactly — and write fast; you're racing the clock.

Keeping a Journal

One good way to collect topics for writing, as well as simply to keep track of your intellectual and emotional self, is to keep a journal or diary. A journal records the adventures of your own mind from day to day. Write about things you've done, things you've heard or seen, things you've thought. Take notes on your reading. Copy out strikingly good — or bad — passages. Question your own ideas and those of others. Update your thinking. For example, try to account for new attitudes toward something you wrote about a day or a week earlier. Your journal will be full of things you can and will want to write about. In fact, you will already be writing about them in the journal itself.

DETERMINING YOUR READERS

The occasion for a piece of writing often determines who is going to read it and what your purpose is in writing it. You write a diary for (usually) your own eyes only. If you write a letter, you have an audience of one, or of a few specific people. If you write a memo or a monthly report, you again have a small number of readers, probably ones you know fairly well. If you write for a club newsletter you may have a larger number of readers, but your special *purpose* will still define them for you.

But when you write for a larger, more remote audience, your readers are more difficult to define — especially if your purpose is less built-in. The larger your audience, the more diverse will be your readers' backgrounds and attitudes. On such occasions, then, it is even more important that you keep at the front of your mind both your *readers* and your *purpose*.

Constructing a Reader Profile

A profile is a side view, often merely in outline, that lets you identify an object or a face. It leaves out minor features in favour of more obvious ones. Try drawing up a "profile" of your potential readers. Think of the ways in which both individuals and groups of people can differ:

age	biases
income	affiliations
social class	cultural assumptions
education	ethnic origin
occupation	nationality
experience	superstitions
sex	goals
values	special interests

To construct a profile of those who will be your readers, try to see which kinds of differences are important for your topic and your purpose. Sex, age, and occupation are perhaps obvious enough, but some of the others may be just as important. Consider "values," for example, or "biases", or "cultural assumptions": can you say how your readers will feel about such contemporary issues as law and order, the progressive income tax, abortion, human rights and property rights, the family, funding for education, technological change, and censorship? How you see your readers reacting to such issues will help you determine such things as the kinds of examples you can use, perhaps even the kinds of language.

Here is a profile drawn up by a university student for a projected essay directed at fellow students majoring in English:

- age: 20-25 (average 21; a few older, but only a few)
- income: $2,000-$12,000 (very few fully subsidized)
- social class: middle to upper middle
- education: 3-5 years at university
- occupation: student (some also work at various jobs)
- sex: 55% female
- experience (travel, work, hobbies, etc.): varied (avoid easy assumptions); quite a few have travelled, not just to the US but overseas
- values: tend to be slightly more liberal than the population at large; tend to be people- rather than object-oriented; less materialistic; politically, probably leftish, though many quite conservative
- biases: tend to be suspicious of math, science, and technology (though many are all for some of its products, perhaps taking them for granted)
- ethnic origins: mostly white-Anglo-Saxon-Protestant, but not over-whelmingly; most (but not all) of their parents have English as first language
- goals: most hope for professional careers
- special interests: common interest in literature

The more you know about your readers, the more effectively you can choose among the available alternatives. If you know how strongly your readers feel about a particular issue, you'll know how much evidence you need in order to persuade them to change their minds. If you can gauge their attitudes toward your topic, you'll know whether you can risk humour. If you know how much they already know about something, you'll know how much information you have to supply. Too much background and detail will bore your readers; too little will confuse them or lose them.

> KNOW YOUR READERS.
> UNDERSTAND YOUR READERS.
> WRITE FOR YOUR READERS.

Project 1-b

Construct a reader profile of one or more of the following:

- the cabinet ministers in your province
- the law-enforcement personnel in your community
- readers of the Toronto *Globe and Mail*
- your own classmates
- guitar players (or violin players)
- tourists in New Zealand (or Hawaii)
- supporters of the Hamilton Tiger-Cats
- Sunday shoppers
- small farmers in Manitoba
- immigrants to Canada from eastern European countries (or Asian countries, or African)

Project 1-c

Examine two or three recent issues of one of the following magazines. Look at the kinds of advertising as well as the kinds of articles they contain. Then draw up a reader profile for it. You may want to try doing the same for a second magazine, one that you expect will have a readership markedly different from that of your first choice.

The Atlantic	*Golf Digest*	*The New Statesman*
The Canadian Forum	*Gourmet*	*The New Yorker*
Canadian Wildlife	*Homemaker*	*Outdoor Life*
Chatelaine	*Maclean's*	*Personal Computing*
Consumer Reports	*Ms*	*Road and Track*
Cosmopolitan	*The Nation*	*Saturday Night*
Fortune	*The National Review*	*TV Guide*

DETERMINING YOUR PURPOSE

Most of the purposes of writing can be classed under one of these four headings:

1. to express yourself
2. to inform others (explain, instruct)
3. to persuade others (convince, argue)
4. to entertain others (interest, amuse)

Often these purposes overlap in a given piece of writing. But usually you will have one or another of them as your *primary* or *overall* purpose. As you write, keep your eye continually on that purpose, and on your readers.

Reasons for Writing

Of course there are also broader motivations behind most writing. For example, professional writers write primarily to make money — but they make it only if what they write has a clear **purpose** of its own and succeeds in fulfilling it. A service-manager in an automobile agency may write a report because the job requires it, and perhaps also to impress a superior and get a raise or a promotion. But the **purpose** of the report itself is to convey certain information.

Similarly, when you write a paper for a particular course you have several reasons for writing it. You write

- to fulfill an assignment and thereby complete the course requirements;
- to learn about the topic assigned;
- to demonstrate to your instructor that you can do the kind of work called for; and probably even
- to impress your instructor with your abilities and thereby earn a good grade.

But each paper will have its own defined purpose: perhaps to **investigate** superstition in the Middle Ages, to **discuss** economic conditions in Latin America, to **analyze** a poem by Tennyson, to **report** on a chemistry experiment, or to **explore** the causes of a historical event. That is, you will have a topic, and you will formulate a thesis (pp. 38-39, 57-55, 101) about that topic. For these reasons, most academic writing will have as its purpose either *informing* or *persuading*. That is, you will usually be writing what are called *exposition* and *argument*.

Or think of Tracy Wheeler, writing her letter applying for a job. As you saw in the Introduction, her MOTIVE was to get a job and make money. Her THESIS was that she was well qualified for the job. Her PURPOSE was to *persuade* the employer to grant an interview. Or it could be illustrated this way:

	PURPOSE	**READER**		**THESIS**
I want	to PERSUADE	the EMPLOYER	that	I AM THE PERSON FOR THE JOB.

Project 1-d

Suppose you asked a number of writers what their purposes were in writing particular pieces, and they replied with the following:

1. to sell something
2. to console someone
3. to interpret a story
4. to give pleasure with a poem
5. to correct a mistaken view
6. to attack someone
7. to share feelings
8. to warn others
9. to praise someone
10. to justify myself

Under which of the four basic overall purposes would you classify each of these?

QUESTIONS TO HELP YOU FOCUS ON READERS AND PURPOSE

The better idea you have of your readers and your purpose, the better you will be able to write for any given occasion. In addition to the questions listed in the Introduction (pp. 2-3, 6), here are a few others that can help you arrive at a clear view of both readers and purpose. Answer them (write your answers down) as fully as you can.

Readers and Topic

How well do my readers know my topic?

What background information do they need?

What do they think or feel about the topic?

Are they likely to be friendly, hostile, or neutral toward it?

Readers and Writer

Do my readers know me at all? How do they feel about me?

How do I want them to feel about me?

What do they expect of me?

Purpose and Readers

Will my readers be aware of my purpose before they begin to read (perhaps because of the occasion)?

Are my readers likely to be receptive to my purpose, or hostile, or neutral?

What do I want this piece of writing to do for my readers?

What do I want my readers to do as a result of reading this piece of writing?

Here are two other questions worth asking:

1. How many readers will I have for this piece? (You can't please everyone. As the saying goes, if you try to please everyone, you'll end up pleasing no one.)

2. How do my readers think of *themselves*? (If you know, you can decide whether to appeal to that image, ignore it, or challenge it.)

After you've drawn up a profile of your readers for a particular piece of writing, write out as complete a statement of your purpose as you can manage. For example:

> I want to *persuade* my classmates and the instructor, by using careful explanation, that the electoral system of Indonesia today is much more democratic than is reported by the European press.

THE SPECIAL PROBLEMS OF THE STUDENT WRITER

Students are often confused about the occasion for their writing assignments. How can you think of "readers" when you are likely writing only for your instructor? Some instructors will ask you to pretend to write for "a general audience." But such advice can't help much, because it's not specific. Others suggest that you write for "an audience of your peers" — that is, your classmates. This suggestion is more helpful, for you can ask yourself specific questions about them.

Still, you know that your instructors will often be your only readers. But keep in mind that readers, like writers, play roles. Your aim is to allow your instructors to assume readers' roles that are comfortable. Most instructors don't *want* to become harsh judges for the purpose of marking up the errors in your writing, but by making the reading unpleasant, you can compel them to take on such roles. Most instructors start out with a neutral or somewhat positive attitude. Try to keep them on your side.

You may, for example, want your readers to take on the role of beginner for the purpose of learning how to do something. Instructors will usually be willing to do that, unless you make it difficult or impossible for them. They *want* to be friendly and willing to learn; they *want* to be receptive (if skeptical). Your task is to let them.

Even if your instructors are specialists and you're just learning about the subject, they will at least be interested in seeing how you handle things. Suppose you're writing a history essay on R. B. Bennett and his attitudes toward the unemployed in the early 1930's. You realize that your instructor knows much more than you do about both Bennett and the plight of the unemployed in those years. Most likely, however, your reader will accept the comfortable role of a sympathetic observer, genuinely interested in the facts you come up with and in how you put them together. But an error of fact or an awkward sentence may force your instructor to shift from willing spectator to unwilling proofreader and judge.

Project 1-e

Just as you create an image of yourself as writer on a given occasion, so do you partly create an image of your readers. That's one reason the beginning of a piece of writing is so important. Think of the times you've quit reading something after a few sentences; you realized that it wasn't intended for you: you rejected the role it invited you to play.

Here are the opening paragraphs of two student "how to" papers on the same topic. What strengths and weaknesses do you find in them? Does one more effectively establish a role for its readers than the other? Why?

```
A.          Italian Spaghetti Sauce—Make Your Own!
```
People often buy their spaghetti sauce ready-made from the grocery store because they feel incapable of making their own. If you are one of these people, here is a recipe which should prove to you that making spaghetti sauce is a lot easier than you think. Just follow these easy instructions and the result of your efforts will be a spaghetti sauce much more delicious than any you could ever get from a can or a jar.

```
B.                    Italian Meat Sauce
```
The secret in making delicious meat sauce, Italian style, is to let the sauce cook slowly over low heat, for 2 hours. The utensils needed are few: 1 medium size saucepan, and 1 wooden spoon. Begin by lightly covering bottom of saucepan with olive oil. Sauté over low heat: 1 small, finely chopped onion and garlic clove, and 1 lb. ground hamburger.

Project 1·f

Choose some incident that happened to you within the last week or two and write a short letter about it to two distinctly different readers, for example a close relative or friend and a radio news-reporter.

NARROWING TO A WORKABLE TOPIC

To be successful, a topic must be

(a) unified, single;

(b) significant enough to be of interest not only to you but also to your readers; and

(c) supportable, capable of being developed in accordance with your purpose.

It must also be

(d) manageable in the time and space you have on a given occasion.

Usually your limits of both time and space will be severe.

Many topics, in the form in which they first occur to you or are assigned to you, will need to be drastically limited. Consider some examples:

Pollution. To try to deal with such a broad subject in only a few pages would mean that you could say only the most vague and general and obvious things. It would be difficult to keep readers interested or to say anything with much point to it. How about *toxic-waste disposal? the threat of acid rain? the future of fossil fuels?* Long articles, even whole books, have been written about such broad topics. For a term paper something like *cleaning up Lake Erie* might be more promising. For an even shorter paper, especially one directed at your fellow students or some other group of local readers, you could narrow it to something like *enforcing the local anti-noise law.*

Education. This is a huge topic, broad enough to have a large library classification all to itself. Try narrowing it: *The back-to-basics movement. Discipline in elementary schools. Teachers.* But even these are too broad, unless perhaps for a long paper. *Teachers,* for instance, might be further narrowed to *red-haired teachers, teachers I have known,* or *my absent-minded chemistry teacher.* Such topics could lend themselves to relatively short papers that were either informative or entertaining, or both. For an argumentative piece you might decide to deal with a contentious issue such as *Should teachers go on strike?*

The difficulty with many topics is that they are too general and abstract (see pp. 147-48). Often simply moving to something more concrete and specific will help narrow a topic to one that will suit your purpose. *Music,* for example, could be narrowed to *sonatas, Dixieland jazz, Christmas carols.* But those are still too broad. For a particular group of readers you might move to something even more specific, such as *Will jazz survive rock and roll?*

A topic like *weather* could be narrowed to something workable like *climate control* or *how hurricanes form* or *the blizzard of '86.*

If you're interested in *sports,* you could narrow that broad concept to something manageable. *Violence in sport,* for example, could be handled in different ways, depending on your readers and your purpose: Are they bothered by it, or not? Are you? Could you be neutral? But since it's still rather broad, you would probably want to narrow it to something much more specific, like *soccer madness* or *the causes of violence in sport* or *the violent Philadephia Flyers of 1976* or *teaching pee-wees how to fight.*

See also p. 33-34.

Project 1-g

Select three of the following general and abstract terms and for each write a short paragraph that defines the term partly by supplying specific and concrete examples.

responsibility	generosity	hope
power	dignity	cruelty
speed	ennui	happiness
friendship	sloth	worry
culture	gratitude	independence

Project 1-h

Comment on the following as potential topics. Keep in mind the five elements of the writing context. Try to imagine occasions on which someone could write about such topics. Are any simply impossible? Do some sound too dull? Why? Could they be made interesting? Which ones sound most promising? Why? Would some be suitable only for a limited audience? Which ones could *you* write about? To what readers? For what purpose? Which topics would need drastic narrowing?

puppy-love	heroism in war
Shakespeare's *Macbeth*	TV programs
the French Revolution	Halley's comet
baking buttermilk biscuits	our high-school play
a mother's love	automobiles
last summer	clip-boards
how the NDP won the federal election	living in a basement apartment
	ethics
my new baby kitten	the Tang dynasty
Solidarity	pop music
tying flies	the standard of living in South Africa
why students should run this school	the function of commas in a novel by Henry James
insect life in South America	the word *the*
fear	pawn moves in chess
fad food	pencils
bricks	lasers
the pleasures of poverty	the canals of Mars
Manitoba painters	architecture in Ontario
my life so far	

Project 1-i

Starting from these five general topics,

sarcasm, marriage, hockey, rock music, clothing fashions,

a group of students came up with the following list of narrowed topics for possible essays:

1. The key to a stable and lasting marriage.
2. The implications of a student's choice of clothing.
3. Defence play in the NHL has deteriorated recently.
4. How one teacher used sarcasm to maintain discipline.
5. Analysis of sarcasm in a political cartoon.
6. Rock isn't the only music teenagers like.
7. The difficulties of keeping up with fashion today.
8. Marriage: This is my mom and dad.
9. African rhythms in rock music.
10. Uses and misuses of sarcasm.
11. The latest fashion trends at the health club.
12. If there is a "language of clothes," what is it saying?

Evaluate these topics. Which are strong, and which weak? Can the weaker ones be improved? Is the purpose of all of them essentially to inform — or do you think that some should have a different primary purpose? What readers would they be aimed at? Would they all be suitable for an audience of your peers — that is, one including you? Do any of them seem still too large for a paper of about 1000 words (four double-spaced typed pages)? If so, could they be narrowed further?

Project 1-j

From the following ten broad topics, choose five, and for each provide

(a) a narrowed topic suitable for a short paper of 500-750 words (two to three typed pages), and

(b) one suitable for a paper of 2000-2500 words (eight to ten typed pages).

For each of the five suggest an appropriate purpose and readership.

movies	morals
transportation	international relations
food	travel
books	health
politics	Canadian history

Project 1-k

Listed below are fifteen topics. All are fairly broad, some more than others. Choose five, and for each provide a narrowed topic for an essay of about five pages that you think would either *entertain* or *persuade*

(a) a group of grade-ten students in Alberta, Saskatchewan, or Manitoba,

(b) a group of high-school teachers in the Maritimes,

(c) a group of elderly people in British Columbia.

forest fires	Newfoundland	superstition
journalism	unions	conformity
campus architecture	beauty	sanitation
television advertising	Picasso	communication
crime	inflation	doubt

CHAPTER 2
Step 2
Finding Material

Ideas, opinions, facts, data — the material that goes into a piece of writing has to come from somewhere. This chapter offers you techniques for generating material about any topic you're writing on. If you're writing an account of a personal experience, you probably have all you need — but you may still need to jog your memory. The techniques discussed in this chapter will help you do that, too.

If you feel that you don't know enough about a topic, these techniques can even guide you toward useful research. (For how to conduct such research, see Chapter 12, "Writing a Research Paper.") But don't resort to sources outside yourself too early, for you may cut off the flow of your own ideas. *Get all you can from your own thinking first*. You often know more than you think you do, but much of it is stored, waiting for these techniques to release it.

THE PRINCIPLE OF SELECTION

Suppose you need about ten basic ideas for a short paper. If you simply take the first ten that come to mind, the paper might succeed in fulfilling your purpose. But if you first find twenty ideas and then use only the best ten, the result will be stronger. And think how much better still it will be if you begin with fifty and select the best ten. It's unlikely that the first ten will be the best ten.

> The more you can discard, the stronger will be
> what you keep.

BRAINSTORMING

Start by **brainstorming** your topic. Sit down with blank sheets of paper and quickly jot down everything that comes to mind about your topic. Don't stop to analyze or evaluate; just get it all written down. Later you can sift and sort, guided by your earlier decisions about purpose and readers; now you want to get on paper as many ideas as you can: facts, opinions, statistics, questions, contexts, relationships, even wild guesses. Don't worry about style or spelling. Let your mind run free and fast. You'll soon have words, phrases, clauses, sentences, perhaps even diagrams and pictures, all over the page. As items accumulate and one idea or train of thought calls up another, you'll begin grouping ideas together, making lists, circling and underlining and starring and joining with arrows. You will already have begun selecting and arranging.

Sometimes it helps to brainstorm with others. Even just two or three people bouncing ideas off one another can generate an astonishing amount of material in a short time.

Project 2-a

(a) Decide on a topic, one that you know something about. Perhaps select one from projects 1-g through 1-k (pp. 25-27). Then try brainstorming it. Give yourself just 15 or 20 minutes — no more. And work fast.

(b) Pick another topic, this time one you don't think you know much about, and brainstorm it in the same way. See if you come up with ideas you didn't know you had.

(c) Now try brainstorming the same topics with one or more other people. Your results will expand.

USING QUESTIONS

You have already used questions to help you focus on the writing context and on your readers and your purpose. Asking questions will also help you gather material.

Rapidly asking questions is similar to brainstorming, but here the process is more systematic. And as with brainstorming, it sometimes helps to work with others. Also as with brainstorming, work fast. Don't stop to criticize, evaluate, ponder, or follow up ideas — not yet. Don't stop to think about the results until all the results are in.

And *write down* whatever answers your questions elicit. You will be generating words, phrases, and sentences that you can use later.

Caution: Save *all* the notes you make while working on a project. You never know what may come in handy later. For example, something you reject during planning may prove useful during revision. DON'T THROW ANYTHING AWAY until you are all through and the finished product has left your hands.

The Reporter's Questions

The newspaper reporter's formula of *Who-What-Where-When-Why* (with a judicious *How* added) works well for some topics:

1. What is it? What is happening?
2. Who is doing it, and to whom?
3. Where and when is it?
4. Why is it? Why is it being done?
5. How is it happening? How or with what is it done?

Answering such questions will yield useful information:

1. *What:* nature, identity, appearance, definition
2. *Who:* human (or non-human) agents or victims, if any
3. *Where* and *When:* setting, or scene
4. *Why:* motivation, causes
5. *How:* method, agency, instrument

Such questions work especially well for *events*. But you can ask such questions of almost any topic. Take for example "Ottawa." "What is it?" is easy: it's a place, a capital city. "Who" questions could produce several sorts of answers, including possibly both agents and victims. So could questions about motivation and method. Such questions could easily help you narrow the topic to, for example, the operation of a single government agency or department.

But go beyond the reporter's fact-finding. Increase the range of questions in order to *generate ideas*, to discover material for writing. Since the reason for asking questions is to prompt your mind and your imagination, the more questions, and the more kinds of questions, the better.

Kinds of Topics

Most topics can be classified into several clearly recognizable categories, such as

> things or objects,
> events or occurrences,
> persons or other creatures,
> places,
> activities or processes,
> ideas, feelings, beliefs, states of mind.

Others can be thought of as natural conditions, man-made institutions, and perhaps some kinds of abstract qualities. Common sense tells you that certain questions are appropriate only to certain kinds of topics. But many questions, with the change of a word or two, are applicable to different kinds of topics.

QUESTIONS ABOUT IDENTITY

If your topic is a thing, an **object**, try such questions as these:

> What is it? Does it exist?
> When and where does (did, will) it exist?
> What is its appearance, etc. (shape, size, colour, feel, smell, taste, sound)?
> Does it move? How does it work?
> Is it unchanging, or does it change or can it be changed?
> Does it have degrees?
> What is it made of?
> What are the main kinds of it?
> Does it have parts? Is it part of anything else?
> What is it like, or unlike? Does it have an opposite?
> Is it unique? Is there or can there be more than one of it?

If your topic is an **event**, some questions will be slightly different. For example:

> What happened? Did (Does, Will) it happen?
> When and where did (does, will) it happen?

If your topic is a **person** or other creature, you will again change some questions a little. For example:

> Who is it? Does she (he, it) exist? When? Where?

If your topic is a **place**:

> Does it exist? Where and when? What happens there?

And so on.

You can also ask special questions in order to get at other ideas about your topic.

QUESTIONS ABOUT CONNECTIONS WITH PEOPLE

Who uses it? Who owns it? Who made it?
Who is associated with it?
Who sees it, hears it, smells it, etc.?
Who respects, fears, likes, dislikes it?

QUESTIONS ABOUT CAUSE AND EFFECT

Why does (did, will) it exist (happen)?
Who or what causes (caused, will cause) it?
What does (did, will, can) it do or cause?
How or for what is it used?
Is it part of a process?
What if it did *not* exist or happen?

QUESTIONS ABOUT TESTIMONY, AUTHORITY, USAGE

What has been said about it? Any useful quotations?
What information about it is there from statistics, precedents, history, past or present actions on it?
Do references to it occur loosely or figuratively — in clichés, common phrases, proverbs, anecdotes, stories?
What can I learn about it from its etymology?

Answering such questions systematically can open up many avenues of thought and development.

Project 2-b

Sometimes it helps to push your mind to what may seem exaggerated lengths. One teacher we know, for example, asks students to list 101 ways to use a brick (What is it for? What can it do?). Here's a start:

A brick makes an effective paperweight.
A brick is handy for smashing a window.
Several bricks and some boards make a good bookcase.
A brick makes an excellent doorstop.
You can practise the shot-put with a brick.
You can pound a brick into brickdust (what could you use brickdust for?).
Bricks, in large numbers, provide jobs for brickmakers and bricklayers.
A brick . . . .

But you take it from there; you need only about 95 more (and make the 101st use that of building walls).

Project 2-c

List as many uses as you can think of for one or more of the following. Try to reach at least 50 for each.

a paper clip	a tennis ball
a wire coat-hanger	a styrofoam cup
a wooden match	a potato
a clothes-pin	Australia

FINDING MATERIAL AND TOPIC-NARROWING

Suppose that in a geography course you have chosen or been assigned the topic "energy resources in Canada." That's already narrowed somewhat from the broader topic "energy," but you may want to narrow it further, perhaps to focus on one kind of energy or on one region of the country, or even on one kind in one region.

Run your narrowed topic ("hydro power in Quebec") through all the questions you can. For example:

When and where does it happen?
How does it work? Is it part of a larger process?
Who is involved with it?
What or who causes it? What does it cause?
Can it be changed?

The answers to such questions could provide you with a solid core of material on the narrowed topic. But don't stop there. Pretend you hadn't narrowed the topic; apply questions also to the large general topic "energy." If you do, you'll probably ask some that you'd be unlikely to direct at the narrowed topic:

Does it have an opposite?
What is its appearance? What is it like?
What can I learn from its etymology?
What has been said about it?

Here are some answers to these questions from a session with a small class, including as resources a regular dictionary and a dictionary of quotations:

- Energy's opposite is lethargy, weakness, impotence, powerlessness. (Are conservationists and consumers powerless against big governments and big companies?)
- Metaphorically, it is something large, muscular. Its colour is probably red. It looks like oil wells and power lines and waterfalls (white?) and gymnasts and kids (no energy shortage there!) and hurricanes (tidal power?).

- Etymology: it's from the Greek *energeia,* coined by Aristotle from *energos,* "active, at work," from *en,* "at," and *ergon,* "work," the same root that the word for units of energy, *ergs,* derives from.
- "Energy is eternal delight." (William Blake)
- "Power when wielded by abnormal energy is the most serious of facts." (Henry Adams)

Such material can at least enable you to inject some extra sparkle into your writing, for example with quotations and metaphors. Answers and ideas like these might provide you with a good way to begin or end a paper (see pp. 95-100). They might even suggest whole new approaches to the topic.

So leave your options open. Ask a wide range of questions that will generate a variety of ideas, contexts, relationships. Further, things you can say about a large topic may well be applicable to a narrowed version of it.

Project 2-d

In a good standard dictionary or in an etymological dictionary, look up the histories of five of the following words. Show how you might use each etymology in an essay.

fear	harmony	luck	nemesis
education	calligraphy	garbage	dormitory
parents	pollution	food	whisky

Project 2-e

Select three words from the following list and, in one or more dictionaries of quotations, find and copy out at least two quotations using each of them. Show how you might use each quotation in an essay.

moon	horses	luck	hate
trust	science	river	power
pain	spring	books	Canada

Cross-Fertilizing: Shifting Categories

You may find that some questions don't help much with some topics. You may even think that asking only a few questions makes the job easier. But remember: the reason for taking a topic through this step is to discover ideas you didn't know you had — not only obvious ideas but unexpected ones as well.

One way to broaden your range of discovery is to think of your topic in unusual ways, to look at it from fresh perspectives. Ask questions that common sense tells you are appropriate to certain kinds of topics — and then forget about common sense. If your topic is a **place**, think of it also as an **object**, or a **process**. If your topic is an **idea**, think of it also as a **place**, a **person**, an **object**. And so on. By deliberately asking questions that are *not* logically appropriate, you may get some surprisingly useful ideas.

For this reason we can rejoice that many topics fit into more than one category. Is "education," for example, an institution, like a high school or university, or is it a process, like climbing a mountain? While you're looking for material, think of it in both ways. Could it be thought of as an event? a place? an idea? a natural condition?

Consider another topic: "Ottawa." Obviously it's a **place**. But start asking some unlikely questions about it:

> What caused it? Is it part of a process? How does it work? What colour is it? Is it part of something? What does it do? Does it change? To whom is it important? What does it mean? What does it weigh? Does it have a personality?

Before long you begin thinking of Ottawa not only as a place, a city, but as the heart (or head) of Canada; as the seat of government; as a place where decisions are made that affect us all; as a sort of presence, whatever party is in power; as part of the process called democracy; as a person or agent (Ottawa demands money); as a heavy weight the taxpayer must shoulder; even as an idea, or state of mind. You could even see it as an activity. Try it as a verb: what might it mean "to Ottawa" something or someone?

When we treated "energy" as an object and asked what it looked like, we got several potentially useful ideas. We asked a class to think of the abstract topic "hate" in different ways; here are some of their suggestions:

- Hate as **object**: red, because of anger, passion, danger; purple, because of an enraged person's face (and, punningly, "ultra-violent"); yellow, because hate is like a disease; green, because hate is sometimes caused by envy (Old English *hete* meant both "hate" and "envy"); something heavy, a burden.
- Hate as **activity**: something people enjoy, like a hobby.
- Hate as **condition**: part of human nature, built into us.
- Hate as **place**: If it were a city, what would it look like?

Metaphors and Similes

As you see, asking questions such as "What is it like?" produces not only literal comparisons but also figurative ones, such as thinking of "hate" as something concrete, a physical burden that weighs down some people, or as a disease. Or personify it as some sort of creature: how would it look in a horror movie?

Some would say that hate is *like* a poison in the system of a person or community; that would be a **simile**, a stated or explicit comparison, using the word *like*. Or you could say it *is* a poison; that would be an implicit comparison, a **metaphor**, an assumption that the two things were identical. Or you could decide that hate was like food: some people seem to thrive on it (simile). Or you may have heard someone say, "I ran into a wall of hatred" (metaphor).

If you look for common phrases in which the word occurs, you will come up with "a pet hate" and (another personification — a kind of metaphor) "blind hatred." And the latter might lead to interesting comparisons with such common sayings as "Love is blind" and "Justice is blind." (Such clichés are dangerous, however, unless you are doing something fresh with them, as you *would* be when making such comparisons. See pp. 152-53.)

Project 2-f

Choose five of the following, and come up with at least two figurative comparisons for each of them. Include some examples of simile, metaphor, and personification.

garbage	swimming	fear	student life
education	blood	music	spring
pollution	Calgary	traffic	relatives

Look over your results, choose the ones you like best, and write a short paper — a two- or three-paragraph sketch — in which you make use of them.

Random Association

Another way to bounce your mind out of the ruts of standardized or clichéd thinking is **random association**. Put your topic, or a key word from it, beside another word or idea and try to make sense of the association or combination. You may stir up a useful line of thought that wouldn't otherwise occur to you. Think of it as grabbing a word out of thin air and throwing it at your topic to see if the collision sends off any sparks.

You can find useful words by opening a dictionary at random and putting your finger on the page. Or you can use other kinds of books; nonfiction usually works best. Or you can do it with numbers. We tried

288, 21, and 2. Opening a handy book to page 288, we found the second word in the twenty-first line to be *value*, a promising word to put beside almost any topic. It could raise a whole set of questions like "What is it worth? To whom?"

You can think of other ways to get something to throw at your topic. Grab a handful of letters from a word-game and see what words you can make from them; or glance out the window and focus on the first object your eye lights upon.

Occasionally you'll hit a word — like a technical term — that obviously won't do you any good. Then just move along the line or down the page until you hit a better one. Or try for a new word. But don't give up too soon: even an *and* or a *the* or an *if* might send off a spark if you give it a chance.

Project 2-g

Choose one number from each column and then open any appropriate book to find the indicated word. See what happens when you strike that word against some of the suggested topics or words listed in earlier exercises in this section, or a topic you're working on.

Page	Line	Word
288	21	2
17	3	9
101	12	6
53	25	7
190	8	4

One Question Leads to Another

Don't stop with the questions listed above. Make up questions about your topic. Let the answer to one question lead to another question, and so on. Pile up the answers. Let your material grow — and your topic narrow. As it narrows, you'll find it easier to get more ideas about it.

For example, a student begins with the large topic "education" and narrows it to a couple of possibilities, "methods of teaching" and "methods of learning." She doesn't feel comfortable with it yet, and she's not sure about readers and purpose, either. She keeps asking questions that enable her to narrow it further, to get more and more specific:

What methods of teaching have I been exposed to?
What method has worked best for me?
Which is more important, class or home study?

And so on. Such questions lead to others, more focussed:

> What methods of study work best for me?
> At what time of day do I study best?
> What part of the school year is the hardest?
> Which teachers do I feel most grateful to?
> How important are all the notes I take?

And so on. Soon she's asking even more specific, focussed questions — and producing increasingly specific answers:

> What's the best way to take notes?
> How many times do I have to reread a chapter?
> Do I contribute enough in the classroom?
> Why is the exam period especially difficult?

Judging from the way the questions and answers are going, it looks as though she's more interested in "methods of learning" than in "methods of teaching" — and perhaps also more qualified to say something useful about them. Her focus has narrowed down to herself, her experience as a student. She decides that her *readers* will be her fellow students — maybe she can even get something in the school paper. She finds herself focussing on the question about the exam period.

Her *purpose*, she decides, will be to help her readers by making suggestions from her own experience. Maybe she could ask, "How do I prepare for an exam?" A **thesis question** is beginning to emerge: "What can I tell my classmates about preparing for exams?"

Sharpening the Thesis Question

First she tries expressing her thesis question more economically:

> How should students prepare for an exam?

But then she asks herself if she can usefully tell others how to prepare for "an" exam. Students face many kinds of exams, and she can't cover them all. Maybe she can broaden her topic again and consider "exams," or "the exam period" itself. She rephrases the thesis question once more:

> What is the best way for students to prepare themselves for the final examination period?

It's longer again, but clear and solid; when she decides how she's going to answer it, she'll have a **thesis statement**.

Topic, Thesis Question, and Thesis Statement

Eventually you will arrive at a **thesis**, a statement of the main point you intend to make about your narrowed topic. But during these early steps, especially as you ask questions to help you find material, your thesis is more likely to emerge as a **question** than as a **statement**. That is, as you zero in on what you want to say about your topic, you begin formulating a question that will help guide you through the rest of the writing process.

For example, with a narrowed topic like "computers in the schools," you could formulate this thesis question:

How do computers help students in secondary school?

For a topic about marathon running, a thesis question could take this shape:

What is the best way to train for a marathon?

As you begin to think of possible ways of answering such questions, you might find them growing into **statements**:

topic:	computers
narrower topic:	computers in the classroom
narrowed topic:	computers in secondary school
thesis question:	How can computers most help students in secondary school?
thesis statement:	Computers in secondary-school classrooms help students understand mathematical concepts.
topic:	running a marathon
narrowed topic:	training for marathon running
thesis question:	How should one train for a marathon?
thesis statement:	Training for marathon running breaks down into three phases.

The next chapter discusses thesis statements further (see pp. 55-57).

Project 2-h

The strategies in this chapter will help you narrow your topic, focus on readers and purpose, begin formulating a thesis, and even perhaps begin working out schemes of organization and development (the subjects of the next chapters). They are designed to help you find ideas that might not occur to you otherwise. With these techniques you can hammer your square peg of a topic into unlikely round-holed categories and discover unexpected similarities, differences, and associations. Even if you come up with only a few ideas, keep questioning. Something may turn up, something may spark a train of thought, some absurd answer may suggest a useful contrast or a new direction.

For experiment and practice, take the same topics you used for brainstorming (Project 2-a) and run each through as many questions as possible. Don't think of our lists as complete: make up other questions that might be useful. Try cross-fertilizing and random association. Conclude by formulating two possible thesis questions for each topic.

CHAPTER 3
Step 3
Organizing Your Material: Planning Development and Constructing an Outline

From your planning work during Steps 1 and 2 you have
   a narrowed topic,
   a strong sense of your readers and your purpose,
   a number of ideas about the topic, and
   at least a tentative thesis question.

The next step is to decide how to **develop** your material and how to **arrange** it into a unified and coherent whole. In the first two steps you concentrate on *what* to write; now you begin to concentrate on *how* to write it.

THE SUB-STEPS OF PLANNING DEVELOPMENT AND ARRANGEMENT

As you work out how to develop and organize your project, you go through a series of sub-steps:

- Decide on your main method of development.
- Formulate a thesis statement.
- Arrange your material.
- Construct a working outline.

These sub-steps may not occur in this order; indeed they may all go on simultaneously. The nature of Step 3 will largely depend on your working habits and on the length and complexity of a particular project. For example, as you look over the material you have generated, you may find that patterns are already emerging. A method of development and a scheme of organization may suggest themselves right away. (But be careful: the first arrangement that occurs to you may not be the best one.) You may already have a thesis question that can easily be turned into a tentative thesis statement. And you may have made some notes to yourself about possible ways of developing your ideas. If your material is already taking shape in these ways, perhaps you can simply write down some headings for your main groups of ideas and use them as a working outline.

But if you haven't yet reached such a point, you'll have to make a conscious effort to find an order for your material before you begin writing your draft. The aim of Step 3 is to help you do that. Go through these sub-steps in whatever order your inclinations and the nature of your material dictate; you'll see that they overlap each other.

DECIDE ON YOUR MAIN METHOD OF DEVELOPMENT

As your project takes shape, you begin to see it as made up of sections, subsections, even paragraphs. You need to decide on the best **method of development** for the piece as a whole and for each of its parts.

The principal methods of development are as follows:

- **analysis:** You can *analyze* or divide all or part of your topic.
- **description:** You can *describe* an object, person, or scene.
- **narration:** You can *narrate* a sequence of events, tell a story.
- **example and illustration:** You can provide *examples and illustrations* to support a general statement.
- **classification:** You can *classify* items in your material.
- **definition:** You can *define* words or ideas.
- **comparison and contrast:** You can *compare and contrast* one or more things with one or more others.
- **process:** You can *analyze a process* in order to explain it.
- **cause and effect:** You can search out and discuss *causes and effects*.

These methods of development reflect some of the main ways people think. There are other, less formal methods, but these are the ones you are likely to use most often.

ONE OVERALL METHOD

For most of your writing projects, you will choose one of these methods as the main one for developing your topic. And the method you choose will largely determine the overall organization of your paper.

OTHER METHODS FOR THE PARTS

For the various parts of your paper, both small and large, you will use other methods as well. For instance, if **comparison and contrast** is your overall method, you could develop some parts by giving **examples**, and you could develop one of those by **narrating** a personal experience. In a set of instructions on how to follow a step-by-step **process**, you might discuss **causes and effects** in a paragraph explaining why a step must be performed in a particular way. You can help **define** something by placing it in its **class**, by providing **illustrations** of it, by **comparing or contrasting** it with something else, or by **analyzing** it into its parts.

Deciding Which Methods of Development to Use

Questions that help you find material can also help you choose an appropriate method of development. For example, "What is it?" might lead you to **describe** an object or **define** a term. Or suppose you are writing about Christmas carols and have arrived at this thesis question: "What kinds of Christmas carols are there?" The phrase *what kinds of* immediately suggests **classifying**. Look again at the thesis question generated at the end of the preceding chapter:

> What is the best way for students to prepare themselves for the final examination period?

The project is taking the form of a recommended schedule for students to follow. Looking at the phrase *best way to prepare*, the writer begins to think of her material as calling for an **analysis** of the **process** of getting through the exam period, a sort of "how to" paper.

Briefly consider each of the individual methods (the next chapter provides further advice on using them):

ANALYSIS (see also pp. 67-68)

One common way of dealing with a topic is to divide it up into its component parts. If questions like the following have enabled you to get a grip on your topic, ty using **analysis** as your principal method of development:

- Does it have parts?
- Can I break it down into subdivisions?
- Does it have degrees?
- What are the relations among its parts?

Analysis will sometimes be the simplest, most obvious method of developing a topic. For example, to explain how an electric motor works you could begin by explaining its parts. To inform readers who know little about personal computers, you would probably discuss the various components one by one: central processing unit, keyboard, monitor, printer, modem; and you would likely further subdivide some of tose units in ordr to explain them.

Analysis is also an integral part of some of the other methods, especially **process** and **cause and effect**.

Organizing Analyses

Once you have decided on **analysis** as your controlling method, you need only find the best order for the various parts and pieces. Usually common sense and logic will be sufficient guides, especially if you keep in mind both your purpose and the needs of your readers; the pieces will easily fall into order. Sometimes, however — especially if your purpose is to persuade — you will want to use what is called "climactic order," saving the largest or most important part for last.

DESCRIPTION (see also pp. 68-70)

Description seldom occurs by itself. It is most often used in support of other methods. Consider using **description** for parts of your project — or possibly even as the main method — if in your earlier planning you found such questions as these productive:

- What is its appearance, etc. (size, shape, sound, etc.)?
- Does it have parts? Of what is it a part?
- Does it change or is it constant?
- Is it similar to something else?
- What is its environment like?

Objective and Subjective Description

Every description needs both an *observer* and *someone or something observed*. Think of these as the ends of a scale running from **subjective** to **objective**. Most descriptions can be placed somewhere on this scale:

observer   object

$\longleftarrow\!\!\!\longrightarrow$

(subjective)   (objective)

If you focus on the object or scene itself, independent of your feelings, the description will be objective. Write objective descriptions when your purpose is mainly to impart information, for example in a technical report. If your purpose calls for not only the details of an object or scene but also, or even primarily, your feelings about it, write a more subjective description: select the details you want to include or emphasize, and use metaphors and other emotionally coloured language.

Organizing Descriptions

Order the parts in a way that reflects the arrangement in space of the object or scene. Maintain a consistent point of view by showing the object or scene either (a) as it would appear from a fixed point in space or (b) as it would appear to an observer moving around or through it.

For objective description, this method works well:

1. Begin with a brief overview of the object or scene.
2. Develop it analytically; divide it into its parts.
3. Discuss each part in turn in as much detail as your purpose requires. A long or complex description could devote a paragraph to each part; in a shorter, simpler description, a sentence for each may be enough.

Subjective descriptions often use a similar layout, but by their nature they are more flexible, depending on the particular emphases the writer desires.

Project 3-a

Describe an area you know well — for example, a small town, a local park, the neighbourhood you live in, where you work, where you spend your summer holidays. Include both natural and human-made features (for example, as they contrast or harmonize with each other). Work from direct observation if you can. Use the point of view of an observer walking through the area, and organize your material accordingly.

Project 3-b

(a) Write a one-paragraph physical description of someone you know. Write from observation if possible (do you have a willing roommate?), or perhaps from a good full-length photograph. Be entirely objective, as if you were writing a police bulletin on a missing person or a wanted criminal. Organize by moving from head to foot.

(b) Write another one-paragraph description of the same person. This time let subjective impressions and personal knowledge colour your description and guide your ordering of details. What is your purpose? Who might be your readers?

NARRATION (see also pp. 70-71)

In writing whose purpose is to inform, narration, like description, is most often used in support of some other overall method. Sometimes a brief narrative — an anecdote — is a good way to begin a paper. But you can use narrative as your overall method. For example, you could narrate a personal experience to illustrate some point about life. And when you are explaining a process or a cause-effect relation, you may decide to use a narrative as a frame.

Consider using **narration** to develop all or part of a paper if questions like these have stimulated your thinking:

- What happened?
- Did it happen?
- How did it happen?
- What happened there?
- When and where did it happen?
- What was it like?

We've all grown up listening to, reading, and telling stories, and we all appreciate a well-told story, one whose details and proportions and pacing all contribute to its overall effect. If you are using narrative to present or illustrate a point, the same principles apply as when you are telling a story primarily to interest or amuse.

Organizing Narratives

Since narration recounts events or actions as they progress through time, *chronology* is central to it: first this happened, and then that, and then something else. But you can step out of a strict chronological sequence by using a brief flashback or flash-forward, as movies sometimes do. Something out of sequence — for example an exciting bit of action at the beginning of a narrative — can grab a reader's attention.

Let your purpose, your thesis, and your sense of your readers guide you in selecting and ordering incidents. If you use a narrative as an example, choose details that add up to something genuinely exemplary.

Project 3-c

(a) Write a short narrative (about 200 words) using strict chronological order, with the climax — the punch line, as it were — in the final sentence.

(b) Write another narrative about the same event, but start somewhere in the middle and use a flashback to bring in the earlier events. Again, save the climax for the end.

(c) Try it again, beginning with the climax: how can you keep readers interested once you've revealed the climax?

EXAMPLE AND ILLUSTRATION (see also p. 71)

Using examples and illustrations is perhaps the most common and powerful method of explaining something. Because our minds depend on sense perception, we need specific and concrete examples (see pp. 147-48). When you provide such examples of an idea, you show that you understand it. And so will your reader.

If questions like the following have helped you generate ideas, and especially if your topic is partly abstract or general, consider developing all or part of it by providing **examples and illustrations**:

- What is it? What does it do? What is it used for?
- When and where, in what contexts, does it appear?
- What are the main kinds of it?
- What is it like?
- What are some examples of it?
- What has been said or done about it?
- Does it occur in any common phrases or proverbs?

Examples provide a straightforward way to support or clarify a point. But keep in mind two criteria as you go through your material looking for examples to use:

1. Use *enough* examples, but not too many. Consider the following, from a student's paper on meaning in language:

> There is no "natural" name for anything except as speakers of a language determine it, and then it seems right and natural to speakers of that language only. For example, the concept "girl" is rendered as *Mädel* in German, *fille* in French, *ragazza* in Italian, and *korizzi* in Greek. All five words designate equally a female child.

Here the writer decided to cite four examples, besides *girl*. He could have listed dozens more, of course, but that would have become tedious. One or two examples may not be enough to support his statement well. Three or four is a good number. But if your purpose is to clarify — to explain or define — rather than to support or demonstrate, one well-chosen example or illustration may be enough.

2. Use *representative* examples. Choose examples that are representative rather than unique or unusual. If you know three people who own a certain kind of car, but only one of them likes it, it would scarcely be fair to cite that one driver as proof that people like the car.

Organizing Examples and Illustrations

If you use a series of examples or illustrations, decide on the best order for them. Think about your *purpose*: it is your best guide. And remember that *climactic order*, putting the strongest last, is usually effective. If you aren't sure, try out different arrangements to see which will work best, or perhaps try them out on a friend.

CLASSIFICATION (see also p. 72)

As you narrow a topic, you may find it useful to consider it

1. as a member of a class (badminton as one of many sports), or
2. as a whole made up of a number of similar parts (the various kinds of racquet sports).

When you deal with an object or idea in terms of other things like it, you are **classifying.** When you classify,

1. you move from a group of similar individual items to a category or class that contains them; or
2. you move from a whole (a class or category) to its parts (the group of similar items that it contains).

Suppose your planning notes include a list of twenty movies. You could classify them to see what groups they fall into and what that might lead you to discover about them. But if you began with the large topic "movies," you might divide it into its parts, "kinds of movies," and then fill up each group or sub-class with the names of individual movies.

But say you've classified movies into three categories: adventure, comedy, and drama. If the topic is still too big, you might decide to focus on adventure movies alone. You could then reclassify the ones in that category by dividing them into subgroups according to some other criterion. Or you could *analyze* the adventure movie itself as a form: break it up into its parts to see what makes it tick, and use the individual movies in that class as specific examples.

If you find questions like these especially productive, consider developing your topic by means of **classification**:

- What kinds of it are there?
- Can it be divided into groups of similar things?
- What other things are like it?
- Is it a member of a larger class?
- What goes with it?
- Does it have an opposite?
- In what contexts does it occur?

Classifying with a Purpose

When you create categories or adopt those of other people, think about your *purpose*. What questions do you want your categories to answer? What problems do you want them to solve?

For example, suppose you want to discuss television programs and have narrowed your topic to "violence on television." In order to examine television violence and say something about its nature and distribution, you try using the standard classification of television fare into sports, adventure, drama, comedy, news, and children's programs. But when you start taking notes, you find significant levels of violence in some programs in each category. So you decide to create a new set of categories that will better serve your purpose. For instance, you could classify programs according to their different kinds or degrees or amounts of violence, or according to whether their violence is accidental or intentional, or whether it's mere sensationalism or essential to the plot or news report.

Suppose that you want to give tourists an idea of the kinds of restaurants in your area. Rather than list and categorize every eatery in town, you could list the main kinds (Oriental, French, Italian; seafood, steak; vegetarian; etc.) and include a *representative* sampling of places under each heading, perhaps with an added note about price for each place. If you think your readers will be more concerned about cost than about the kind of food served, you could classify the restaurants according to price and add a word or two for each to indicate the kind.

The scheme of classification you use depends on your *purpose* and on how you perceive the needs of your *readers*.

Organizing Classifications

As with examples and illustrations, if your classified items or groups don't immediately fall into a good order, look for connections between the parts. Try putting major ones first and last. Above all, think about how the purpose of each part relates to your overall *purpose*.

Project 3-d

(a) Choose one of the following headings and list ten to fifteen specific items that belong under it. Then classify the items into at least three categories. Include a statement explaining the purpose of the scheme you use.

winter sports	musical instruments	game fish
forest products	university courses	automobiles
religious faiths	computer programs	video movies

(b) Then try reclassifying the same items according to another scheme, for a different purpose.

DEFINITION (see also pp. 72-74)

Without definitions, communication between writers and readers would often break down. You define a key term or concept at the beginning of a paper to ensure that your readers understand you. If you need to use a technical term, you define it for them. Sometimes you will use definition as the overall method of development — for example in a paper that answers a thesis question like "What is 'responsible government,' anyway?" or "What do we mean when we speak of 'privacy' in our daily lives?"

If you find such questions as these useful in generating material, consider using **definition** to develop all or part of a writing project:

- What is it? Does it exist?
- Of what is it a part?
- When and where (in what contexts) does it occur?
- What is it like, or unlike? Does it have an opposite?
- Will my readers know this term?
- What information is there from etymology?

Organizing Definitions

If you are using formal definition (see pp. 72-73), first specify the larger class or *genus* to which an item belongs and then point out the features that distinguish it from other members of that class. If you are defining by analysis or by listing members of a class (see p. 73), you need only decide on the most effective order for dealing with the parts or listing the representative members.

COMPARISON AND CONTRAST (see also pp. 74-77)

The mind delights in finding similarities in things that seem different and differences in things that seem alike. You **compare** and **contrast** when you want to show how one person, object, or idea is like or unlike another. If questions like the following have been productive, consider using **comparison and contrast**:

- What is it like? What is it unlike? Is it unique?
- Is it like or unlike several other things?
- How does it differ from similar things?
- Does it have an opposite?

Comparison can help you explain something by showing that it is like something else. For example, you could explain the concept of interest by comparing it to rent: just as one returns a rented tool to the shop and pays for its use, so one returns the principle of a loan to the lender and pays interest for its use. Because the features of similarity are quite close, the comparison clarifies the point nicely.

You use **contrast** to explain how one thing differs from another that is already familiar to your readers. Contrast works best when there are enough similarities to make a difference revealing; it wouldn't help much to contrast two things that are different in almost every way. There would be little point, for example, in contrasting airplanes with bicycles as means of transportation. But you could usefully contrast airplanes with ships or trains or buses.

Using Appropriate Features

When comparing and contrasting, *choose appropriate features*. Think of your purpose. We've all heard that you can't compare apples and oranges. But you can if your purpose is to discuss their desirability as snacks or as parts of a colourful centrepiece. If you compare cars to find out which would provide the best and cheapest transportation, you would consider such features as weight, age, model, and fuel economy; colour would be irrelevant. But for deciding which to use in a photograph for an advertisement, colour would be important.

Similarly, *concentrate on major features*. Don't waste your own or your readers' time on trivial similarities and differences.

Project 3-e

Provide a few features of similarity and difference for two of the sets of items below. For each set, specify your purpose and the basis of comparison or contrast.

Example: hiking and skiing. Purpose: to argue that hiking is better. Basis: features of cost, convenience, and pleasure. Similarities: Both are healthful outdoor activities. Differences: Hiking is less expensive, can be done in any season and in more places, and offers better opportunities for companionship and enjoying nature.

> the St. Lawrence and the Rhine
> hunting and fishing
> country music and rock music
> rowboats and canoes
> poker and gin rummy
> reproducing sound on tape and on disc
> Mexican, Chinese, and Greek cuisines
> hockey, soccer, and rugby

Organizing Comparisons and Contrasts

Basically your have two choices of arrangement:

1. item by item
2. feature by feature

For the first, you discuss all of one item and then all of the other. If you're comparing only two items, however, this method may lead to a "broken-backed" discussion that reads like two separate pieces. You may also have to repeat in the second part points you've already made in the first.

It's often smoother and more economical to discuss the two items feature by feature. For example, you might want to explain that two cameras are alike in their viewfinders, lens mounts, and rewind mechanisms but differ in their lenses and film-speed indicators. Using this method, you could first discuss the viewfinders of both cameras, then their rewind mechanisms, then their lens mounts, then their film-speed indicators, and conclude with the differences in their lenses, the feature you think most significant.

Here is how the two methods look in outline form:

Item by Item	*Feature by Feature*
Camera A	Viewfinders
Viewfinder	Camera A
Rewind mechanism	Camera B
Lens mount	Rewind mechanisms
Film-speed indicator	Camera A
Lens	Camera B
Camera B	Lens mounts
Viewfinder	Camera A
Rewind mechanism	Camera B
Lens mount	Film-speed indicators
Film-speed indicator	Camera A
Lens	Camera B
	Lenses
	Camera A
	Camera B

If you have six or more features to discuss, however, the feature-by-feature method may lead to what is called the "ping-pong" effect. For such topics, the item-by-item method may well be clearer. The item-by-item method may also be better when you are comparing more than just two items. Test the strengths and weaknesses of each method before you decide which one to use.

Project 3-f

List three pairs of topics that can be developed by comparison and contrast. Here are some examples:

> home-cooked food and restaurant food
> trail bikes and mountain bikes
> living with parents and living on your own
> hydro and nuclear power
> team sports and individual sports

But draw on your own experience. For each pair you list, construct a tentative outline. If possible use the feature-by-feature method, but try one with a large number of features (say 9 or 10) and use the item-by-item method.

PROCESS (see also pp. 77-78)

Some topics are obviously processes: baking a cake, repairing an engine, travelling from one city to another, studying for an exam, osmosis, the conduct of a battle. Clearly process analysis is the logical way to develop such topics. But you may also find it useful to consider something seemingly solid and constant as part of a process. How about a tree, for example, or a pond? An insect? A golf ball? A stone? Is an individual human being a process or a thing? A machine may embody a process, but might it also be part of some larger process?

If questions like the following have prompted your thinking about a topic, consider developing all or part of it by examining one or more of the **processes** involved:

- What happens? Where does it happen?
- Why does it exist or happen?
- Who is associated with it?
- How or for what is it used?
- Does it move? How does it work?
- Is it part of a larger process or system?
- Does it include any sub processes?
- What if it didn't exist or happen?

You analyze a process to explain how something works, or how something happens or happened. If you write instructions to tell a reader how to do something, you analyze a process. Processes that lend themselves to such analysis consist of a series of steps, actions, or events leading to a specific result. You can use process analysis to explain mental actions (how to solve a quadratic equation), physical actions (how digestion works, how to clean a squid), historical events (how Hitler came to power), or natural occurrences (how a hurricane forms).

Organizing Process Analyses

Plan carefully. Whether you are giving instructions on how to wax skis or describing the events that led up to the Russian Revolution, be extra careful in your planning.

First analyze the process into separate steps that you can discuss in order. If there are many small steps, group them into a number of more easily manageable stages. Try to keep the number of main divisions between three and seven (see the note on p. 58).

For instructions, follow chronological order, and don't skip over any steps. For such topics as historical events, it is possible to use flash-backs and flash-forwards, as in other narratives (see pp. 46, 70). If the topic is a large or complex one, you may have to do some telescoping or condensing of time and events; but try not to falsify the facts or to omit anything important.

Project 3-g
Write a brief set of instructions on how to do one of the following. Be prepared to have your instructions read out to someone who must then try to follow them.

blowing up a balloon	setting up a chess-board
peeling an onion	using a manual can-opener
playing tic-tac-toe	drawing a rhombus
applying mascara	putting on a jacket

CAUSE AND EFFECT (see also pp. 78-80)

As with narration and process analysis, when you discuss causes and effects you work with relationships across time. A narrative tells *what*, process analysis shows *how*, and cause-and-effect analysis explains *why*. If you have found questions like these promising, consider developing some or all of your project by loking for **causes** and **effects**:

- Why does it exist or happen? Who or what causes it?
- What does it cause? For what is it used?
- Can it be changed?
- Is it a part of a larger process?
- What if it didn't exist or happen?

Much of what you learn in school has to do with causation: the results of mixing nitric acid with zinc; what caused the Crimean War; the effect of climate on a culture; why cities are declining in population, and what the political and economic consequences will be. And you devote a good deal of time outside the classroom to matters of causation: why the car keeps stalling; how the strike will affect your holidays; why a friend was sarcastic; the causes of a sudden headache.

But people aren't always right about causes. Sometimes what they think was a cause is only incidental, or maybe it is itself only a result of another, more fundamental cause. For example, in what sense is it true to say that lightning *causes* thunder or that a green light *causes* traffic to resume? Further, a number of causes may combine to produce a certain effect, and it may be that all of them must be present for the effect to occur.

Caution: As you examine the possible causes of an event, beware of the *post hoc* fallacy (*post hoc, ergo propter hoc* : "after this, therefore because of this"). Just because one event follows another, the first is not necessarily the cause of the second. You would reject a claim that the amber light of a traffic signal somehow *causes* the red light. But what about the hockey fan who always wears his red hat to the games because his team won the first time he wore it? The *post hoc* fallacy is behind most superstitions.

Organizing Cause-and-Effect Relations

Depending on your purpose and on the nature of your topic and the material you've generated for it, you can

1. start with an effect and try to explain its cause or causes, or
2. start with a cause and try to show or predict its effect or effects.

Just as an effect may have more than one cause, so may a cause have several effects. You could even find yourself dealing with a number of interconnected effects. Or you might find that the best way to treat your topic is to begin in the present, then explore past causes, and then predict future consequences. In any event, the more complex the relations are, the more careful you have to be to keep them sorted out for your readers.

Project 3-h

Some proverbs use figurative language to assert cause-and-effect relations. Choose two of those following and state each in non-metaphorical terms, and then comment briefly on its adequacy as a statement of cause and effect.

Where there's smoke, there's fire.
Pride goeth before a fall.
Too many cooks spoil the broth.
A stitch in time saves nine.
Spare the rod and spoil the child.
A rolling stone gathers no moss.
Still waters run deep.

FORMULATE A THESIS STATEMENT

> **Note:** If you have already formulated a thesis statement, check it again after deciding on your methods of development. You may now be able to refine it further.

A **thesis** is an assertion, a statement about your narrowed topic, one that the ideas you have generated will explain or support. Your thesis is the *controlling idea* of your project, the point that it is all about. You may not formulate your thesis fully and finally until you've done two or three drafts, but you need at least a preliminary or tentative one to guide you as you draft and revise. If gathering material and narrowing the topic have led you to a thesis **question**, now turn it into a **statement** that answers that question. If you have already decided what your strategies of development are going to be, it should be even easier to formulate a thesis statement.

Here for example is the thesis question for a student's paper on the topic of "Politics and the Olympic Games":

> Can the Olympic games be kept free of politics?

As he continued to examine and sort out his material, the student answered his question with the following statement:

> Despite the efforts of the organizers, politics have strongly affected the Olympic games, notably in recent years in Mexico City, Munich, and Moscow.

This fully formulated thesis offers a specific assertion about the topic and at the same time suggests how the material can be developed and arranged.

The Form of the Thesis Statement

Suppose you have chosen DNA for a topic and have narrowed it to "recent research on recombinant DNA." A thesis developed from this topic might look like this:

> Recent research on recombinant DNA raises serious ethical issues for biologists.

For a **thesis** you want a **statement**, a complete sentence. Try to construct a thesis sentence with your narrowed topic as the subject part and your assertion about it as the predicate part. Here, *recent research on recombinant DNA* is the subject part of the sentence, and *raises serious ethical issues for biologists* is its predicate.

Further, frame your thesis statement as either a SIMPLE or a COMPLEX sentence. Avoid compound sentences (see p. 299). For example, consider this compound sentence: "Recent research in recombinant DNA has been startling; biologists are being forced to re-examine the ethics of their entire field." This sentence won't work as a thesis to set up an outline, because each of its two independent clauses tries to dominate. Rephrase such a statement until you have just one independent clause with everything else subordinated to it; for example: "The startling new research on recombinant DNA is forcing biologists to re-examine the ethics of their entire field." (See also the examples in the preceding chapter, pp. 38-39.)

Project 3-i

Choose two of the following topics, narrow each to something you know about and could handle in three or four pages, and for each compose two thesis statements that suggest different methods of development. (Identify the methods.)

rock bands	student clubs	fashion magazines
sports	the Arctic	cable television
orchestras	computers	a practical education

Project 3-j

Combine each of the following groups of sentences into a possible thesis statement. Remember, no compound sentences.

1.a) Careful planning is necessary for wilderness exploration.
   b) Accidents happen easily in mountainous country.
   c) Rivers claim lives every year.
   d) Winter can be particularly dangerous.

2.a) Canada should be careful about its exploitation of northern resources.
   b) Mineral resources may be less plentiful than expected.

3.a) Students should not neglect their physical health because of the pressure of mental work.
   b) A program of regular exercise or participation in sport is important for students.
   c) One's physical health influences one's intellectual functions.

4.a) Organic foods are usually more expensive than other foods.
   b) Chemical additives in foods can, according to some people, be bad for one's health.

5.a) Kite-flying is a pleasant pastime.
   b) Outdoor activities are healthful.
   c) Kite-flying is an inexpensive hobby.
   d) People usually fly kites in spring, the prettiest season.

ARRANGE YOUR MATERIAL

The methods of development themselves often suggest effective arrangements, as the preceding discussions show. Further, as your thesis statement becomes more specific, it may suggest an effective order, as does the one about politics and the Olympic games just above. The planning for the piece on the exam period went from a thesis question:

> What is the best way for students to prepare themselves for the final examination period?

to a preliminary thesis statement:

> Students can best prepare for the exam period by carefully planning their daily study schedules, including some self-indulgence.

The form of this statement suggests an arrangement for the parts, though what the second part will include isn't yet clear. And the apparent two-part structure is dangerous: having only two parts risks producing a badly split or broken-backed essay; having more than seven parts risks overburdening your reader:

Try to select and organize your material so that your essay has *at least three* major parts and *no more than seven.*

And remember, often the final form of the thesis statement won't come until during revising. Only during work on the second draft did the student finish finding her material and arrive at a final wording of her thesis — and as you see, she avoided the problem of having only two parts:

> To handle the exam period, carefully construct and follow a study schedule, making sure to allow time for enough sleep, proper food and exercise, and a little pampering.

CONSTRUCT A WORKING OUTLINE

Sometimes you may need to postpone this step until you have worked through a draft or two. But if your planning seems sufficient, draw up some sort of outline to help guide you as you draft. A thesis statement orients you; an outline gives you a map to follow. An outline can help

- by indicating clearly where you have to go;
- by breaking a project into smaller units that you can handle one at a time;
- by giving you a sense of the relative proportions of the parts of your project, including which parts are the main ones and which are subordinate, and whether the ideas at each level are themselves coordinate — that is, parallel, of similar importance;
- by letting you see at a glance if you have left out anything necessary or put in anything unnecessary.

With your project mapped out, you can concentrate on stringing sentences together rather than worry about organization.

Caution: DON'T settle on a firm organization too early. You can't be sure a given order is best until you try it. Be prepared to make changes — to shift items around, to add further items, to delete items — as you write and revise, for you will likely continue to discover new material and new approaches. An outline is not a straitjacket.

> STAY FLEXIBLE: change your outline, and even your thesis if necessary, in order to accommodate good ideas that come along as you draft and revise.

A rough outline of the paper on "Politics and the Olympic Games" might look like this:

Three recent Olympics suggest that it is difficult if not impossible to keep politics out:
1. What happened in Mexico City in 1968
2. What happened in Munich in 1972
3. What happened (or didn't happen) in Moscow in 1980

A more detailed outline may also reflect the ways you've chosen to develop your topic. Here for example is a student's outline for a short paper: the main headings show the classification of expenses into three categories, and under each are the examples that will explain it. This is an example of a "topic" outline, using words or short phrases for the various headings and subheadings:

THESIS STATEMENT: Although students are subject to a variety of pressures, the main one for many is financial.
BEGINNING: Work 4 months at low-paying job to support 12 months; part-time work detracts from study.
   I. School expenses
       A. Tuition
       B. Texts
       C. Other (lab fees, supplies)
  II. Living expenses
       A. Housing
       B. Transportation
       C. Food and clothing (usually low priority)
 III. Other expenses (necessary for morale)
       A. Trips home
       B. Entertainment
ENDING: Need for thrift; educational value?

Note: Don't worry about beginnings and endings until after you've written a draft or two. If you have any ideas for them, jot them down, as here — but don't try to refine them now. (See pp. 64 and 95-100.)

Here is another example. For the paper on the exam period, the student eventually constructed this more formal kind of outline, called a "sentence" outline:

> How to Prepare for the Exam Period
>
> T.S.: To handle the exam period, carefully construct and follow a study schedule, making sure to allow time for enough sleep, proper food and exercise, and a little pampering.
>   I. Draw up a study schedule.
>   A. Establish course priorities.
>   B. Be flexible, but firm.
>   II. Don't shortchange yourself on sleep.
>   III. Food: don't forget that the mind needs fuel too.
>   IV. Get some exercise, for both mind and body.
>   V. Self-indulgence: pamper yourself a bit for psychological stability.
>   A. Take breaks.
>   B. Meet friends.
>   C. Go to a movie.

Kinds of Outlines

The kind of outline you use will depend on the kind of project you're working on. A rough list of points may be enough for a small and relatively simple project. But as length and complexity increase, a more elaborate and formal outline is usually a safer guide. But remember: if you construct a sentence outline, DON'T let its apparent completeness and stability keep you from changing it when you get new ideas. Not even this kind of outline should be a straitjacket.

Note: See also Chapter 10, pp. 192-93, for the mechanical and other conventions of outlines.

Project 3-k

Here is a student's topic outline for a short essay. Examine it critically. What are its weaknesses? How would you revise it to make it better?

> T.S.: Strikes in essential public services are harmful to the public.
>   — The postal strike last summer
>   — small businesses ruined
>   — people in remote areas who depend on mail
>   — phones cut off because of unpaid bills
>   — my driver's licence and social insurance card held up
>   — Ambulance workers on strike (but only briefly)
>   — danger of emergencies ignored
>   — affects firefighters and other groups who have to do the work

Project 3-l

This assignment lets you review the principles of planning.

(a) From the following broad topics, choose three and narrow each to two different topics. Specify the readers and purpose for each, and the length of the proposed paper.

travel	summer jobs	surprise
politics	using money wisely	mining
fruit	leisure time	tact

(b) Choose one of the resulting pairs of topics and for each do at least some brainstorming in order to gather material.

(c) For each topic construct two thesis statements.

(d) Designate the principal method of development you would use for each thesis statement.

(e) For each thesis statement, draw up at least an informal outline showing the major divisions. If your proposal is for a longer paper, go to at least one level of subheading. Indicate any secondary methods of development you think it likely you would use for parts of the paper.

CHAPTER 4
Step 4
Developing Your Material:
Writing the First Draft

PLANNING AND DRAFTING

How you write a draft depends partly on the occasion and on your working habits. If the topic is difficult and you have only a rough outline, you can use one or more drafts both to generate material and to find the right form for it. Some writers deliberately use the first couple of drafts as part of their planning: they need to get it all written out so they can see where they are heading. As the English writer E. M. Forster once put it, "How do I know what I think until I see what I say?"

If your planning is virtually complete and you have a detailed sentence outline, drafting will be relatively mechanical. If your notes from the first three steps are generous, you may already have what amounts to a rough draft.

But even with many notes and a detailed outline, you may not fully realize what you want to say or what shape the project is going to take until you've written a draft or two. Always leave the door open for possible improvements.

Slow and Fast Drafting

The first draft is often called a *rough* draft. How rough it is will depend not only on the occasion but also on whether you are a fast or a slow writer. Think of fast writers as *hares* and slow writers as *tortoises*. Some people are hares by nature, and some are tortoises. In the fable the tortoise won because "slow and steady wins the race." But sometimes the fast drafter will win.

Slow drafters seldom leave a sentence untouched. They rearrange, try different words, different punctuation. They delete words, insert new words, then delete some of those. They check spelling and grammar. They like to see one part pretty well polished before they move on to the next.

Fast drafters, on the other hand, don't pause to consider details. However much planning they've done, they treat drafting almost like brainstorming. They don't want anything to interrupt the flow of their thinking. And they know that when they finish a draft, they can take all the time they want for revising it.

These are the extremes. Each method has its advantages. Consider them carefully and try to decide where you are on the spectrum, and where you would like to be.

ADVANTAGES OF SLOW DRAFTING

1. The satisfaction some writers get out of neat rows and well-stitched lines helps keep them going.

2. The discipline of searching for the right word or the right arrangement of words may help you see more clearly what you mean, or that something needs changing.

3. Tortoises who have planned carefully feel that they always know where they are and where they are going. They don't like the sometimes feverish uncertainty of the hare's progress. They will end up with smoother drafts than will the hares. In effect, tortoises combine the steps of drafting and revising — or at least some of the revising: even tortoises should devote careful attention to revising, though their drafts may need less of it.

ADVANTAGES OF FAST DRAFTING

1. As we point out in earlier chapters, the physical act of writing can itself be a process of discovery. Putting words on paper, making sentences about something, often leads to new ideas and insights. You are still discovering material. Stopping to fuss over individual words and sentences may block the flow of new ideas.

2. Hares are often more efficient in the long run, and more open to improvements. Imagine yourself drafting slowly and meticulously. What if you suddenly get a new idea, halfway through the draft, and have to scrap much of what you have so carefully done? If you resist

the change as being too much trouble, you may sacrifice quality. It is easier to change sentences or drop paragraphs if you haven't invested time in polishing them.

3. Many writers get a strong feeling of satisfaction from finishing a draft, a completed chunk of writing, however rough it may be. Such a psychological boost can give you the momentum to carry on with revising.

However you arrive at it, then, and at whatever speed, you need something by way of a draft, something you can apply your revising strategies to in the next step.

HINTS FOR DRAFTING

Getting Started

Most writers know the experience of sitting and staring at that blank first page. The longer you stare the more frustrating it becomes, and the more difficult it is to get those first words down. Here are some suggestions to help you avoid this unpleasant experience:

1. *Review your outline and your notes.* Look for an idea or phrase that you can use as a springboard.

2. *Think of a title.* If you haven't yet thought of a title, now is a good time to try for at least a tentative one. Even if you decide to change it later, it can help now: getting even that small bit onto the white page can start your ideas flowing.

3. *Don't worry about the introduction; write it later.* Beginnings are difficult for most writers. Rather than waste time, skip it and start with the first point on your outline. When you've written a draft or two you will have a clearer sense of your paper; you'll know just what needs introducing. Even if you do get some sort of introduction down at the start, you'll probably have to change it later. But do write down your *thesis*, however stiff and heavy it may be at this point; it may be a good springboard from which to dive into the draft.

4. *Try "free-writing."* Since the act of writing is itself generative, just start writing. Write your title or your thesis statement or the first main heading from your outline, over and over again. This technique is sometimes called "pump-priming." Suddenly things begin to flow. Ideas you didn't even know you had will start pouring onto the page — especially if you've thought a lot about your topic.

Keeping Going

Momentum helps you write. Try to finish your first draft at one sitting. Avoid interruptions. Some suggestions:

1. If you hit a problem, don't worry about it (easier, of course, if you are a hare rather than a tortoise). You can't think of a transition between two major parts? You need another supporting example but can't think of one? Leave a blank space and come back and work on it later. You can't decide between two words? Put them both down and choose between them later. Don't lose momentum.

2. If you get stuck at the beginning of a new paragraph, look over the last two or three. Often you'll find a simile or metaphor you can continue with. Or you may notice a word or phrase that you can repeat; maybe you can set up a contrast. Get your momentum back.

3. If you can't avoid interruptions, do this: When you return to your draft after an unexpected break, read slowly through all or most of what you've written, especially the last paragraph or two. It should help you recapture your momentum and get started again.

4. If you're working on something long, do this: When you take a break or quit for the day or to go to a class, stop where you know exactly what you're going to write next — for example, after a transitional paragraph that sets up the next idea, or after a topic sentence that automatically calls up the rest of the paragraph (see p. 104). When you return, your momentum will be there waiting for you.

Changing Course

Because you know that you will be writing more than one draft, you can feel free to change things as you go along. If you get a new idea, or see a new way of arranging or developing your material, or find a whole new chunk of material to put in — fine: go ahead and make whatever changes you want. You can evaluate them later.

Think of your outline as a road map and of drafting as a journey. You expect to follow the route you have marked on the map. But if as you're driving along you spot something interesting down a side road, feel free to explore it. If it turns out to be a mirage, a digression, you can return to the main road. But if it's solid and stays interesting, keep following it. It could even lead to other interesting and unexpected adventures you would have missed by stubbornly sticking to the original route. You may have to follow the new route all the way to the end before you can be sure, but if it turns out better than the original, stay with it and change your map accordingly.

One of the virtues of an outline is that if you make any changes in it, you will make them consciously. Without a map, you can easily get onto a wrong road without knowing it. But your reader would know.

The Mechanics of the First Draft

How you put your first draft on paper affects the ease and quality of your revising. You have several choices:

- Write in longhand; ink wears better than pencil.
- Type.
- Write in longhand and then type a clean copy for revising.
- Use a word-processor. Many people find writing with a word-processor a comfortable way to compose a first draft as well as to correct and revise. (See **Note** below.)
- Dictate a draft into a tape recorder and then type it or have it typed for a working copy. Dictation usually induces a more natural, conversational tone and sentence structure. Some people also find it easier to get started and keep going if they're talking rather than writing.

Type or use a word-processor if possible. It is easier to work with typed or printed copy than with handwritten copy — easier to see words, phrases, sentences, and punctuation that might need changing, easier to spot spelling errors, and easier to judge where paragraph breaks belong.

Leave plenty of space. Whether you type or write by hand, double- or triple-space. Some writers even quadruple-space. You will probably want to rewrite or insert whole sentences, even paragraphs. For the same reason, leave generous margins all around. The more space, the freer you'll feel to make changes. The space invites improvements, whereas a single-spaced marginless page discourages even small changes.

Write on one side only. You may want to spread out successive pages so that you can look them over. And you can add a long sentence or even a paragraph by writing it on the back and putting an arrow where it is to be inserted.

Note: If you have access to and can use a word-processor, take advantage of it; or if you have an opportunity to learn to use one, it would be well worth your time. These machines are designed to help you revise. With a good program it is easy to make all sorts of changes: to add or delete words and sentences and paragraphs; to move words or sentences or paragraphs from one place to another; to put in or take out punctuation marks or paragraph breaks; to format and reformat your lines and paragraphs and whole documents; and — if you decide you don't like what you've done — to put things back the way they were. And all without having to retype pages.

Project 4-a

Experiment with fast and slow drafting. Write a few short rough drafts to get a feel for how different speeds affect what you do. Find out whether you're a hare or a tortoise or somewhere in between, and whether different topics can call for different approaches. Here are some topics that shouldn't need more than a few moments of brainstorming by way of planning. You can think of others, if you need to.

> something I ate yesterday
> how _____ behaved toward me yesterday
> how I felt when I got up this morning
> my roommate
> my favourite extra-curricular activity
> why I like (don't like) dogs (cats)
> why I watch (don't watch much) television

USING THE DIFFERENT METHODS OF DEVELOPMENT

In Chapter 3 we discuss how to decide which methods of development to use and offer some suggestions about organizing material. Here we briefly discuss the methods further and offer a few more suggestions and examples, as well as some exercises to practise with.

Analysis (see also pp. 43-44)

SYNTHESIS FOLLOWING ANALYSIS

Analysis is breaking something into its component parts. But when you divide something in order to discuss it, your purpose may dictate that you put the parts back together again after explaining them. That is, you'll want to leave your readers with a sense of the whole, not just the parts. You want to restore the unity and integrity of the original. And that means you **synthesize** what you have **analyzed**.

After explaining the parts of a motor, you will at least briefly say something about the motor as a whole and how it functions. After analyzing a government, you will say a few words about it in its entirety. After you analyze a poem to show how it achieves its effects, you will put the pieces back together again so that your readers can appreciate the poem as a whole with enriched awareness. After you analyze a process and discuss the several steps in order, you can end by referring once again to the whole process and its importance or usefulness.

Sometimes this synthesis will be implicit, too obvious to mention. But usually you will want to end with some kind of mention of the original whole by way of wrap-up.

Project 4-b

Write a short paper (500-700 words) based on an analysis of a typical day in your life. Perhaps yesterday will do. Divide the day into its constituent parts as well as you can and use each part as the topic of a section of your paper. (Try to keep the number under seven.) After you've gathered your material, use your notes to help you formulate a thesis statement, and use it to guide you in deciding how to order the parts. End with at least a brief synthesis.

Description (see also pp. 44-45)

OBJECTIVE DESCRIPTION

When you write objective description, your purpose is to inform. Aim for accuracy and economy, as in this passage from an article in *Canadian Geographic*:

> Rattlesnake fangs are hollow and act as dual hypodermic syringes. In their normal resting position, when the mouth is closed, they are folded backwards and up against the roof of the mouth. They are actually movable bone covered by sheaths of skin and have a pronounced curve which aids in penetration (somewhat like a surgeon's suturing needle), a kind of "folding in" once the fang has entered its victim.
>
> (Malcolm Stark, "Rattlesnakes: All They Ask Is a Little Respect," June/July 1986)

The details and language are selected to enable readers to get a clear idea of the fangs and how they work. The metaphors or similes serve primarily to clarify the explanation, not to convey impressions or feelings.

SUBJECTIVE DESCRIPTION

Subjective descriptions are especially useful when your main purpose is expressive or persuasive. Here is an example; the student's feelings about the scene come through clearly:

Stumbling around a shipyard for the first time is both exciting and scary. Everything seems to happen in a daze. Through billows of steam and smoke, black and gritty, erupts a terrifying din. Everywhere metal pounding, grinders screaming, welders snarling. Sparks shoot through the air and land hissing on the ground. Men rush here and there shouting at each other. The motion makes you dizzy. The whole place groans and gnashes. Overhead a crane swings its neck a hundred yards and drops its cargo onto the greasy floor. Men cling to scaffolds suspended from the sides of monster ships. You find yourself up against the wall, hands on ears, searching for a way out of this pandemonium.

The writer has selected and treated his details in order to convey what is called a "dominant impression," that of the apparent demonic madness of the scene.

ADJECTIVES

When writing descriptions, don't overuse adjectives. The above example uses a few descriptive adjectives, such as *scary*, *gritty*, and *greasy*, but most of the force of the passage comes from the specific nouns and strong verbs. In contrast, here is the beginning of another student's description that depends too heavily on descriptive adjectives (shown in italics):

As the school term drew to a close, the *fertile, sandy* soil of the strawberry farms south of town filled with *thick, long* rows of *leafy, strawberry-laden* plants.

POINT OF VIEW

Be sure to maintain a consistent point of view. A good objective description will describe the object or scene as it would appear to most neutral viewers. In a description nearer the subjective end of the scale, the details depend more upon the selective eyes and ears of the writer. Both kinds, however, require you to keep the point of view consistent. Here, for example, is a fairly subjective description; notice how the student keeps her readers oriented as she moves from detail to detail:

Standing forlornly in the centre of the table is a coffee mug. It is mustardy-coloured, with faint speckles of deep brown scattered about the sides. Around the rim is a wide band of chocolate brown where little splashes of colour, which have escaped from beneath the band, drip down the sides like icing on a freshly frosted cake. A splash of brown also runs down the handle of the mug in one bold stripe. As you near the mug and peer into its depths, you can see swirls of coffee-stain etched into the sides — reminders of its long service. Moisture inside and a slight aroma of coffee mark its recent abandonment.

Project 4-c

Select a simple object from among your possessions — a chess piece, a spool of thread, a golf ball, a rosebud, a spoon, a pencil, an eraser, a coin. These are only suggestions; the point is that the object should be something small and simple so that you can treat it thoroughly in a short space. First write an *objective* description of it (as you might for a science lab), and then write a *subjective* description of it (specify your readers and purpose), each in a single paragraph of not more than 200 words.

Narration (see also p. 46)

Consider *pacing and proportion*. Pace your narrative so that it focusses on what is important for your purpose. Slow down for important details. Omit whatever isn't genuinely needed. Especially, make sure the beginning is not too long and detailed. An overdeveloped beginning can make the rest seem to rush to the end and cause readers to miss the point.

If you use a flashback or flash-forward, don't mystify or otherwise annoy your readers by staying with it too long: get to — or back to — the main chronology fairly quickly.

As with description, maintain a consistent point of view.

NARRATION COUPLED WITH DESCRIPTION

Narration and description are often so closely bound together that you can't tell where one leaves off and the other begins. In any event, it's rare to find a narrative without at least some description in it. Notice how the student intertwines narration and description in the following paragraph:

> Usually I run down to the beach when the tide's out. Something about the smooth wet sand always makes me run faster: I can feel my feet sink and hear the water spurting out from beneath my sneakers. Sometimes I take along Cyrano, the neighbours' mongrel. He thrashes wildly through the surf and tries to eat the foam. He's a crazy dog at the best of times, but at the beach he goes nuts. Once I reach the gun tower, I turn around to survey our footprints — or pawprints — staring back at me. By this time Cyrano is exhausted from his battle with the breakers, and lies down in the sand for a pant and a slobber. After a five-minute rest, the two of us head home, Cyrano dying of thirst from swallowing too many salt-water waves, and me secure in the knowledge that this beats pumping iron in the gym any day.

Project 4-d

Write a narrative of personal experience: tell about something memorable that happened to you when you were much younger. Mix in as much description as you need. Aim for between 500 and 1000 words (two to four typed pages).

Example and Illustration (see also p. 47)

When you use good examples, your readers will be confident that you know what you're talking about. For instance, think how you feel about the writer's authority as you read the following passage:

> In every society children model their behaviour on that of their elders, particularly their parents. Bushman children in the Kalahari desert play elaborate games to help them develop the agility and stealth they need in order to be successful hunters later in life. In Beirut, Lebanon, children constantly play war games that reflect with bizarre accuracy the horrors they see around them. Clearly, children's games are often rehearsals for future real-life situations. The tragedy, as they almost always discover, is that the reality is a lot less fun than the fantasy.

GENERAL TO SPECIFIC TO GENERAL; DOWNSHIFTING

The preceding passage also illustrates another of the ways people often think and write: note how the student begins with a generalization, then provides specific examples to clarify and support it, and then moves on to a further generalization based on those examples. Much effective writing swings back and forth like this from general to specific and back to general again. Examples give life and nourishment to generalizations; generalizations give order and coherence to discrete facts.

A related technique, called "downshifting," moves from the general to a series of increasingly specific points.

Project 4-e

Compose a paragraph of five to seven sentences that develops one of the following topics by moving back and forth from general to specific. Try to both begin and end with general statements, with the specifics in the middle.

owning a cat	a recent hockey game
a local newspaper	where you eat lunch
leisure time	foreign languages
formal clothing	crossword puzzles
rock musicians	horror movies

Try it again, using downshifting.

Classification (see also pp. 48-49)

When you have established a principle of classification that suits your purpose, make that purpose clear to your readers. In the following paragraph, for example, the student writer clearly sets out the principle of classification she discovered for her own use of language:

> As one who is basically the same on nearly all occasions, I find it difficult to draw real distinctions among my various identities and the way my language presents those roles. However, though my language doesn't change much, I have discovered three main areas of difference: (1) in what I say, (2) in how I say it, and (3) in what I don't say. Curiously, the language I *don't* use best reflects the identity I am assuming at the time.

This introductory paragraph ends by focussing on the part of the classification the writer intends to emphasize.

Project 4-f

Look around your room or neighbourhood and make a list of

seven ⎰ green / square / tasteful / tasty / small / broken / crossed ⎰ things

Write a paper about the things in one of these groups. OR write a paper about some things that turn up in more than one group. In the first or second sentence, indicate the purpose for your classification.

Definition (see also pp. 49-50)

KINDS OF DEFINITION

Formal Definition

The most familiar kind of definition, the one we're used to seeing in dictionaries, depends on our awareness of things as belonging in classes. It specifies the larger class to which an item belongs (the *genus*) and then provides the features that distinguish it from other members of that class (the *differentiae*). Philosophers and scientists and lawyers favour this kind of defining because it is both clear and precise. Here, from a student's paper, is a passage that uses formal definition:

Erosion is a geological process wherein natural forces wear away
landforms. For example, wind and waves from the sea gradually wear
away the face of a cliff. Or wind, rain, changes in temperature, and
glaciers cause mountains to erode.

The larger class here is "geological process"; what differentiates erosion
from other geological processes includes "natural forces" which "wear
away landforms." The writer then clarifies the definition by providing
examples.

Defining by Pointing

Sometimes the simplest way to define something is to point to it:

"What's a carburetor?"
"That thing right there" — pointing — "on the engine."

In writing we can come close to this kind of pointing by using careful
description. Dictionaries do something similar when they provide pictures or diagrams as parts of definitions. And so can you, for example
when you're writing an advertisement or giving directions or defining
something technical or scientific.

Defining by Context

You can sometimes define a term by locating it in its context, in a
framework already familiar to your readers. If for example your readers
know what the Mesozoic era is, you could define the Cretaceous period
as "the first of the three periods of the Mesozoic era."

Defining by Analysis

Often you can define something in terms of its parts and how they work
together. For example, you could partly define a carburetor this way:

A carburetor is a device on an internal combustion engine, controlled
by the throttle, that by means of a valve mixes air with a spray of
gasoline to produce a vapour that will ignite in the cylinder.

Defining by Listing Members of a Class

One way to define the grammatical term *article* is to point out that the
class *article* has only three members: *a, an,* and *the.* You could define
the provinces of Canada by listing their names. But you can seldom
be exhaustive; usually you can list only representative members of a
class. For example, you could give an idea of the grammatical term
preposition by pointing out that "Prepositions are words such as *into,
of, on, among, about, under.*"

Defining with Appositives

One of the most common and useful informal methods of defining is
to provide an **appositive**, a word or phrase renaming or further
identifying a term. Appositives are often set off with commas, like this:

Nathan, *the man in charge of the committee,* reported that no money
was left for the project.

But you can also enclose the appositive in parentheses or sometimes even dashes, like this:

> In narrative and descriptive writing, avoid an overdependence on adjectives *(words that modify nouns)* and adverbs *(words that modify verbs, adjectives, and other adverbs).*

This technique is smooth and efficient. It's often a good way to define technical terms without making readers pause to absorb a sentence or two of definition. (Note that under "Formal Definition," above, we reverse this method, putting the technical terms *genus* and *differentiae* in parentheses.)

Negative Definition

Sometimes you can help define something by pointing out what it is *not* — useful when you are trying to correct a mistaken view. For example, in a piece on gardening you could point out that the Jerusalem artichoke is not really an artichoke but rather a kind of sunflower. (Note that this operation also uses both classification and comparison and contrast.) Negative definition is seldom enough by itself; use it along with other methods.

Project 4-g

Briefly define five of the following terms. Use a different method or combination of methods for each. Do not merely copy out dictionary definitions. (Does etymology help with any of these terms?)

ansate cross	lute	rhombus
chapati	Marilyn Monroe	riot
comedian	metronome	surd
conifer	mitre	transitive verb
green	mountain	twilight
heat pump	prime number	winch

Comparison and Contrast (see also pp. 50-52)

If comparison and contrast is your overall method of development, keep your eye on three things as you work your way through your draft:

1. The features you are using: are they as appropriate and important as you thought earlier? Don't hesitate to scrap or replace any that raise doubts in your mind as you try to work with them.

2. The method of organization you chose: is it working out as well as you thought it would? If you have misgivings, try the other method to see if it works better. (See pp. 51-52.)

3. Similarities and differences: which are turning out to be more important for your purpose?

Here, from George Woodcock's *Canada and the Canadians*, is an example of a passage using comparison and contrast:

> Thus the pattern of man's relationship with the land in Canada, though it appears to have changed radically, is fundamentally little altered. Mechanical developments mean that far fewer men are occupied in the fields, woods and mines, and one's impression that the land outside the cities is emptier than before is not erroneous: 1,100,000 men worked on Canada's farms in 1931 as against 650,000 in 1961. But in balance Canada's well-being is still dependent on raw materials rather than on skills, and even in the eyes of its planners the sophistication of its technology is still no more important than the continued confrontation of the wild land that will bring into use its vast untouched resources of water power and find a way to exploit the mineral wealth that lies under the Barren Land of the far north and the icy islands of the arctic.
>
> (Toronto: Macmillan, 1970), p. 119.

Project 4-h

In a paragraph or two compare and contrast the items in one of these pairs (note that you will also be defining):

fear and paranoia	precision and pedantry
envy and jealousy	design and scheme
pride and vanity	economy and frugality
banal and boring	crass and coarse
boor and lout	moral and ethical

COMPARING WITH METAPHOR AND ANALOGY

Metaphor (see also pp. 35-36)

When you express similarities figuratively rather than literally, you are using **metaphor.** "That wasn't a hockey game; it was a street riot." The speaker doesn't mean that the police had to be called in to restore order but that too much roughing and fighting spoiled the game.

The power of metaphors lies partly in their linking of two things not usually thought of as similar. The metaphor in the preceding paragraph links street riots and that particular hockey game as examples of the abstract idea of violent disorder. An explicit comparison would identify the common abstract feature: "The game was spoiled by roughing and fighting, like a street riot." A metaphor allows you to leave it unexpressed.

A further strength of metaphors is that they offer you another way of making your writing more specific and concrete (see pp. 147-48). Note for example how in the following sentence a student uses metaphor to make a point more forceful because more concrete:

> Many economic and cultural developments have been forged in the automotive foundry of North America.

Caution: When you use metaphors, be careful not to combine them incongruously. Here's a student's "mixed" metaphor:

> The road ahead was studded with pitfalls.

Studs stick up; pitfalls are holes. The many dead or dying metaphors in the language — the kind that so often turn up as clichés (see pp. 152-53) — can trip you up if you aren't careful, as they did the politician who said this:

> If this idea ever catches fire, it will snowball across the land.

Analogy

When you continue a metaphor (or simile) over several sentences or even paragraphs, you build up an **analogy**. In the following passage, the writer uses the analogy of jugglers to help explain and clarify his point about the work teachers do:

> The people who work in public schools are almost not teachers at all. They are jugglers. They have a variety of different functions, many of which are in conflict with one another. The success of the teacher depends on the ability to keep all of the balls in the air without dropping any. The capable "teacher" is on the ball—professional failure may mean only that the teacher has dropped the ball.
>
> (Anthony Burton, *The Horn and the Beanstalk: Problems and Possibilities in Canadian Education* [Toronto: Holt, 1972], pp. 30-31.)

When you use analogy, cite several points of similarity. The more points (within reason), the better the analogy. And be sure to cite appropriate, significant similarities: pointing out that both radishes and tomatoes are usually red wouldn't help clarify or establish anything about the food value of either. (See also p. 209.)

Project 4-i

Select one of the topics in column A below and see how many points of comparison you can discover in drawing out an analogy with one or more of the items in column B. Then try it again with a different item from column A.

A	B
applying for a loan	baking bread
courtship	a fast-food restaurant
Middle East diplomacy	a horror movie
modern art	portaging a canoe
provincial politics	a rock concert
psychological testing	snowmobiling
writing a letter of apology	a video-game arcade
being nice to one's elders	cabinetmaking

Process (see also pp. 53-54)

As with narration, a process analysis explains events that follow one another in time. Here for example is part of a student's explanation of how trees are turned into paper:

> The pulp operators blow the chips into vats, called digesters, which are huge pressure-cookers not much different from the ones used at home, only much larger, sometimes ten to fifteen storeys high. In the digester, the chips are mixed with strong chemicals that break them down under pressure and high temperatures, separating the cellulose fibres from the natural turpentines, resins, and other substances that grow together to make a tree in the forest. The cellulose, which is what paper is, is screened out and the rest of the material is burned as fuel in huge boilers that generate the steam for the pulp process and electricity for power. The method used to screen the cellulose reclaims the chemicals so that they can be used again and again, resulting in minimal waste.

WRITING INSTRUCTIONS

The preceding paragraph explains how something *is done*; readers aren't meant to go out and do it themselves. When you write instructions, however, telling a reader *how to do* something, you're also analyzing a process. You're familiar with the basic features of instructions; the process is laid out step by step, and the verbs are imperative:

> Next insert Tab A in Slot B.
> Then stir the sauce briskly over low heat.
> Turn left at the light and drive three blocks.

Much of this book, since its main purpose is to explain the steps in the process of writing, is developed by process analysis.

If you're writing a set of instructions, follow these steps:

1. Write the introduction. State your purpose, and include any necessary background information or theory (for example, list any necessary equipment).

2. List the steps in order. Don't omit any, even if you think they're obvious.

3. Develop each step. (This is the body of your paper.) Try to put major steps in paragraphs by themselves and sub-steps in sentences by themselves.

4. Write the conclusion — perhaps a brief summary, or an evaluation of the results; or remind your readers of the importance or usefulness of the process you've analyzed.

Project 4-j

Write a paper of 500-1000 words explaining how to do — and enjoy — something people used to do, but now rarely do, such as churning butter, harnessing a team, making root-beer, dancing a waltz, making soap. These are only suggestions; write on a topic that genuinely interests you.

Project 4-k

For readers who know nothing about the game (suppose they are from Mars), explain how to play and do reasonably well at one of the following: badminton, racquetball, checkers, Frisbee, pinochle, croquet, Parcheesi, backgammon. Aim for between 1000 and 1500 words.

Project 4-l

Use an extended analogy (a paragraph or two) to explain one of the following processes to an audience of ten-year-olds:

inflation	pruning trees	how atoms combine
digestion	photosynthesis	using a telephone
osmosis	rocket propulsion	reed instruments

Cause and Effect (see also pp. 54-55)

As we say earlier, cause-and-effect relations can be complicated and therefore hard to handle. As you work through your draft, check your analyses for clarity, accuracy, and effective organization. For example, are you primarily moving from cause to effect or from effect to cause? Should you be? Here are some other specific things to look out for:

• Don't mistake a minor cause or a coincidental circumstance for a major cause.

• Don't go too far back in your tracing of causation. (Depending on your cosmology, everything *can* be traced back to either the Big Bang or the Creator.)

• Don't claim *A* as a cause of *B* if both *A* and *B* are parallel effects of some other cause.

From his book *Basin and Range,* here is a passage by John McPhee. He wanted to know how gold gets into mountains before it leaches out into creeks. He was aware that the old-time prospecters knew it was associated with quartz. His account follows:

> . . . gold is not merely rare. It can be said to love itself. It is, with platinum, the noblest of the noble metals—those which resist combination with other elements. Gold wants to be free. In cool crust rock, it generally is free. At very high temperatures, however, it will go into compounds; and the gold that is among the magmatic fluids in certain pockets of interior earth may be combined, for example, with chlorine. Gold chloride is "modestly" soluble, and will dissolve in water that comes down and circulates in the magma. The water picks up many other elements, too: potassium, sodium, silicon. Heated, the solution rises into fissures in hard crust rock, where the cooling gold breaks away from the chlorine and—in specks, in flakes, in nuggets even larger than the eggs of geese—falls out of the water as metal. Silicon precipitates, too, filling up the fissures and enveloping the gold with veins of silicon dioxide, which is quartz.
>
> (New York: Farrar, 1981), pp. 32-33.

Project 4-m

Examine the following passage from a paper that deals with parents overindulging their children. In your judgment, has the writer adequately sorted out and presented the causes and effects in such circumstances?

> Many parents try to make up for the material things that they lacked in their own childhoods by constantly giving to their own children. In fact, they are only reliving their own adolescent years through the eyes and feelings of their children. But they give too little attention to the adverse effects of this overindulgence. Many children raised in such circumstances become pompous, selfish adults, who have not felt the gratifying experience of sharing or the rewards of their own accomplishments. How much better it would be for parents to cut down on giving, thus granting their children a purpose for using their own initiative, and thereby aiding independence.

Project 4-n

Write a short piece (about 500 words) analyzing one of your own superstitions. For what reasons do you persist in it? Or, if you think you are free of superstition, try to explain why — but expect to be challenged, for few people are without at least one or two small superstitions. (For this paper, avoid the obvious ones having to do with ladders, black cats, and the number 13.)

Project 4-o

For a paper of about 1000 words, choose one of the topics below and examine the causal relations involved. Apply the principles of cause and effect carefully. Keep your line of reasoning clear, and make the account lively and interesting for a reader who may be skeptical.

Why jazz (rock, punk, country) is increasing (decreasing) in popularity.
Why I chose to continue my education.
Why there are fewer (more) jobs in the field of _____.
Why more money is spent on _____ than on _____.
Why movies are better (worse) than they used to be.
Why I sometimes neglect my studies.
Why I chose to leave _____.

Project 4-p

In a paper of about 1000 words, explain the events that led up to some crisis or turning point in your life. Note that you will be analyzing both *process* and *causes and effects*.

CHAPTER 5
Step 5
Revising

When you finish writing the first draft, you turn to the most important step in the writing process: **revising**. As you plan and draft, you no doubt also do some revising: you change a few things, you add a few things, you delete a few things. Now you turn your full attention to revising.

Some inexperienced writers — even some relatively fast drafters — feel that they're nearly done when they finish the first draft. All that's left, they think, is a little polishing and proofreading. Some also seem to think that having to revise is a sign of weakness, a result of failing to get it right the first time. But revising is much more than mere proofreading. And it is not a curse visited upon poor writers; rather it is a blessing, a major opportunity to improve the quality of a piece of writing. As Canadian author and editor Robert Fulford puts it, there are three rules to writing: "Rewrite. Rewrite. Rewrite."

Here is a rough timetable that will work for most writing projects. The proportions will of course differ on different occasions. For example, if you are assigned a writing project whose topic and purpose and development are already laid out, you will spend less time planning. But don't cut time from revising.

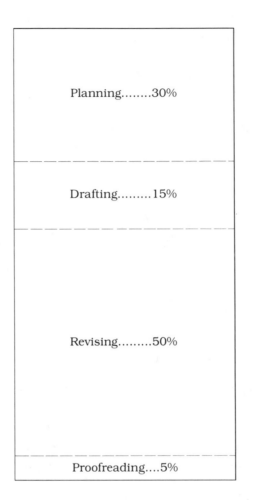

Planning........30%

Drafting.........15%

Revising.........50%

Proofreading....5%

Practical hint: When revising, don't blot things out so that you can't read them. Just draw a single line through whatever you change, so that you can still read it. Later on you may want to change it back, or lift a passage and use it elsewhere. If you blot it out, you've lost it.

THE STAGES OF REVISING

Don't try to revise everything at once. Even experienced writers make several sweeps through their drafts, focussing on one thing at a time. Some revise a dozen or more times. You should make *at least* these four separate sweeps:

Sweep 1: the whole essay and its paragraphs
Sweep 2: sentences — clarity, economy, vigour
Sweep 3: words and phrases — clarity, economy, vigour
Sweep 4: punctuation

You can seldom deal with one of these wholly apart from the others. But in each sweep, *concentrate* on *one* of them.

> Chapters 6 through 10 constitute a HANDBOOK to guide you in performing those sweeps effectively. Use them carefully.

Cooling-off Period

Sometimes it's useful to read through a draft right away to see how it "feels." But don't try to do much with it yet. Usually it's better to put it aside for a while before you begin revising. When it's fresh in your mind, you can't be objective about it; you're too close to it to see it well. Let it cool off for a couple of days — longer if possible.

A SAMPLE PAPER: BEFORE AND AFTER

To illustrate the importance of revising, here is a student's draft of a paper. Its modest purpose is to convey the feelings of the writer during the events she narrates and describes. Finding material was easy: she could call on memory and select the details she needed. Straight chronological order fit her purpose. Her outline would be a simple list of the main details: the setting, the wind, the water, the lightning and thunder, the aftermath. The draft went smoothly, and after a little tinkering, everything seemed settled. Here is how her draft read at that point:

The Sudden Storm

(1)   One day last summer during a peaceful evening, we were relaxing, reading the mail, when a storm came. The sun suddenly disappeared as if it's switch had been pulled. A roll of thunder superseded the laughter of children outside. At first we didn't pay any attention, for thunder storms are a common occurence during Ontario summers. This one had its own ideas, however.

(2)   Now, by the window, I am suprised by the velocity of the wind; evident by the helpless flailing of the Lombardi Poplars next door. These trees were at the mercy of the wind. I was certain they'd be snapped in half or totally uprooted at any second. My next realization was that the lawn was under an inch and a half of water. A muddy torrent was rushing down the slope of the lawn past our windows. Where was it coming from; how deep would it get? Could it get into the house?

(3)   The river kept coming and the rain continued to pelt. At that moment the sky was lit up by lightening and the building shook from resonating claps of thunder! They were now right over head. This display was repeated several times in rapid succession. I felt exposed near the window, as if the lightening was looking for someone to strike. As I retreated back to the saftey of the room, the next blow struck and the lights went out.

(4)   As we sat listening, afraid of what might occur next, the thunder became slowly more distant untill it was inaudible. Then the sun burst forth, and the children returned to their games. The birds sung a thankful tune and hopped about the lawn looking for worms. That peaceful calm of a summer evening had returned. The storm was over. The only reminder was the debris scattered about the lawn where the water had left it as it disappeared back into the earth.

Some inexperienced writers might leave it at that. Others would at least proofread and catch the ten spelling errors and the problem with tense in the second paragraph. But this student cared about her writing. She had saved time for thorough revising. After letting the piece cool off a while, she returned to it and went through it several more times, looking not only for errors to correct but for other ways to improve it. She found several. At the end of the process, she presented this version:

A Summer Storm

(1)   It happened last summer on a peaceful evening, which began like any other in July. We were relaxing, reading the day's mail, when the storm hit. The sun went out like a turned-off light, and the rolling thunder took over from the laughing taunts of the neighbourhood children. At first we paid little attention; thunderstorms are a common enough occurrence in Ontario summers. But this was something different.

(2)   Now at the living room window, I was surprised by the wind's velocity: the towering Lombardy poplars next door flailed helplessly. I was sure that any second they'd be snapped in half or uprooted.

(3)   I suddenly realized that the lawn had disappeared under an inch and a half of water. A muddy river was torrenting down the slope of the lawn past the window. Where was it coming from? How deep would it get? Could it get in the house?

(4)   The rain kept pelting and the river kept coming. Then for a moment the sky whitened with lightning and the house shook from the resonating claps of thunder, now right overhead. This display was repeated several times in quick succession, like a string of firecrackers. I felt exposed at the window, as if the lightning were seeking someone to spear. And just as I retreated into the safety of the room, the next blow struck and the lights went out.

(5)   We sat listening, fearing what might happen next; the thunder became slowly more distant, until it was no longer audible. The sun burst forth as quickly as it had vanished, the children returned to their games, the birds sang a thankful tune while reaping the harvest of worms; the calm of a summer evening had returned. The only reminders of the storm were a styrofoam cup and a few bits of paper strewn about the lawn where the departing water had abandoned them.

The earlier draft (proofread carefully) would please many instructors. They would pass it, with some suggestions for improving the style. But writers who would stop at that point would not be carrying the process of writing to its end. This writer spent about 70% of her time on revising. The result was something she could present with confidence. And instructors would be likely to reward her for it.

Project 5-a

Go through the two versions with care. Try to answer the following questions about some of the changes:

1. Why is the new title better?
2. How is the less abrupt opening sentence an improvement?
3. What can you say about the changes in the punctuation of the opening paragraph?
4. What is the effect of combining the sentences in the opening paragraph?
5. Why is the final sentence of the opening paragraph more effective in the revised version?
6. Why do you think the writer broke the original second paragraph into two?
7. Comment on the changes in diction in the new paragraphs 2 and 3.
8. In what way is the first sentence of the new paragraph 4 an improvement over the earlier version?
9. Try to justify the following changes in the revised paragraph 4:
   a. *was lit up* —> *whitened*
   b. *rapid* —> *quick*
   c. *looking for* —> *seeking*
   d. the new connective *and just* at the beginning of the last sentence of the paragraph
10. Try to justify the following changes in the final paragraph:
    a. dropping the initial *As*
    b. *occur* —> *happen*
    c. *debris* —> *a styrofoam cup and a few bits of paper*
    d. *The storm was over* —> *of the storm*

The writer made several other changes. Try to account for them. Do you think each an improvement? Why or why not?

Project 5-b

Do it yourself. Write a brief description — 250-350 words — of a scene vivid enough that you remember it in some detail. It can be a simple scene or event; it needn't be something cataclysmic or monumental. Avoid melodrama. Try to evoke in the reader the kind of feelings you had at the time. Use as much narrative as necessary. And *revise carefully.*

TONE AND STYLE

Throughout the writing process, but especially during the several sweeps of revising, you will be concerned with the way you present yourself, the way your readers perceive you. Or think of it as how your readers will *hear* you.

By the time they leave high school, most people have learned to adapt their speech to the occasion. They know which **tone of voice** to use for which subjects and which listeners. And by listening to the tone of voice, most people can tell how a speaker feels about the topic of conversation and about them as listeners.

Similarly, experienced writers have learned what **tone** to adopt for a given occasion. A letter to a close friend that you dash off while on holiday will have a tone quite different from that of a note of condolence to a co-worker who has lost a close relative.

The term **style** refers to the selection of language used to convey such tones. Different styles convey different tones. The letter to a friend would no doubt use a lively conversational style, whereas the note of condolence would require a more sober, perhaps even formal style.

CONTROLLING YOUR STYLE

Experienced writers almost instinctively adopt a style appropriate to the occasion. And as you learn how to control your style consciously, you can guard against inappropriate tones and you can alter a dominant tone for a special effect. For example, in the chatty letter you could use bits of formality in a humorous way; in the note of condolence you could decide to use a touch of colloquial style so as not to sound too distant and stuffy.

As you revise a piece of writing, stop and think now and then about the tone you want to adopt and maintain. Here are a few simple ways to control your style:

To make your style **More Formal**, use		To make your style **More Informal, Colloquial**, use
bigger, less common	WORDS	shorter, simpler, more everyday
less	COLLOQUIALISM, SLANG	more
fewer	CONTRACTIONS	more
less	*YOU* and *I*	more
longer, more complex, more variety of kinds	SENTENCES	shorter, simpler, less variety of kinds
longer, more complex	PARAGRAPHS	shorter, simpler

Note that the distinction between formal and informal is not a matter of *better* or *worse*, but simply of *difference*. The best style on any given occasion is the one that will best accomplish your purpose. There are times when a colloquial style is far more effective than a formal one.

Just as you can control the relative formality of your style, so can you control its intricacy and liveliness. In a note of condolence, for example, you would want to avoid anything fancy. But in a sports column you'd probably want your style to be both colloquial and lively.

To make your style **Quieter, Sober, More Subdued**, use		To make your style **Livelier, Fancier, More Poetic**, use
quieter, less lively	VERBS	more vigorous and vivid
more	*BE* and *HAVE*	less
less specific and concrete	NOUNS	more specific and concrete
fewer, less variety	MODIFIERS	more, and more variety
fewer	METAPHORS	more
fewer	SOUND PATTERNS	more
less	RHYTHM	more
less	PARALLELISM and BALANCE	more
less variety	SENTENCE LENGTH	more variety

Most technical, academic, and public prose uses a moderate style. It avoids the extremes both of flat, dull sobriety and stiffness and of excessive liveliness and intricacy, just as it avoids extremes both of ponderous formality and of street-corner slanginess. Usually you will aim for a moderate style, about midway between the two sets of extremes. But whenever you want, you can use these techniques to adjust your style either way on either scale.

Project 5-c

A particular style is often appropriate to a particular topic, of course. But sometimes a topic can be handled in different ways according to the circumstances. In the following three paragraphs a student demonstrates how a single topic can be treated for three different kinds of occasion. Examine the techniques the writer uses to change the style. What kinds of publications could these different pieces appear in? Does the purpose change along with the change in readers? Try your own hand at something similar.

Automotive Dependency: A Change in Attitude

Automobiles form an integral component of North American life. Such a pervasive automotive society has developed around the expanding use of these individual transportation units that it would be difficult to imagine modern North America without the ubiquitous motorcar. Many new economic and cultural developments have been forged in the automotive foundry of North American society. The list includes motels, drive-in theatres, drive-in restaurants, drive-through banks, and even drive-in churches. The zenith of the automotive age occurred in the mid-twentieth century. In the 1950's and 1960's parking lots and freeways, both engendered by the automotive revolution, became synonymous with general economic progress. Even today some younger members of society revere particular models and devote a great deal of time to their maintenance and restoration. But in 1973 an event occurred that began to alter the automotive mentality of North America: the increase in the price of world crude oil. Presently a new attitude towards automobiles appeared. Gone were the days of luxurious but inefficient automobiles. North American society began demanding efficient, more compact, and higher quality automotive products.

Thinking Small

Cars are an important part of North American society. We all rely on them to a large extent as our primary means of transportation. Try to imagine what life would be like without our horseless carriages. Difficult, isn't it? For our social and economic structure has developed around the use of the automobile. Motels and drive-in banks, restaurants, and movie theatres are all examples of the automotive culture. During the 1950's and 60's the parking lot became a symbol of progress. In the USA billions of

dollars were spent on massive interstate freeways that web
throughout the country. Some young men even go so far as to
worship some particular models as if they were gods. But
unfortunately (or fortunately?) all this may be coming to an
end. The price hikes in world oil that occurred in 1973
have dramatically changed attitudes toward cars in North
America. Where bigger, faster, flashier was once the norm
for automotive design, people started looking for smaller,
better built, and more efficient cars.

No More Big Wheels

     In North America cars rule. What would we do without
them? We'd be up the creek, that's what! We depend upon
our wheels for almost everything we do. We travel from
motel to motel, eat at drive-in restaurants, bank at
drive-in banks, and even worship at drive-in churches--in
sunny, funny California, anyway--all because of the boom
in cars. In fact the whole continent's daily life
revolves around these beasts. This motor madness has
gone so far that some guys make a particular model like a
'Vette or a Mustang their golden calf. The seas of
blacktop called parking lots and the thousands of miles
of U.S. interstate freeways became symbols of progress in
the 50's and 60's. But the bubble burst in 1973 when gas
prices shot up. This changed everybody's feelings about
our four-wheeled friends. Where once we all wanted
snarling, gleaming gas-pigs, now we're crying for
econo-boxes.

> **Note:** Chapters 6 through 10 include "marking
> symbols" in the margins beside discussions of
> specific points. Instructors may use these
> symbols on papers they return for correction and
> revision. If you revise carefully, you should catch
> errors and weaknesses before you hand a paper
> in. (A complete list of the marking symbols is on
> the inside of the back cover.)

The Handbook

CHAPTER 6
Revising the Whole Paper and Its Paragraphs

THE WHOLE PAPER

When you start revising in earnest — either right after finishing the rough draft or after a cooling-off period — concentrate first on the large matters. Here are some questions to help you focus on the paper as a whole:

1. Unity: Are all the parts relevant to your purpose?

u

The parts may all be good in themselves, but if one of them doesn't contribute to your purpose, it weakens the whole. Suppose you're trying to persuade people to drive smaller cars. You can point to such advantages as lower initial cost, lower operating cost, easier handling and parking. But if you know a lot about cars, you could get carried away and overload the paper. Some data about fuel economy and braking distances and repair bills would be in order; but statistics about displacement, carburetion, and torque might confuse readers rather than impress them. If you distract them from your main point, you weaken your case.

2. Have you left anything out?

Put yourself in your readers' place. Read your draft as they would. Check for assumptions that they may want explained. In the rush of drafting, did you slight any points? For example, when explaining a process you know well, you may have left out a step that is obvious to you but that would be missed by someone unfamiliar with the process. Have you used any technical terms that need defining?

Did you leave any gaps so as not to break the momentum of drafting? Fill them in now. A transition between parts? A figure or date or other fact you left to look up later?

3. Are your points accurate and sufficiently explained?

You may find that you put in as fact something you now find questionable. Check it, and correct it if necessary, or explain it enough to keep your readers from questioning it.

You may even discover that a part of your discussion no longer makes sense. This is a common experience: something that seemed clear while you were drafting is no longer clear. Rethink the point, find out what went wrong, and rewrite it. Maybe add an example or two, or a diagram or table or chart to clarify a complex explanation. If you can't restore it to clarity, get rid of it.

4. Are your points in the best order?

Is the arrangement of your material as effective as you thought it would be when you decided on it? Is your opening point sufficiently interesting? Is your closing point sufficiently climactic? Or perhaps you discovered a new idea while drafting and put it in. Check its effect on the whole. If it disturbs the flow or changes the emphasis on other points, you may have to do some rearranging.

5. Are the main ideas sufficiently emphasized?

Position is one way to get emphasis; others are repetition and proportion. For example, you may decide to repeat a point toward the end, both to emphasize it and to keep your readers oriented. Or you might decide that an important point needs more detail, not just to clarify it but also to keep it from being overshadowed by its surroundings.

Or you might emphasize a point by putting it in a short paragraph by itself.

You might even decide to use a graphic device like a numbered or indented list, or extra white space, or even — in some kinds of writing— lines or boxes to set someting off.

BEGINNINGS AND ENDINGS

When you write a first draft, don't worry much about the beginning or the ending; you're interested in getting the main body of your ideas down. But during the first sweep of revising, draft at least a tentative beginning and ending.

HOW LONG?

There's no rule about how long beginnings and endings should be in relation to the rest of a paper. Even so, some teachers and texts recommend "the five-paragraph essay":

Paragraph 1	Introduction
Paragraph 2	Body, Part I
Paragraph 3	Body, Part II
Paragraph 4	Body, Part III
Paragraph 5	Conclusion

The "Introduction" and the "Conclusion" each take up about one-fifth of the whole, framing three other paragraphs of similar length. There's nothing wrong with this formula if it fits the occasion: that is, if the topic has three main points of equal weight and the occasion calls for a substantial opening and an equally substantial closing. For most of your writing, however, you will find it restricting. Rather than impose such a structure on your material, let the material and the occasion determine the structure.

Think of **beginnings** and **endings** rather than of "Introductions" and "Conclusions." Not all projects need formal introductions and formal conclusions. But every piece of writing needs to begin and end.

Here is a more flexible way to think of how long to make beginnings and endings:

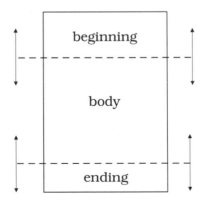

The dotted lines can slide up and down according to the needs of a piece of writing. The ending doesn't have to be the same length as the beginning; as the diagram suggests, the beginning is often about twice as long as the ending.

Beginnings

The beginning can make or break a piece of writing because it is (after the title) the first part readers see. Take some pains with it.

BASIC PRINCIPLES

An effective beginning does at least two things:

- It identifies your topic.
- It involves your readers.

Beyond this, and depending on the occasion, it may also

- state your thesis, and even indicate how you will proceed;
- establish your tone;
- identify the occasion, suggesting roles for you and your readers;
- provide needed background.

Not every beginning needs to do all this. You can often take the occasion for granted, for example with a business memo or an essay examination. But usually you'll want to think about these principles in order to make your beginnings as effective as possible.

Identify your topic, and state all or part of your thesis. Even if the title identifies your topic, the beginning must still do so. And because readers want to know what they're getting into, identify your topic and at least suggest your thesis by the end of the first paragraph or the start of the second.

Establish the tone you intend to use throughout. Think of your beginning as a contract with your readers. You not only announce your topic and suggest your approach; you also commit yourself to a style. Readers expect you to maintain a reasonably uniform tone of voice throughout a piece of writing. You might want to open humorously and then turn serious (though not the other way around — except perhaps for an effective ending), but avoid other major shifts. For example, if you open with formal words and phrases, don't suddenly become informally casual. If you begin with mostly short sentences, don't shift to mostly long ones later.

We don't mean that you have to write with a monotonous sameness of style throughout. You can vary your style, even shift your tone dramatically now and then, for interest and emphasis. But generally stick close to the base-line you establish at the outset.

Identify the occasion; suggest roles for yourself and your readers. If it isn't clear already, let your readers know why you are writing and why they should be reading. In a sense you're offering them a role to play. They honour the contract by accepting the role and continuing to read. (See pp. 23-24).

Arouse your readers' interest. Even if you have a guaranteed audience, you still want them to be interested in what you write. A good title can spark interest, but that is mainly the job of the beginning. Some suggestions:

• Arouse curiosity (but don't puzzle readers too long; for example, provide any necessary background information fairly quickly, and define unusual or technical terms).

• Point out the importance of the topic (that is, its importance for you and your readers).

• Open with something concrete and vivid; or at least get specific as soon as possible.

• Begin concisely; don't waste your readers' time.

• Avoid opening with a string of long sentences; consider starting with a two- or three-word sentence, or with a long sentence followed by a short one.

KINDS OF BEGINNINGS

Short papers usually have short, direct beginnings. Longer papers can have — or even need — longer, more elaborate ones. A twenty-five page paper may use an "introduction" of two or three paragraphs. But unless circumstances require otherwise, use shorter, relatively direct beginnings.

Here are some effective ways to begin:

• Directly state your thesis or purpose.

• Set up an opposing idea that you can then refute.

• Open with a general statement and then gradually narrow it until you state your thesis in specific terms.

• Define one or more key terms in your topic or thesis.

• Provide some historical or factual background, or a setting for your discussion, or (for a report or a research paper) a summary of previous work on the subject.

• Open with a quotation or proverb related to your topic.

• Ask a question that will arouse your readers' curiosity. Or use a series of questions leading to your thesis. Sometimes you can put your thesis in the form of a question, one that the rest of your paper will answer.

• Start with a brief narration or description of something to serve as an illustration (a vivid sketch, a lively anecdote, a dramatic incident, a few lines of dialogue).

- Open with a striking or unusual fact or statistic that bears on your topic. Or use a sensational statement, astriking analogy, a dire prediction. But don't prolong or labour it; keep it brief, and let it speak for itself.
- Draw a contrast. For example point out a change ("I used to think so-and-so, but now I think such-and-such").
- Refer to some widely shared attitude or experience.
- Refer to some well-known person or some historical or recent event that you can make pertinent to your topic. But be sure it's one your readers will recognize.
- Use a careful combination of two or more of these kinds.

BEGINNINGS TO AVOID

- Don't start too far back. If you're writing about modern sports cars, don't start with the invention of the wheel. Above all, avoid the formula "When man first...." You can of course open with a *brief* reference to something in the past, for example by way of contrast or analogy.
- Don't use the overworn "dictionary" beginning ("Webster says" or "According to Webster" or "The dictionary says"). Put definitions in your own words and direct them toward your topic ("Altruism, the habit of being unselfish, of thinking first of others, is becoming rarer, especially among people packed into large cities.")
- Don't introduce a quotation with the limply passive "It has been said that...." Say who says it: "Many high-school kids these days say...."
- Don't devote your entire opening sentence to an obvious fact ("Many people these days find it hard to make ends meet." "Brian Mulroney became Prime Minister in 1984." "Peanut butter is rich in protein."). If you want to begin with such a fact, make it *part* of a statement, perhaps of your thesis: "More and more adults are discovering that peanut butter is rich in protein."
- Unless you're following a prescribed format, for example in some scientific or other report, don't begin by telling your readers what you're going to do: "In this essay I will discuss three aspects of the computer revolution." Instead, do it; find a more direct way: "Nearly everyone agrees that computers are changing our lives. But they don't agree about three potentially serious problems."
- Don't apologize ("Although I am no expert on the Russian Imperial court in the 1850's and will probably do a poor job of explaining it...."), and don't complain ("Since I must try to make sense of the difference between type A and type E bonds in order to satisfy this

assignment...."). What role do such openings ask readers to assume? What reader would want to continue reading?

- Don't burden your readers with an overlong beginning. Such beginnings sometimes result from trying to write a formal "Introduction." Sometimes they result from warming up, shadowboxing, as a way of getting ready to begin; sometimes discarding a first paragraph will let you find your true beginning. If your draft has an overlong introduction, rethink your plan, for you may have mistaken for introductory material what should be part of the body.

Endings

First impressions are important, but final impressions are even more important. The closing words are what readers take away with them. A strong ending won't save a weak paper, but a weak ending can ruin an otherwise strong paper.

BASIC PRINCIPLES

An effective ending accomplishes the following:

- It completes the contract made by the beginning.
- It conveys the "sense" or "feel" of an ending.
- It leaves no questions to be asked.
- It keeps readers interested until the final word.

Sometimes you can convey a sense of completion with a shift in tone, a slight heightening or lowering of style. And though endings usually should be strong, you can sometimes be just as effective by ending quietly. Sometimes it is better just to stop when you feel you've said what you had to say; the worst kind of ending is a flat, tacked-on one.

KINDS OF ENDINGS

As with beginnings, the longer and more complicated the paper, the longer the ending it will support or even need. Here are some of the ways you can end:

- Restate your thesis, usually at the beginning of the ending. If the ending is short, it may be little more than your thesis restated, or possibly even stated in full for the first time.
- Answer the question "So what?" To keep your readers from asking such a question, spell out the more important implications of what your paper has demonstrated.
- Summarize the main points of an argument or explanation or the main steps of a process. But be sure your paper is long enough and

complex enough to need a summary: don't summarize a short and easily remembered paper.

PARTICULAR STRATEGIES FOR ENDINGS

Called-for endings: The overall purpose or method of development of a paper often suggests an appropriate ending:

- A *narrative* usually culminates in a climax of some sort.
- An *analysis* often calls for a closing *synthesis*.
- A description of a *process* might end with an evaluation of the process or a re-emphasis of its purpose and usefulness.
- An analysis of *causes* and *effects* could build to a climax pinpointing the main cause or the main effect.
- A *comparison* or *contrast* might end by pulling together the main features of similarity or difference, or perhaps with an evaluation based on the comparison.
- A thesis-*illustration* paper can end with one final important illustration or example.
- A technical *report* might end with a formal summary of the major points or with a set of recommendations.
- A process of *inductive reasoning* leads to a final generalization based on the particulars discussed.
- A process of *deductive reasoning* leads to a final conclusion based on the starting premises.
- An *argument* can end with a call to action, or at least a modest suggestion or recommendation, or just by disposing of one final opposition point (see p. 208).

Frames and echoes: Frequently a beginning and an ending work together to frame a piece of writing. The frame will be more effective if you make the relationship explicit:

- If the beginning includes one or more questions, end by providing the answer(s).
- The echo effect: pick up something from the beginning or even from the title; repeat a word or phrase or sentence or metaphor or analogy or quotation.

Endings with clinchers: Like beginnings, endings can use specific devices to produce a sharp effect. Some go nicely with beginnings to make frames or echoes. For example:

- An anecdote, perhaps referring back to the beginning.
- An allusion, perhaps referring to something in the beginning.

- A quotation or proverb or aphorism, perhaps one that picks up an idea from the beginning. But don't jut tack it on at the end; integrate it into your own sentence, or at least follow it with your own final comment.

- An ironic or otherwise surprising twist, perhaps some kind of sharp contrast or unexpected analogy.

- A question or speculation or prediction that provokes further thought on the topic.

- Something humorous. If the occasion permits, some sort of light touch — a joke, a witticism, a play on words — can make an effective ending. But don't end with a joke if it will clash with the topic or tone; be especially careful about sarcasm, for that can ruin the overall effect by leaving an unpleasant taste in readers' mouths.

ENDINGS TO AVOID

- Don't label or announce an ending as such. Unless you are writing a business or technical report that requires it, don't start your ending with "In conclusion...." or "In summary....." or even "Thus we see that...." In non-technical writing such formulas sound stiff and artificial. You can announce an ending more quietly with a *so* or *then* tucked into the sentence ("The result, then, is clear." "And so it turns out that...."). You could, however, follow a long discussion with something like this: "Several conclusions emerge from these experiments. The first, and the easiest to act on, is...."

- Don't end with an apology or a complaint or with some qualifying remark that contradicts your main point.

- Don't irritate your readers with an afterthought or a minor detail that you couldn't fit in elsewhere.

- Don't introduce wholly new ideas in your ending. Make sure that anything fresh you bring in is linked to or builds on what has gone before.

- Don't end too abruptly. A snappy ending can be effective, but don't jar your readers or leave them dangling.

- Don't *merely* restate your thesis at the end; restate it in a new way, one that incorporates the new light you've shed on it. Similarly, except in a scientific or other report with a set format, don't end with a *mere* summary or a *mere* recapitulation. Respect your readers' intelligence.

- Don't exaggerate. If you've made a small matter clear or proved a small point, don't come on grandly at the end as if you'd done much more (the "ta-TAH" crescendo). Don't claim more than you've accomplished. If anything, be modest. And always be wary of absolutes.

A Note on the Form and Placement of the Thesis

You will almost always want to include your thesis in your paper, but it needn't be in the same form as in the outline. There you wanted a careful statement to use as a blueprint for constructing your essay; a stiff, heavy sentence was appropriate. Now you may want to express it more smoothly.

As for where to put it: You will most often put it near the beginning. Occasionally you may want to put it only near the end; some topics invite this kind of suspenseful technique. Or adopt the most common practice: state it both near the beginning and near the end.

If your thesis has two or more parts, they may appear in different places, for example one near the beginning and one about the middle; the end could tie them together.

Rarely — for example in a piece of pure description or narration — your thesis may not need stating at all.

___

Project 6-a

Examine the beginnings and endings of at least ten pieces from a recent anthology of nonfictional prose. Try to identify what kind each is, what devices or strategies each uses. How many consist of whole paragraphs? Are any longer than one paragraph? Can you always tell exactly where the beginning ends or the ending begins? Do any pieces simply start or stop, with no discernibly separate beginning or ending?

Project 6-b

In dictionaries of proverbs and quotations, find ten that you could use in a title or in a beginning or ending. Try twisting some or using them ironically. For example, could the old saw about pouring oil on troubled waters be given an ironic application in these days of disastrous oil spills? Could you somehow combine two proverbs, for example "He who hesitates is lost" and "Look before you leap"?

Project 6-c

Construct a proposition for a possible argument (see Chapter 11) and write two beginnings for it. Assume that half your readers will be people who don't agree with your position.

Project 6-d

Choose one of the narrowed topics you came up with for Project 1-j or 1-k (p. 27) and write at least five different possible beginnings, using different strategies. Then write a possible ending to go with each beginning.

___

PARAGRAPHS

Imagine trying to read a book or even just an essay that had not been divided into paragraphs. The main purpose of paragraphing is to help your readers through your paper. Revise your paragraphs as much as necessary to bring them into line with the principles discussed in this section.

There are three basic kinds of paragraphs:

1. substantive paragraphs
2. beginning and ending paragraphs
3. transitional paragraphs

Since most paragraphs are **substantive**, most of this section focusses on them.

Substantive Paragraphs

A substantive paragraph develops a single idea. It is built up of smaller parts — sentences — just as a paper is made of paragraphs. Therefore many principles that apply to longer compositions also apply to single paragraphs. For example a substantive paragraph often has a *topic sentence* stating its controlling idea, just as a paper has its *thesis statement.* Here is a student's paragraph; note how the first sentence sets up the general idea that the rest of the paragraph supports with narrative details:

> Gerry Sorenson's form was hair-raising but she managed to capture the Gold Medal at the World Alpine Ski Championships in Schladming, Austria. Excitement (and anxiety) began to build as she leaped over a metre in the air bursting from the starting gate. By the time she had screamed past the ninth gate and gone into her crouch, the crowd knew she meant business. Skis scraping and chattering against the icy slope, she crouched even lower to get up more speed. Exploding over the final jump, she touched down a split second before rounding the last gate, already tasting victory. As she shot across the finish line, her hands flew up in triumph. Another Crazy Canuck had done it.

Paragraph Length

There is no ideal or "correct" length for all paragraphs. A paragraph can have one word or hundreds. It can contain one sentence or dozens. The longer and more formal a paper is, the longer its paragraphs are likely to be, because it will be developing larger ideas than an informal paper. But one reason for dividing prose into paragraphs in the first place is to make it easier to read; you can often improve even formal writing by dividing it into shorter paragraphs.

CHECKING AND REVISING PARAGRAPH LENGTH

Most modern nonfictional prose uses paragraphs of between 4 and 9 sentences and between 75 and 225 words. The student's paragraph above, for example, has 118 words in 7 sentences.

Short Paragraphs

If a paragraph is less than 4 sentences or 75 words long, check to see if it is sufficiently developed. A short transitional or beginning or ending paragraph is fine, but a short *substantive* paragraph may need revising in one of the following four ways:

1. *Develop it further.* Provide more examples to support its controlling idea. Or add a couple of sentences that are more specific than what you've already written.

2. *Combine it with the paragraph just before or after it, or both.* Often a string of short paragraphs needs to be combined under one topic sentence.

3. *Find a home for it in another paragraph.* If it provides only one example, it may have got out of sequence. See if you can fit it in elsewhere.

4. *Delete it.* If you can't develop it, combine it, or move it, you may decide to cut it out altogether. Perhaps it's only a digression: check your outline.

If you decide to keep such a short paragraph, you should be able to justify it in one of these three ways:

1. You want to set off a point in a short paragraph in order to give it special emphasis.

2. The sentence or sentences are unusually long, adding up to over 75 words. (See if you can say the same thing better with 4 or more shorter sentences).

3. You have a special reason for short paragraphs. For example you may want to set off the steps in a process.

Long Paragraphs

A paragraph of 10 or more sentences or of more than about 250 words may be difficult for readers. See if you can divide it into two shorter paragraphs. Try to find a place where a clear break falls—perhaps the beginning of an extended example. If you decide to keep such a paragraph, you should be able to justify it in one of these three ways:

1. It has to be long to develop its single idea adequately; dividing it would destroy its unity.
2. It is long because you want to emphasize the importance of its topic.
3. It has more than 10 sentences because you have deliberately chosen to use a number of short sentences.

The Parts of a Paragraph

THE TOPIC SENTENCE

Many paragraphs begin with a topic sentence that announces the controlling idea, what the paragraph will be about. It helps readers keep track of what's going on. A good first sentence does four jobs:

1. It introduces the main idea of the paragraph.
2. It begins developing the idea, or at least narrows it.
3. It refers to the overall topic of the paper.
4. It provides a transition from the preceding paragraph.

Sometimes a topic sentence can cover two or three paragraphs, especially if it has two or three parts. In a narrative most paragraphs won't have topic sentences.

Sometimes you can make the second or third sentence of a paragraph the topic sentence, or even end with it. Once in a while a paragraph's main idea will be so clearly *implied* that readers can infer it without needing a topic sentence.

Many of the principles and devices discussed under "Beginnings" apply also to paragraphs (see pp. 95-98). Usually you'll begin them with a sentence that identifies the topic and also tells readers what to expect. For example, after a general statement your readers will expect specifics of some kind. After a question they will expect an answer. After a sentence that sets up subdivisions they will expect detailed treatment of those subdivisions.

The Second Sentence

The work of the topic sentence is often spread over the first two sentences of a paragraph. The second sentence partly restates the topic and partly develops it. In the following example, the student sets up her general topic in the first sentence and then uses the second sentence to narrow it to the more specific topic of the paragraph:

> It seems that everywhere we shop today, the pressure is on us to buy, buy, buy. With the high-pressure and subliminal sales tactics that stores use, it is hard for the average shopper to resist the temptation to spend. Slogans such as "Sale—50% off!" and "Limited Time Offer!" often cause us to come home with several unnecessary—and often unwanted—items. The

policy of "buy now, pay later," which most stores are constantly advertising, further encourages this impulse buying. Although you probably don't need or can't afford that cute striped dress, it is so easy to pull a credit card out of your wallet to pay for it. It is easy because you don't have to worry about the bill coming until the end of the month.

THE BODY

The body of a paragraph develops its topic, usually by one of the methods discussed in Chapter 3. For example a paragraph working mainly by **analysis** might have a topic sentence specifying a division into three, and the body would then briefly discuss the three parts:

X has three Y's.
| Part 1 |
| Part 2 |
| Part 3 |

Here are abstract paragraph models for th other main methods of development:

Description
Object
| Feature |
| Feature |
| Feature |

Narration
A story about X
| Event |
| Event |
| Event |

Example and Illustration
Generalization
| Example |
| Example |
| Example |

Classification
Main Heading
| Subcategory |
| Subcategory |
| Subcategory |

Definition
Larger Class
| Distinguishing Feature |
| Distinguishing Feature |
| Distinguishing Feature |

Process Analysis
Main Step
| Substep 1 |
| Substep 2 |
| Substep 3 |

Comparison and Contrast
Feature A
| Item 1 |
| Item 2 |

(If the details are at all complex, the two items can be treated in separate paragraphs.)

Feature B
| Item 1 |
| Item 2 |

Cause and Effect

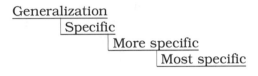

Effect
| Contributing cause 1 |
| Contributing cause 2 |
| Contributing cause 3 |

Cause
| Effect 1 |
| Effect 2 |
| Effect 3 |

The "downshifting" paragraph, moving from a generalization through increasing levels of specificity:

Generalization
| Specific |
| More specific |
| Most specific |

Whichever method or methods you use for a given paragraph, make sure that you do **develop** the paragraph. Few things can weaken a paper as easily as insufficiently developed paragraphs. Make sure your paragraphs *go somewhere.*

THE ENDING

Like a good ending to a whole paper, a good paragraph ending gives readers a satisfying sense of completion. You can try some of the techniques we suggest in the section on endings (see pp. 98-100). For example, one way to end a paragraph is to refer back to or partly restate the topic sentence.

But you don't always have to conclude a paragraph explicitly. Many paragraphs will end naturally, without your having to round them off. It is often better simply to let a paragraph stop rather than to tack on a tail.

Two other suggestions about paragraph endings:

1. *End strongly.* Don't let a paragraph dribble away at the end; avoid final words and phrases that are trivial, vague, or otherwise weak—for example *in a way, among other things, sometimes, generally,* the pronoun *this.*

2. *Don't try to include a specific transition to the next paragraph.* Such a coupling at the end of a **substantive** paragraph deflects its course and dissipates its energy. It is the job of *the beginning of the next paragraph* to provide a transition.

u

Paragraph Unity

Check each paragraph for unity. If a paragraph seems to shift from one topic to another — a sort of broken-backed paragraph — try dividing it into two, each with its own topic sentence.

Readers expect a paragraph to deal with one idea and to develop it by illustrating, defining, analyzing, explaining, or in some other way developing or supporting it. And they expect that idea to be evident, often announced in a topic sentence early in the paragraph. If a topic sentence states a paragraph's central idea clearly, and if that idea controls every sentence in the paragraph, readers will see and feel the paragraph's unity.

Paragraph Coherence

Check to see that the sentences within your paragraphs stick together, cohere. A break in continuity will jolt readers. If a paragraph is *unified,* the sentences will usually stick together of their own accord. They often follow an obvious pattern or movement set up by the method of development: for example, item X-item Y, question-answer, pro-con; general to specific, small to large, simple to complex; chronological order, spatial order; parallel structure.

But sometimes they need help. If you find that a paragraph's coherence needs to be made more evident, here are some ways to do it. You will have used some of these devices in your draft; now decide whether you need any more.

USING TRANSITIONAL TERMS

Many common words and phrases are available to help connect sentences:

To move from general to specific; to introduce examples or details

for example	namely	for one thing
as an example	such as	for another
for instance	that is	specifically
to illustrate	the following	in particular
as an illustration	in fact	in essence

To add a point or introduce a comparison

and	nor	furthermore	similarly
also	moreover	as well	equally
besides	another	as well as	in the same way
too	a second point	likewise	the same as
next	in addition	like	by comparison
or	further	just as	again

To emphasize a point

especially	particularly	more important	certainly
above all	to repeat	most important	surely
most of all	in fact	mostly	primarily
in particular	indeed	unquestionably	chiefly

coh

tr

To restate a point

in other words	in brief	again
to put it another way	in short	to repeat
in simpler terms	in effect	that is

To introduce a contrast or qualification or concession

but	generally	although	to be sure
however	in general	otherwise	no doubt
occasionally	in spite of	yet	doubtless
usually	despite	conversely	certainly
provided	surely	unlike	admittedly
whereas	nevertheless	rather	I admit
after all	nonetheless	if	of course
on the other hand	anyway	unless	in a sense
on the contrary	in any event	even though	granted
in contrast	still	even if	naturally
by contrast	though	all the same	it is true

To show cause or effect

as a result	consequently	thus
because	accordingly	therefore
since	for	so
for that reason	hence	and so
it follows that	then	(*Don't overuse these last two.*)

To show connections in time

at the same time	since	shortly	when
at this time	until	soon	thereafter
simultaneously	formerly	immediately	lately
while	before	in time	subsequently
now	earlier	in the future	last
nowadays	previously	later	at last
meanwhile	hitherto	afterward	eventually
in the meantime	once	ago	ultimately
at present	tomorrow	in the past	final
at times	next	then	finally

To show connections in space

above	across	distant
below	adjacent	in the distance
under	near	in the background
behind	nearby	here
in front of	beyond	there
in the foreground	far	elsewhere
on (at, to) the left	far away	opposite
on (at, to) the right	farther	beside

To show sequence

> first, second, third, etc.
> first, secondly, thirdly, etc. (do not use *firstly*)
> in the first place, in the second place, etc.
> at first, to begin with; next, also, then; at last, finally, at the end

To end

on the whole	final	therefore
all in all	lastly	accordingly
altogether	as a result	hence
so	in short	thus
finally	then	consequently

USING PERSONAL PRONOUNS

If you refer to a person or a thing by name at the beginning of a paragraph, it is natural to substitute pronouns for the name in the rest of the paragraph:

> Emily Carr . . . . She . . . . of her . . . . And when she . . . .
> My family . . . . They . . . . to them . . . .
> The truck . . . . It . . . . on its side . . . .

The continuity is clear. Toward the end of the paragraph you might want to use the name itself again.

USING DEMONSTRATIVES

You can establish strong coherence by using the words *this, that, these,* and *those* to refer back to some earlier point in a paragraph:

> Building the railroad. . . . *That* project. . . . *That* massive achievement. . . .
> The Fathers of Confederation . . . . *Those* men . . . .*That* body of men . . . .

You can use them without a following noun if the reference is close and clear:

> Modern economic theories . . . . *These* are . . . .

But if there is even the slightest chance that your readers won't be sure what the word is referring to, provide a noun that will make your meaning clear:

> That *fact*; This *plan*; These *theories*; Those *ideas*

See also p. 124.

USING OTHER WORDS

Similarly, you can use other common words (indefinite pronouns, enumerators) that refer back to specific points and thereby help readers keep track of your ideas:

some	all	such	either	each
many	several	so	neither	one, first, *etc.*

REPEATING

Repeating key words, phrases, or even ideas is one of the best and most conventional ways to tie a paragraph together. Of course, unnecessary repetition is weak. But if you use a different word just for variety, you are more likely to puzzle readers than help them. But don't *just* repeat. Make sure your paragraph is moving, developing. Don't make the mistake of some student writers: don't repeat the topic two or three times in slightly different words but at the same level of generality. Get specific.

Project 6-e

Examine some paragraphs from nonfictional prose you are currently reading or studying. Point out everything that contributes to their coherence. Identify the techniques. Here is a student's paragraph to start with:

> The most corrupt piece of literature existing today is not the violent comic book or the pornographic novel. Rather, this debauching classic is the woman's fashion magazine. As she leafs through page after glossy page of anorexic models with immobile hair and faultless complexions, even the most confident female is susceptible to feelings of inadequacy. The modern woman is not infallible yet, according to *Vogue* and *Cosmopolitan,* she should appear to be. It is distressing that in a society of emerging opportunities for women, an intrinsic element of their success is still physical beauty. Until this myth is eradicated, the full potential of women will not be realized.

CHECKING OVERALL UNITY AND COHERENCE

You have looked at the whole draft to see if its parts hang together. Now recheck the unity and coherence of the whole piece by looking at *the first sentence of each paragraph.*

• Does it in some way remind readers of your overall topic or thesis? If it does, and if the paragraph develops that opening sentence, your paper will be unified because all its paragraphs focus on some aspect of its overall topic.

• Does it provide some kind of transition from the preceding paragraph? If it does, your paragraphs will stick to each other and the paper as a whole will be coherent.

Even if the first sentence isn't the topic sentence, or states only part of the topic, it will usually still in some way reflect the essay's topic and establish transition.

Transitional Paragraphs

Transitional paragraphs form bridges between the larger parts of a piece of writing. Such paragraphs are usually short—one or two sentences. Unless you're working on a fairly long and complicated piece, you probably won't need any transitional paragraphs; the openings of your substantive paragraphs will take care of coherence.

When you decide you need a transitional paragraph to keep your readers oriented as you move from one large block of material to another, think of it as doing two things:

1. It glances back at what has gone before (perhaps by briefly recapping it).
2. It briefly introduces what is to come (perhaps by stating or restating part of a complex thesis).

Here for example is a one-sentence transitional paragraph from a paper on setting up and stocking an aquarium:

> Once you have all the necessary equipment, the work of setting up the tank begins.

It could have been made the first sentence of the next paragraph, but setting it off by itself more clearly marks the shift from the first to the second part of the process.

Beginning and Ending Paragraphs

As we point out earlier, neither the beginning nor the ending of a paper has to take up a whole paragraph. But it may. In a longer paper, a full paragraph usually works well as a beginning or an ending.

In shorter papers, the beginning or ending is often part of a paragraph that is also developing one of your ideas. An opening paragraph might spend two or three sentences getting the paper going and then start developing your first point. Similarly, a final paragraph might start out as a normal substantive paragraph, developing your last point, and then in the last sentence or two bring both the paragraph and the paper to a satisfying close.

Emphasis in Paragraphs

| *emph* |

You can emphasize a point in a paragraph in one or more of the following ways:

1. **Vary the length of your sentences.** Consider the following:

> (1) The life of a student is hard. (2) It is hard because there is too much work and not enough time. (3) Many people, however, think just the opposite is true. (4) They think students spend most of their time

protesting, carousing, and getting into all sorts of trouble. (5) I must admit that these people are not entirely mistaken, for there are students who come to university solely to have a good time. (6) But I hardly think this characterizes most students. (7) It certainly doesn't characterize those who take their studies seriously. (8) It doesn't characterize me.

The shortest sentences — 1, 6, and 8 — are most emphasized. Sentence 6 is especially strong because of its contrast with 5, which itself is emphasized by being longest.

2. Repeat a word or phrase. Note in the sample paragraph above how repetition helps emphasize the topic, *students* (and *studies*), and how repetition of *characterize(s)* toward the end helps build to a climax in that final short sentence.

3. Put your important points last or first. The end is the most emphatic position in a paragraph, the beginning the second most emphatic. In the student's paragraph quoted above, the last sentence is the most emphasized not only because it is the shortest but also because it is at the end. Similarly, the opening sentence is not only the second shortest but is also in the second most emphatic position. Length and position work together.

4. Make a point in a different style. In the paragraph quoted above, the first and last sentences are emphasized by being the only *simple* sentences (having only one subject and predicate). And note how the following achieves emphasis:

> Nothing pleases me more than to learn that the efforts of our employees are so much appreciated. Many people get in touch with us when they have complaints, but seldom does anyone take the time to say something nice. It's always pleasing to hear from one of our many, many customers who are satisfied. Your kind words helped make my day.

The writer emphasizes the last sentence not only by putting it last and making it short, but also by shifting, in the final three words, from a somewhat formal to a colloquial style, emphasizing the closing touch of personal warmth.

5. Set off a point typographically. You can set off a word or a phrase or even a whole sentence in several ways: You can underline it. You can PRINT IT IN CAPITALS. With some typewriters and word-processors you can *italicize it* or **put it in boldface**. You can set it off with white space before and after, or by indenting it, or even by putting it in a box. But DON'T use any of these mechanical devices often. And when you do use one, use it with care. Be sure the occasion calls for it — for example technical reports, instructions, advertising, bulletins, memos, and the like. These devices occur less frequently in academic essays.

Project 6-f

(a) Write a paragraph of 150-200 words using one of the following, or another one you make up, as an opening topic sentence. Develop the paragraph any way you want.

> Pop singers aren't what they used to be.
> Getting to campus is sometimes more interesting than being there.
> People change as the seasons change.
> Fast-food outlets deserve a better press.
> Changing a tire isn't as hard as you may think.

(b) Rewrite the paragraph so that the topic sentence, revised if necessary, comes somewhere about the middle.

(c) Rewrite it again so that the topic sentence comes last.

(d) Can you rewrite it so that the topic is only *implied*?

Project 6-g

Take apart a paragraph from writing you've done recently. Scramble the sentences, and then let someone try to put them back in their original order. If it proves difficult, it may be a sign that the paragraph's coherence was weak.

Project 6-h

In a paper of about 1000 words, compare and contrast the items in one of the following pairs:

> two modern paintings or sculptures by different artists
> two current films of the same genre
> two reviews of a recent best-selling novel
> two pieces of professional landscaping in your community
> two new cars of similar size and price

Your purpose is to judge relative quality; you will essentially be writing argumentatively. For this project, draw up an outline consisting of the opening sentences for each paragraph just as you intend to write them in the paper. If you need to change your outline during drafting and revising, submit both versions.

CHAPTER 7
Revising Sentences

> The best way to check individual sentences is to read your draft BACKWARD, one sentence at a time. That way you won't get caught up in the flow of meaning from sentence to sentence. You'll be able to inspect each sentence for itself, and therefore be better able to see what needs revising.

Note: For further definitions and examples of the technical terms used in the following discussions, see the Glossary of Terms at the end of the book (pp. 296-308).

MAJOR SENTENCES, MINOR SENTENCES, AND FRAGMENTS

Major Sentences

Major sentences are the standard, normal, everyday sentences that make up almost all writing. A major sentence contains at least a **subject** and a **predicate**, an actor and an action:

    S   **P**
Birds // sing.

Both subject and predicate can be expanded with modifying words and phrases and clauses into a much longer sentence:

> All those lovely little yellow-green *birds* that come from the forest // will *sing* their hearts out on a bright summer morning until we wish they would stop.

Fragments

A **fragment** is a group of words that is *not* a complete unit. Note that the above example ends with six words that include two subject-predicate combinations:

> until *we* // *wish*   *they* // *would stop*

Nevertheless you would not start this group of words with a capital letter and end it with a period, because you recognize that it is a *part* of the larger sentence. It is not complete in itself. If you did set it off it would be a **fragment.** Consider another example:

> He treated his employees badly *because he thought of them more as machines than as human beings.*

The *because*-clause is a **subordinate** or **dependent** clause. It **depends** on the clause that precedes it, and should not be treated as if it were a sentence by itself, like this:

> **FRAG:**   He treated his employees badly. *Because he thought of them more as machines than as human beings.*

The first part of this is a major sentence; it is an **independent** clause. The second part, even though it contains a subject and a verb *(he thought),* is not a major sentence. Like the word *until* in the first example above, the word *because* is a **subordinator** that marks the clause as **subordinate** or **dependent**.

TWO WAYS TO CHECK FOR FRAGMENTS

If you're not sure whether a group of words is a fragment or a regular sentence, try these two quick checks:

1. *Check the subject and predicate.* Here is an example of a fragment that is not even a clause, but only a phrase:

> **FRAG:**   I couldn't understand Rourke's gloom. *He being the player with the most points.*

The writer was misled by the word *being,* taking it for a verb to go with *He.* But it is not a verb. It is derived from the verb *be,* but it is a present participle; it cannot function by itself as a main verb, with a subject.

If you're not sure, see if the word can be changed to go with either a singular or plural subject. True verbs (in the present tense) can:

> *I am* here; *we are* here.
> *She is* here; *they are* here.
> *He feels* happy; *they feel* happy.

The test here is *he being.* Change singular *he* to plural *they* and you'll see that *being* stays the same.

2. *Try moving the suspect group of words.* Fragments almost always get stuck in after the main or independent clauses they should be attached to. When you find something like this in your draft:

> DRAFT: The glaze was flawed by a number of small cracks. *The pot having been fired at too high a temperature.*

try reversing the order of the two parts. When such a phrase comes first, it will clearly be a part of the sentence; you won't want to separate it; you'll join it to the rest with a comma:

> REVISED: *The pot having been fired at too high a temperature,* the glaze was flawed by a number of small cracks.

An earlier example, with a fragmentary clause, would work the same way:

> *Because he thought of them more as machines than as human beings,* he treated his employees badly.

Once you see that the group of words should *not* be detached, you can decide whether to put it before or after.

Minor Sentences

A **minor sentence** differs from a **fragment** in that it is satisfyingly complete. A minor sentence may be

• an exclamation or other interjection:

> *Aha! Nonsense! Surely not! Ouch! Good heavens!*
> *Big deal. Well, well.*

• an answer to a question:

> When do we leave? *Tomorrow morning.*
> How does it make one feel? *Lousy.*
> Now what can be done? *Very little.*
> Why did he treat his employees so badly? *Because he thought of them more as machines than as human beings.*

In this last example, the *because*-clause, which otherwise would be a fragment, is acceptable. Why? *Because it is the answer to a preceding question,* one not more than a sentence or two away.

- **a question**:

  Why?
  Why the gloomy expression?
  Why diet? To lose weight. (Two minor sentences.)

- **a proverbial or other common expression:**

  The more the merrier.
  The sooner the better.
  Easy come, easy go.
  Once burned, twice shy.

Writers who can control style also use other kinds of minor sentences effectively. An example from a student's paper:

> So what's so hard about a job interview? That's the attitude I took, and look where it got me. *Broke.*

And here's how another student began a short paper:

> *Money, money, money.* It makes the world go round.

If the context permits — that is, depending on your readers and your purpose — by all means use an occasional minor sentence for emphasis or stylistic effect. But do so *consciously,* not accidentally. Your instructor might ask you to label a minor sentence to show that you are being deliberate, not careless.

Caution: Check the final sentence of your essay and of each of its paragraphs to make sure it's a major or minor sentence. Sometimes the desire to end a paragraph or a paper with something different or catchy leads to a fragment.

Project 7-a

Revise the following to get rid of fragments. If a word or group of words is an acceptable minor sentence, leave it.

1. What is the book about? How various people express themselves throughout the world.
2. Many people think that three square meals a day is correct. Whereas four or five meals may be more appropriate.
3. The star players get their share of publicity. Except for Alan Taylor, being a player who receives no recognition but is always doing a commendable job.
4. Here the reader sees the young boy as compared to the old man. The innocent youth as compared to the seasoned victim.
5. He asked me why I looked so awful. I told him. Because I stayed out too late the night before.
6. A man's club, until recently, was considered to be the last male bastion. Exclusive. Dignified. Men only. But no more.
7. He was constantly searching. Searching for love and meaning.

8. Most of the students took some time off to enjoy themselves. Although for some homework was their lives and they spent hours every day doing it.

9. People ask what they as individuals can do about the state of the economy. The experts' answer: little or nothing.

10. Attach the end of the tape to the heel on the back side of the blade. That is, on the reverse side of the curve.

11. Once the trial had begun, it continued every day until sentence was passed. The exception being Sunday.

12. You will have a faraway look in your eyes. And a faraway sound in your voice.

13. Each time I go back to the old neighbourhood, it feels more and more like a prison camp. Because wherever I look, all I can see is high chain-link fences.

CLARITY

cl

Following are some of the main problems that can interfere with the clarity of your sentences.

Sense and Nonsense

A sentence should make sense. Read each sentence critically to make sure it does. Here especially a cooling-off period can help: a sentence you've written quite recently will *seem* to say what you meant it to, but after a few hours — or a few days — you may be able to see that it doesn't. For example:

> DRAFT: The trip takes just over a week, depending on how fast one wants to travel.

This could only puzzle readers. A little thought enabled the student to revise it from nonsense to sense:

> REVISED: The trip can take anywhere from five to ten days, depending on how fast you travel.

ALIGNMENT

al

A particular kind of lapse in sense occurs when two elements of a sentence — most often subject and verb — don't make good sense together. Again, such slips are hard to catch: since *you* know what you mean, what you've written will look all right. But look carefully. Consider this sentence:

> The *price* of even a modest house these days is simply too *costly* for most families who are just starting out.

A *price* can be *high*, but it's the *house* that is *costly.* The intervening string of words clouded the connection between *price* and *costly.* But even words that are side by side can be misaligned, as in the phrase *at a young age*, rather than *at an early age.* Here's a student's sentence:

DRAFT: The new defence policy consisted of several changes.

Obviously a *policy* can't *consist* solely of *changes.* The writer found the problem in the verb:

REVISED: The new defence policy *included* several changes.

Project 7-b
Revise the following sentences to get rid of poor alignment.

1. The pace of this scene moves very quickly.
2. The platforms are usually an overestimation of the party's promises.
3. There are five sports in the curriculum from which you can choose which one you want to do.
4. Another method of selling goods is the idea of contests with exotic prizes.
5. Repair bills usually cost more than two hundred dollars.
6. My move to Qu'Appelle was a difficult and transitional period in my life.
7. They are an extreme form of crash dieting which is a large amount of weight loss in a short time.

Modifiers

A **modifier** is a word, phrase, or clause that changes or adds to the meaning of another word, phrase, or clause. The following table illustrates a variety of modifiers:

word or phrase modified		example
nouns:	report	an *excellent* report
	speed	with *surprising* speed
	article	the article *in the paper*
	shed	the shed *that was destroyed*
pronoun:	he	*Giving up,* he . . . .
verbs:	disappeared	*rapidly* disappeared
	would reveal	would *usually* reveal
	had arrived	had arrived *on Friday*
adjective:	difficult	*unexpectedly* difficult
adverb:	slowly	*very* slowly

Generally, modifiers cause few problems. But two specific misuses of them can cause confusion: the **misplaced modifier** and the **dangling modifier**. These you need to guard against.

MISPLACED MODIFIERS

mm

A modifier too far from what it modifies can obscure the meaning of a sentence. A magazine report included the following sentence:

> There were strong calls for an immediate ceasefire in the UN Security Council.

Was there a shootout in the Council? The phrase *in the UN Security Council* belongs either at the beginning of the sentence or after the word *calls.* Here is another example:

> DRAFT: The winter camper is usually active, so wool is good to wear *which can be worn in layers.*

To clear up this awkward sentence, revise it to get the misplaced *which*-clause next to *wool,* the word it modifies:

> REVISED: Because they are usually active, winter campers should wear wool, *which can be worn in layers.*

READ ALOUD. It is easy to overlook this kind of awkwardness unless you read each sentence *aloud.* The trouble might well strike your ear rather than your eye.

Be particularly careful with these little words:

only	nearly	hardly	just
merely	always	scarcely	even

Put them where they will make your intended meaning clear to your reader. In conversation, few would misunderstand this sentence:

> DRAFT: He only suggested three rules for us to follow.

But in writing, unless you actually mean that "He only *suggested* them; he didn't *insist* on them," you should put the word *only* right in front of what it modifies:

> REVISED: He suggested only three rules for us to follow.

Split Infinitives

split

Another kind of misplaced modifier is an adverb that unnecessarily splits an infinitive:

> **SPLIT:** He did his best *to* politely and even charmingly *refuse* their offer.

An **infinitive** is a verb preceded by the little word *to*:

    to refuse   to write   to walk   to control   to see

There's no law against splitting an infinitive. Sometimes it can't be avoided:

    It was impossible *to* more than *guess* at her intentions.

Where else could *more than* go? But usually it's better to keep the *to* and the verb together. Here for instance is a split infinitive that will sound awkward to most readers:

    DRAFT: Once his followers have left, Laertes starts *to* laboriously *strut* toward Claudius.

The modifier will be less awkward after the infinitive:

    REVISED: Once his followers have left, Laertes starts to strut laboriously toward Claudius.

Project 7-c

Revise the following sentences to get rid of misplaced modifiers.

1. These reporters only relate stories that are important to them.
2. This will continue the rapport you have had with her until the end of the sale.
3. His obvious intention was to extravagantly praise his own relatives.
4. All forms of media are biased, in one way or another, closing the door on objective journalism.
5. They discussed building a new church for five days.
6. Vegetation fights and overwhelms Europeans and their attempts to spread civilization throughout the story.
7. We finally found the bracelet she had lost under the bed.

DANGLING MODIFIERS

dm

A **dangling modifier** is a word or phrase (often participial) that either has no word to modify sensibly or doesn't clearly attach to the word it is meant to modify. That is, it "dangles" because it apparently has nothing to hook onto. Usually the writer has the word in mind, but hasn't put it in the sentence. Watch especially for sentences that begin with an *-ing* phrase and that don't name the actor-subject:

    DRAFT: While leaving the house, the phone rang.

The phone left the house? The problem here is that the phrase *While leaving the house* has nothing to modify. It dangles. But in the reader's mind it attaches itself to the nearest available noun, *phone,* producing the humour. You can revise such a sentence in two ways:

1. Either provide the actor (noun or pronoun) for the phrase to modify:

    REVISED: While leaving the house, *I* heard the phone ring.

2. or change the phrase to a clause with the actor as its subject:

> REVISED: As *I* was leaving the house, the phone rang.

Another example:

> DRAFT: Once viewed from every angle, voters get to know the candidates quite well.

Here the phrase *Once viewed from every angle* is meant to modify the word *candidates*. But it still dangles; it wants to attach itself to the noun *voters*, both because that noun is nearer and because it is the subject of the sentence. Again you have a choice of two ways to revise:

1. Either put the right noun first:

> REVISED: Once viewed from every angle, *the candidates* become well-known to the voters.

2. or change the phrase to a clause that won't dangle:

> REVISED: Once *they* have viewed them from every angle, voters get to know the candidates quite well.

Project 7-d
Revise the following sentences to get rid of dangling modifiers.

1. While paying the fine, the clerk laughed and asked me why I hadn't parked across the street.
2. If after watching for two hours, the cow still hasn't given birth, call the vet.
3. Basketball is a very fast-paced and entertaining sport, and by presenting it to the public, there are many advantages.
4. Looking at the slope through the eyes of an inexperienced skier, it seemed impossibly steep and dangerous.
5. By holding on to a kickboard, the leg movements can be learned.
6. Being of more shallow content than night-time drama, I am able to concentrate on the educational message more easily.
7. Once at my mother's house, the view of the city and the ocean is spectacular.

Weak or Ambiguous Reference

ref

which and this
Check your draft to see if you've used the pronouns *which* and *this*. If you have, make sure you've used them clearly. For example:

> DRAFT: Many joggers neglect such things as warm-ups and cool-downs, *which* could be dangerous.

What is dangerous? Most readers will soon figure out that *which* is meant to refer to the whole preceding clause and not just to *warm-ups* or *cool-downs.* But don't distract your readers by making them pause to figure out what goes with what. Often the best way to revise such a sentence is simply to provide the appropriate **noun**:

REVISED: Many joggers neglect such things as warm-ups and cool-downs; such *neglect* could be dangerous.

Or you could get rid of the problem by rearranging:

REVISED: It could be dangerous for joggers to neglect such things as warm-ups and cool-downs.

This

When you find that you've begun a sentence with the pronoun *This,* you can almost always improve matters by either revising to get rid it or at least supplying a noun to make its reference specifically clear. Ask yourself: This *what?* This *fact,* This *idea,* This *program,* This . . . ? (See also p. 109.)

and this

Be particularly wary if you find that you've used the two words *and this* together. For example someone could have written the above sentence this way:

Many joggers neglect such things as warm-ups and cool-downs, *and this* could be dangerous.

At least provide a noun (*and this neglect*). Better yet, revise to get rid of *and this,* for it almost always amounts to loose coordination (see pp. 131-32) as well as weak reference.

it

Even the simple little pronoun *it* can cause trouble:

DRAFT: A person's opinions seldom change. If they do,*it* is usually caused by some disaster.

Some readers would wonder what *it* refers to. The writer had the word *change* in mind, but in the first sentence *change* is a verb, not a noun. Consider your readers, even if you have to add a word or two:

REVISED: A person's opinions seldom change. If they do, the change is usually caused by some disaster.

Project 7-e

Revise the following sentences to get rid of weak or ambiguous reference.

1. Most people seem to believe that federal money will solve any problem; however, this is not true.
2. Flick your wrist forward during the release to give the ball backspin, which sometimes keeps it from bouncing off the rim.

3. The roads were improved by trying to straighten them out; new surfaces were tried to accomplish this.
4. After hundreds of miles of use, road dirt works into the unit which could cause premature wear.
5. Grace Poole is not surprised by his visit, and this is odd because Rochester does not see his wife very often.
6. The highest value in science is objectivity, which enables the public to trust the opinions of scientists.
7. I decided that her heart was in the right place. This was clear because this was the only time she was actually rude to me, this being when I tried to hide my mistake.

Agreement

Check carefully for slips in **agreement**: subject-nouns must **agree with**, correspond to, their predicate-verbs; and pronouns must **agree with** the nouns they refer to.

SUBJECT-VERB AGREEMENT

Make sure that verbs agree in **number** (are appropriately **singular** or **plural**) with their subjects. Be especially careful in the following four circumstances:

1. *When other words — such as a prepositional phrase — come between the subject and the verb:*

    The main *point* of all her recent speeches *is* (not *are*) that we should support the coalition.

The singular *is* agrees with its subject noun, *point*, not with the intervening plural word *speeches*.

2. *When the subject includes more than one noun:*

    The *groom and* the *best man were* (not *was*) an hour late.

Clearly the phrase *The groom and the best man* includes more than one person and requires the plural form of the verb. But don't be confused by such phrases as *in addition to* and *as well as*: they aren't conjunctions like *and*; rather they are similar to the preposition *like*. In the following, the subject is *groom* and remains singular:

    The *groom*, as well as the best man, *was* an hour late.

3. *When singular subjects are joined by "or":* the verb should always be singular:

    Either Sally or her brother *is* going to cover for me.

If only one of the two is singular, the verb agrees with the nearest one:

> Either Sally or her brothers *are* going to cover for me.

4. When a sentence begins with "There" or "Here":

> There *were* still seven *chapters* to read.
> There *are* over thirty *people* in the room.
> Here *are* the *recipes* you asked for.

The subjects (*chapters, people, recipes*) follow the verbs, but the verbs must still be plural to agree with them.

Project 7-f
Revise the following sentences to get rid of errors in subject-verb agreement.

1. The choice of methods for producing young oysters involve two considerations.
2. Recently there have been a flood of little machines.
3. What society does notice, however, are the people who do not conform.
4. The next major component to stretch are the thighs.
5. The number of people who answered the ad were staggering.
6. A musician thus learns the patience and dedication that goes into mastering a new song.
7. When a bank of these circuits are required, the overall size becomes a problem.
8. The negative view of human nature or the sense of hopelessness about society and life vary from author to author.
9. Change and progress is pushing us ever onwards.
10. The two proposals are basically similar, in that neither are aimed at lowering taxes.

PRONOUN AGREEMENT

A **pronoun** must agree with the word it refers to or stands for — its **antecedent**. Be especially careful with such pronouns as *everyone, no one*, and *anyone*. The element *one* indicates **singular** number. You would never use a plural form of a verb with one of these, and say something like *"Someone are* at the door." Similarly, when you refer to one of them with a pronoun, it too must be singular:

> *Everyone* who wasn't satisfied got *his* (not *their*) money back.

Just as you wouldn't say or write "Everyone who *weren't* satisfied," so you shouldn't use the plural *their*.

But see the next section, "Avoiding Sexist Language."

Project 7-g

Revise the following sentences to get rid of errors in agreement between pronouns and their antecedents.

1. If everyone told the truth about their feelings, society would break down.
2. *The Canadian Food Guide* outlines the amount of carbohydrate one should have daily for their age group.
3. They cannot trust their wives and therefore become suspicious of her behaviour.
4. Every citizen has a right to privacy as long as it does not cause harm to themselves or others.
5. If there is one thing people hate, it's an editor who thinks they know everything.
6. A woman becoming an engineer or a doctor or an executive isn't unusual anymore, for they are all around us.
7. A state of self-confidence is derived from one's ability to accept their deficiencies.

Avoiding Sexist Language

In the example above, using the pronoun *his* to agree with the antecedent *Everyone* raises the problem of sexist language, as does the *his* in the following sentence:

DRAFT: A writer should avoid sexism in *his* use of language.

Fewer and fewer readers these days are willing to accept the masculine pronouns (*he, him, his*) to refer to a singular antecedent (like *everyone* or *a writer*) that doesn't specify gender. Don't lamely accept the ungrammatical *their* as a way out. You can use *he or she, her or his*, and so on:

REVISED: A writer should avoid sexism in *his or her* use of language.

But many readers find that such pairs soon become tedious and annoying. And certainly avoid the unsightly — and never heard — *she/he, his/her, s/he*. You could alternate between masculine and feminine pronouns — but over several pages this too begins to sound gimmicky. Usually the simplest solution is to make the antecedent itself plural; then you don't have to worry about gender:

REVISED: *Writers* should avoid sexism in *their* use of language.
All *those* who weren't satisfied got *their* money back.

You can also use the pronoun *one*: "One should avoid sexism in one's use of language." But that sounds stiff and old-fashioned except on fairly formal occasions. If the occasion permits it and the context is clear, consider using the more informal *you* and *your*:

REVISED: *You* should avoid sexism in *your* use of language.

Often the best solution is to revise the pronouns out — and get a stronger, more economical sentence while you're at it:

> REVISED: A writer (or *Writers*) should avoid using sexist language.

Sexism also appears in language that enforces stereotypes. Not all cooks are women and not all athletes are men. Many men are frail and frivolous; many women are robust and raunchy. Women, as well as men, drive trucks; men, as well as women, take care of children. Therefore

> DRAFT: A *lawyer* should have a good rapport with *his* client.

could just as well be written

> DRAFT: A *lawyer* should have a good rapport with *her* client.

But you can avoid the problem by using the plural or by revising the pronouns out:

> REVISED: *Lawyers* should have a good rapport with *their* clients.
> Lawyers and clients should have a good rapport.
> A lawyer and a client should have a good rapport.

Learn to avoid even implicit sexism. If you refer to *John Smith*, don't in the same context refer to *Ms. Jones*; call her too by her first name. Or refer to them both by surname. Your language reveals the way you perceive the world. Make sure your readers perceive you the way you want them to. You can improve both your prose and your image by removing sexist language whenever you find you've used it.

Project 7-h

Revise the following sentences to get rid of sexism and related problems.

1. Education gives the individual some tools to work with so that he can understand the problems he faces.
2. To open any small business, a man needs a certain amount of capital.
3. Psychologists show that every human being has his/her own mental representation of the world.
4. As man's knowledge grows, his powers over nature increase.
5. But what if the child speaks before he is spoken to ?
6. The optometrist then examines and fits the lens to his patient's eyes.
7. Music has always been an important activity in the lives of men.
8. Most of the troubles in the world are man-made; nature is relatively innocent.

Case

The form a pronoun takes — its **case** — depends on the role it plays in a sentence. *Possessive* pronouns aren't a problem (*my, her, his, your,*

our, their). But make sure you've used the correct case of pronouns acting as *subjects* and *objects* — pronouns like *I* and *me, he* and *him, who* and *whom.*

SUBJECTIVE CASE

If a pronoun is the **subject** of a verb, use the **subjective** form (*I, he, she, we, they, who*):

> *We* (not *Us*) Canadians *are* lucky to live in a country with a plentiful supply of water.

Be especially careful with subjects that have two parts:

> *John and I* (not *me*) *are* still the best of friends.

Don't be thrown off by an intervening *someone thinks* or *believes*:

> He is clearly the one *who* (not *whom*) the Premier thinks *has* the best qualifications.

or by a verb in the passive voice (see pp. 140-41):

> And it was my all-time favourite teacher *who* (not *whom*) *was honoured* by the board when she retired.

OBJECTIVE CASE

If a pronoun is the **object** of a verb or a preposition, use the **objective** form (*me, him, her, us, them, whom*):

> Foreign films and television programs have a strong influence *on us* (not *we*) Canadians.

Again, watch for objects consisting of more than one part:

> The incident *brought* both John and *me* (not *I*) to our senses.

Most people now accept the pronoun *who* in informal speech or writing; but if an occasion requires you to use a more formal style, use *whom* for the objective case:

> *Whom* is the Premier likely *to favour?*

or rephrase the sentence to avoid the problem:

> Which minister is the Premier likely to favour?

Project 7-i

Revise the following sentences to correct errors in the cases of pronouns.

1. Advertisers try to get you and I to buy their products.
2. Whom is going to be given the first chance?
3. But the main reason for the move was my parents' concern for my sister and I.
4. It was either him or me; no one else would dare try it.

5. Dennis and her planned to get married the following month.
6. We all agreed it was time for Mariko and he to stop fighting.
7. Ask not for who the bell tolls.

Shifts

Keep your pronouns consistent in *number* and *person*. Here for example the writer shifted from singular to plural:

DRAFT: Luckily I joined a company that had *its* own training program for *their* employees.

Simply change *their* to *its*. And in the next example the shift is from third person to second person:

DRAFT: Writers must be on *their* toes when revising; *you* have to watch for many things that can go wrong.

Changing *you* to *they* corrects the slip.

MIXED CONSTRUCTIONS

If you shift from one pattern to another in midsentence, you create a **mixed construction**. In the following sentence, for example, the writer shifted from a *both x and y* pattern to an *x as well as y* pattern:

DRAFT: The moderator ordered *both* the heckler *as well as* the speaker to remain quiet.

Once you spot such a mix-up, you can easily fix it by deciding which pattern you want:

REVISED: The moderator ordered *both* the heckler *and* the speaker to remain quiet.

The moderator ordered the speaker *as well as* the heckler to remain quiet.

Project 7-j

Revise the following sentences to get rid of shifts in the person or number of pronouns and in sentence patterns.

1. The advertiser tries to get us to believe that you will be popular if you use the product.
2. I based my entire judgment of people by deciding whether or not I liked the shoes they wore.
3. In this episode, a group of militant policemen takes the law into their own hands.
4. She insisted that one should be permitted to follow one's instincts in such matters, even if it lands you in trouble.
5. This untutored writer, working without benefit of a ghost writer nor editorial guidance, places her world on view.

Comparisons

Check your sentences for any that state comparisons. Make sure each one is complete and makes sense. For example:

> Acme Widgets are more reliable!

"More reliable" than what? Here's another common kind:

> Its engine runs more smoothly than a Mercedes.

To complete the comparison, insert *that of* after *than*. And another:

> DRAFT: The new tanker is longer than any ship afloat.

But the tanker is now itself a "ship afloat"; it can't be longer than itself. Revision makes the comparison clear:

> REVISED: The new tanker is longer than any other ship afloat.
>
> The new tanker is the longest ship afloat.

Project 7-k

Revise the following sentences to get rid of instances of faulty comparison.

1. More people preferred Pepsi to any cola on the market.
2. As for homeowners, the new policy treats them as fairly, if not more fairly, than the one it replaces.
3. Francesca liked Pat more than Jill.
4. These days people are more conscious about their physical appearance.
5. Australia might have been able to recover faster from the recession than by winning the cup.
6. The contrast between my time-frame and theirs was as different as a man returning from years of space travel to find that only a few days had elapsed.
7. The plot was more bizarre than any movie she had seen.

Joining Clauses: Faulty or Loose Coordination

When you decide to join two clauses, use the connector that accurately shows how the clauses are related. Trouble most often occurs with *and* and *but*:

> DRAFT: The weather was almost ideal that day, and our car broke down halfway to Edmonton.

The sentence appears to lack **unity**. The student intended an ironic contrast between her pleasant expectations and what actually happened. Using *but* rather than *and* would make it clearer. In the next example, the coordination is **loose**:

DRAFT: Usually history papers are difficult for me, *and* chemistry reports are much easier.

This sentence could be improved by replacing *and* with either *but* or a semicolon. One more example:

DRAFT: I had forgotten to stop for gas, *and* the engine soon sputtered and died.

This sentence accurately lays out the sequence of events, but the *and* is loose at best. The relation of the two clauses is less one of addition than one of cause and effect. In an informal, conversational piece, you could use the conjunction *so* or even *and so* instead of just *and*. In more formal writing, the relation could be expressed by reversing the clauses and using *for* (or *since* or *because*):

REVISED: The engine soon sputtered and died, *for* I had forgotten to stop for gas.

Or you could indicate causality by beginning with a subordinate *because*-clause:

REVISED: Because I had forgotten to stop for gas, the engine soon sputtered and died.

Project 7-l

Here are some sentences to practise on. Each contains at least one fault discussed in the preceding pages. Revise them to get rid of those problems and any others you see.

1. By reading some good books, it will help in your writing and speaking.
2. No matter how one feels about a particular assignment, you should always do the best you can with it.
3. This proclamation did not solve the problem. Because the pirates would immediately resume their attacks.
4. Hydro is run like a business, and like all businesses a product is supplied to a demanding market.
5. After putting all my energy into fighting the fire for so many hours, the climb back up the hill was a test of muscle and willpower.
6. Coming from high school just three months ago, the university environment is very different. It hardly compares with the first day of high school.
7. The efficiency and speed with which a computer processes data usually pays for itself very quickly.
8. Both passages are very graphic. This is achieved by the author relating his story as a first-hand experience.

9. Nonsmokers are injured as much and, according to some sources, more by cigarette smoke in offices than the actual smokers are.

10. It was threatening to rain, and I decided to leave the gardening until the next day.

11. He merely seems to regard the rules as informal guidelines.

12. Expressionist paintings concentrate on a psychological rather than a natural focus.

13. In each paragraph I examined revealed more clumsy organization.

14. The business has been in my family since its inception.

15. Jean as well as his dog are out in the yard.

16. Not a day passes without noticing someone on radio or television stressing how important it is to be physically fit.

17. The committee was at first unanimous in their decision.

18. The team won five special awards last year, and that's more than any team has ever won.

19. It is this pressure from outside sources that cause me the most trouble.

20. The assignment was unusually heavy, and I managed to finish it two days early.

21. No one complained about having to wait so long for their meal.

22. Although both houses of the US Congress have cast their votes for protectionism, the approach of the two bills differs greatly.

23. Terms such as "brute" and "savage" seems fitting at first, but later we see how inappropriate they are.

24. Advertising gets a lot of flak from consumer groups. Although good advertising, both in print and by word of mouth, helps to maintain high standards.

25. High technology has adversely affected good writing and acting, which is the principal cause of bad movies today.

26. As a child passes through various stages of development, he undergoes various experiences which determine his psychological health.

27. At university I am surrounded by students who want to succeed. This has rubbed off on me, and I am becoming more ambitious.

28. Control over the right hand is even more important than the left.

29. By reviewing Conrad's impressive career as a seaman, it can be seen that he visited most parts of the Malay Archipelago.

30. A full-time student is a difficult role to cope with.

ECONOMY: AVOIDING WORDINESS

w

Nothing is wrong in principle with a long sentence. Use one if that's what you need to fulfill your immediate purpose. But no sentence should use more words than it needs. The most economical form for any particular sentence is not the shortest possible form, but the most effective. **Economy** means avoiding waste.

(In the next chapter, you will find more advice on avoiding wordiness; see pp. 145-47.)

Removing Deadwood

Unnecessary words in sentences are called "deadwood." Prune them out to keep your sentences healthy. For example:

DRAFT: Imagining themselves to be superior beings, vain people act condescendingly toward those they consider to be inferior.

Now a pruned version:

REVISED: Imagining themselves superior, vain people condescend toward those they consider inferior.

No meaning is lost. On the contrary, the meaning is now clearer. Even more could be cut, but there's no need. The object is not to make every sentence sound like a telegram, but to get rid of waste. Here is another, simpler sentence:

DRAFT: The tray is rectangular in shape and predominantly blue in colour.

The deadwood is obvious:

REVISED: The tray is rectangular and predominantly blue.

Reducing Clauses and Phrases

CLAUSES

As you go through your draft, look for chances to reduce clauses to phrases. Relative clauses (beginning with words like *who, which*, and *that*) are often unnecessarily heavy. Especially watch for the "he is a man who" pattern:

DRAFT: My Uncle Ben *is a man who* likes to travel.

You can almost always improve such sentences by simplifying:

REVISED: My Uncle Ben likes to travel.

PHRASES

Hastily drafted sentences sometimes contain unnecessary prepositional phrases. They're especially cluttering when they come in bunches:

DRAFT: The more frequent the author's change *in* style, the less interesting the novel becomes because *of the development of the growing confusion in* the mind *of* the reader.

Revision easily trims all the prepositional phrases:

REVISED: The more often the author changes style, the more confused the reader becomes and the less interesting the novel.

Project 7-m

Revise the following sentences to make them more economical.

1. The hero of the day was a sixteen-year-old teenager.
2. The leaf has an elliptical shape and is light yellow in colour.
3. Irony can be found throughout both novels in several forms.
4. She is a woman who prefers gardening and cooking to other activities that she doesn't enjoy as much.
5. It is a fact that many ex-convicts get back into trouble with the law again.
6. By the end of the novel, it has become a struggle between two great powers, which are America and the Soviet Union.
7. There is a potential danger involved in experiments like this, and I would like to give a short summary of the possible dangers.
8. This is a matter that should be brought to the manager's attention.
9. In the back of my mind I was thinking of some of the things that I'd forgotten in the process of making preparations for going on this trip into the mountains.
10. In the report the committee recommends that the strength of Canada's armed forces should be considerably increased.

Combining Sentences to Reduce Wordiness

Here is a wordy beginning of a draft. Note the mechanical repetition and the overlapping from sentence to sentence:

DRAFT: I have had a few first impressions of this university. Some of my impressions have been favourable. These impressions include those of the setting and the number of services that are available to the student. However, other impressions have not been so favourable. My unfavourable impressions include those of the line-ups and a general confusion about what to do and how to do things for classes.

Combining sentences, the student got rid of the weak repetition and made the paragraph's points much clearer:

REVISED: I have both favourable and unfavourable first impressions of this university. I like the setting, and I'm pleased by the many services available to the student. But I'm not so pleased by all the line-ups, and I'm still confused about what I'm supposed to be doing, especially in getting ready for classes.

Project 7-n

Here are two passages from students' drafts. Revise each by combining sentences to eliminate the unnecessary repetition.

1. Hockey is a fast-moving, exciting sport. It is enjoyed by both the players and the spectators. Although it is one of the most exciting games, it seems to be deteriorating among the professional ranks in the National Hockey League.

2. Dickens's characters do not change so much. An example of this is Joe Gargery, in *Great Expectations.* Joe's character does not change throughout the entire novel even though many things happen to change his life. Examples of these events are Mrs. Joe's being attacked and Pip's going away to the city.

VIGOUR

We don't mean the heading of this section to imply that every sentence has to come on strong, with lights flashing and siren blaring. Quiet sentences can be effective. But even quiet sentences should be vigorous.

Emphasis

Make your sentences say what you want your reader to hear by making sure they emphasize what you want emphasized. There are several ways to emphasize something in a sentence:

• Put the most important points at the end or the beginning.

• Repeat a word or a phrase.

• Shift the style: use a different level of diction, or more elaborate syntax (such as parallelism; see below), or try a minor sentence.

• Make a sentence conspicuously shorter or longer than those surrounding it.

• Usually, put the main idea in a main or independent clause rather than in some subordinate element.

• Depart from normal word order. Since in English the normal order is subject —> predicate, any inversion will stand out. And since an adjective usually precedes the noun it modifies, reversing that order emphasizes the adjective. Here (from a passage cited also in Chapter 4) is a sentence that uses both of these inversions:

> Through billows of steam and smoke, black and gritty, erupts a terrifying din.

• Use punctuation for emphasis. But don't underline or italicize if you can get emphasis in some less obvious and mechanical way. Use exclamation points sparingly if at all. And do NOT use quotation marks for emphasis.

Project 7-o
Compose sentences using various methods of emphasis. Try emphasizing the same word or idea in different ways.

Parallelism

One of the most effective things you can do to make your writing both clearer and more vigorous is to use **parallelism**. A good rule of thumb:

> ELEMENTS THAT **CAN** BE MADE PARALLEL
> **SHOULD** BE MADE PARALLEL

Use parallel forms whenever you list anything, whether the list consists of a series of words, phrases, clauses, or even whole sentences. Here are some examples of parallelism at different levels of sentence structure:

PARALLEL NOUNS: Writers must know at least a little about *grammar, spelling,* and *punctuation.*

PARALLEL ADJECTIVES: The hero is *tall, dark,* and *handsome.*

PARALLEL VERB PHRASES: The assistant will *administer the test, mark the papers,* and *analyze the results.*

PARALLEL INDEPENDENT CLAUSES (OR SENTENCES): *His novels are mainly romantic adventure stories; his poems are mainly lyrical*

PARALLEL SUBORDINATE CLAUSES: The supervisor insists *that you dress properly* and *that you arrive on time.*

PARALLEL INDEPENDENT CLAUSES (OR SENTENCES): *His novels are mainly romantic adventure stories; his poems are mainly lyrical effusions.* (You could choose to separate the clauses with a period. See p. 172)

If you use parallelism your prose will be easier for readers to follow. If you don't make elements parallel where you can, your prose may seem awkward or confusing:

> DRAFT: The aims of the new system are to save time, to conserve energy, and using fewer employees.

Make the last phrase an infinitive like the others:

> REVISED: The aims of the new system are *to save time, to conserve energy,* and *to use fewer employees.*

Notice how you can call attention to the parallelism by repeating the little word *to* at the beginning of each part.

Project 7-p

Compose some sentences like those at the beginning of the discussion of parallelism. Write at least one sentence for each of the different kinds of parallel elements. Or find and transcribe from your reading an example of each kind.

USING CORRELATIVE CONJUNCTIONS

You can often emphasize the parallel elements in a sentence by using a pair of **correlative conjunctions**:

both . . . and	either . . . or
not only . . . but also	neither . . . nor

Such parallel constructions are powerful ways to emphasize similarities and contrasts. Compare the following versions:

> Mr. Domenico gave them his sworn promise *and* a signed statement.
> Mr. Domenico gave them *both* his sworn promise *and* a signed statement.
> Mr. Domenico gave them *not only* his sworn promise *but also* a signed statement.

FAULTY PARALLELISM

ll , fp

Two problems to guard against when you use parallelism:

1. When you use correlative conjunctions, make sure that elements that follow each of the two terms are parallel. If they aren't, the parallelism breaks down, as in this sentence:

> Mr. Domenico gave them
> not only *his sworn promise* [noun phrase]
> but also *signed a statement.* [verb and object]

2. Parallel structure is strong enough to dominate its content. Here a student lets it contradict the sense:

> DRAFT: Both of these kinds of hiking boots provide protection from *water, dirt,* and *other abrasive materials.*

The parallelism makes *water* an "abrasive material," which it isn't. Revising the sentence to clear it up, the student set up a different kind of parallel:

REVISED: Both of these kinds of hiking boots provide protection *from water* and *from dirt and other abrasive materials.*

Note that the repetition of *from* is necessary to avoid the original ambiguity.

Project 7-q
Revise the following sentences to get rid of faulty parallelism.
1. The many forms of advertising include television, newspaper and magazine ads, and by radio.
2. These words not only summarize the views of the evangelist but some religious groups, moralists, and politicians.
3. It is better to try to deal with the results than wasting time trying to reform human nature.
4. A restaurant needs the right combination of capital, a good location, and to excel in service.
5. There are three ways by which this goal can be achieved: through the media, controlling promiscuous activity, and a drug program.
6. I saw the game's outcome as not only dependent on experience and luck but a combination of other things.
7. On the farm she had grown up riding horses, growing fresh vegetables and fresh country air.

Active and Passive Voice

Transitive verbs (those followed by objects) have two **voices**: **active** and **passive**. Verbs in the passive voice can sap the strength of a sentence. You can usually improve a sentence by changing from passive voice to active voice.

ACTIVE VOICE
Active voice is more direct. It follows the most common order for English sentences; the *subject* of the sentence *does* something to an *object*:

subject	**verb**	**object**
actor	*action*	*receiver of the action*
The dog	is chewing	his slipper.
Janet	will play	the guitar.
The demonstrators	shouted	their approval.
One of us	must tell	the truth.
Mr. Bellamy	has found	the missing file.

PASSIVE VOICE

The passive voice turns things around. The receiver of the action becomes the subject of the sentence; the actor becomes a sort of bystander:

subject *receiver of the action*	**verb** *action*	*actor*
His slipper	is being chewed	by the dog.
The guitar	will be played	by Janet.
Approval	was shouted	by the demonstrators.
The truth	must be told	by one of us.
The missing file	has been found	by Mr. Bellamy.

CHANGING FROM PASSIVE VOICE TO ACTIVE VOICE

Note that the passive versions are longer because they add *by* as well as a form of the verb *be*. **To change passive to active, simply reverse the order of the main elements, drop *by*, and drop the *be* verb.** (You'll then have to make the remaining verb the desired tense, but that isn't difficult.)

> Note that the PASSIVE VOICE has nothing to do with PAST TENSE. The phrase *will be played*, for example, is in the passive voice, but it is in future tense.

Project 7-r

Try it yourself with the following sentences. The verbs are all in the passive voice. Change them to the active voice. (We've separated the elements in the first three so that you can see them clearly.)

1. The new paper // was damaged // by the tractor feed.
2. The spoiled paté // was eaten // by all four guests.
3. The best horse // should be ridden // by Zelda Primm.
4. All the ports will be watched by the RCMP.
5. The exchange rate should have been calculated by both clerks.
6. The regatta had been won by an all-female crew.
7. The mail will not be delivered by Stan on Thursday.

USING THE PASSIVE VOICE

The active voice is usually clearer and stronger. But the passive voice does have its uses:

- If you want to emphasize something you can use the passive voice to get it to the beginning or the end of a sentence:

  The guitar will be played by *Janet*. (Instead of by someone else.)
  The truth must be told. (It doesn't matter by whom.)

- Use the passive voice when the *receiver* of the action or the *result* of the action is more important than the actor:

  The missing file has been found. (The fact of the file's being found is what is important; you can leave Mr. Bellamy out of it altogether.)

- Use the passive voice when the *actor* is unknown:

  Sharon was taken to hospital. (*By whom* is unknown, nor does it matter.)

> If you *use* the passive voice, you should *choose* to use it.

MISUSING THE PASSIVE VOICE

Too often, people use the passive voice to evade responsibility or to withhold information unnecessarily. Think how you'd feel if you read this in your school paper:

> It has been decided that students will pay an extra $10.00 fee to the Student Council this year.

What's going on here? You'd probably want to know just *who* "decided": some student bureaucrat? a committee? the administration? The sentence doesn't tell you. Readers often react with similar annoyance to a passive that fails to name the performer of an action.

Furthermore, an unnecessary passive voice will likely be wordy, or lead to misunderstanding, or get tangled up with a dangling modifier (see pp. 122-23), as it does here:

DRAFT: By cutting down on the passive voice in your writing, *habits* of responsibility *are learned.*

Changing to the active voice clears things up, invigorates the sentence, and gets rid of the dangling modifier:

REVISED: By cutting down on the passive voice in your writing, *you learn habits* of responsibility.

pas

Project 7-s

Try converting the passive-voice verbs below to the active voice. Some will be harder to revise than others. Use your imagination and your sense of the context or occasion to fill the gaps. If you decide to leave any verbs in the passive voice, be prepared to defend your decision.

1. These mats were woven by my grandmother, but she didn't dye the yarn herself.
2. You will find the company's policy explained on the enclosed form. If your payment is not received within 30 days, steps will be taken to see that it is collected.
3. Schechter was knocked out at the end of the third round, but it was decided, since he got to his feet shortly after the bell had been rung, to let the fight continue.
4. The meeting was called to order, and the treasurer's report was read.
5. Rules are made to be broken.
6. The minister's motion was ruled out of order, and after some shouting the business of the house was allowed to proceed.
7. Tab A should first be inserted in Slot B, after which Leads W and X should be soldered to Terminals Y and Z.

CHAPTER 8
Revising Words and Phrases

Using a Dictionary

The marking symbol *d* stands for **diction**. Whenever you find it in the margin of a returned paper, start by consulting your **dictionary**. The same goes for other marks associated with words, such as *ww* (wrong word). Dictionaries often give advice about idiom (*id*; see Chapter 14) and usage (*us*; see the last part of this chapter). They also tell you if a word is considered colloquial or slang.

A good dictionary is an indispensable tool for a writer. By "good" we mean one that is reasonably comprehensive and up-to-date — that is, with around 150 000 entries (obviously, not a "pocket" dictionary) and not over ten years old. If you don't own such a dictionary, you might, as a Canadian student, wish to get one of these standard "desk" or "college" dictionaries:

> *Funk & Wagnalls Canadian College Dictionary.* Toronto: Fitzhenry & Whiteside, 1986.
>
> *The Houghton Mifflin Canadian Dictionary of the English Language.* Markham, Ontario: Houghton Mifflin Canada, 1980.
>
> *The Gage Canadian Dictionary.* Toronto: Gage, 1983.

CLARITY: CHOOSING THE RIGHT WORD

Wrong Word

A **wrong word** is often a word that looks or sounds similar to the right word, but isn't the right word. For example, a government advertisement described someone as "one of Canada's leading sculptures." The word *sculptures* looks much like *sculptors*, the word the writer meant. A news story about a bridge collapse included this:

> Seconds later a pickup truck *hurdled* through the air and landed near the car.

At first *hurdled* may look and sound right, but careful revising or proofreading would have changed it to the correct *hurtled*. A student wrote this sentence:

> DRAFT: I call the committee's decision *regretful.*

A committee member may be full of regret (*regretful*), but a decision must be termed *regrettable.*

Note: Some often-confused words are discussed in the Checklist of Usage later in this chapter; others are listed in the section on spelling in Chapter 10, pp. 193-98.

Idiom

A mistake in **idiom** is similar to a **wrong word** choice. For some examples and exercises focussing on this special problem, see Chapter 14.

Denotation and Connotation

Denotation is the specific, direct meaning of a word. **Connotation** is the associative or suggestive meaning of a word. Words that **denote** much the same thing can **connote** quite different things or attitudes. If you choose a word that has a connotation you aren't aware of, you may mislead your readers. Especially check your modifiers.

For example, if you disapproved of someone's being slow to part with money, you might call that person *stingy, cheap, mean, niggardly,* or — less negatively — *parsimonious, tightfisted, close.* If you approved of such saving ways, however, you could use such terms as *thrifty, economical, frugal.* And if you disapproved or approved of someone who was quick to part with money, you could choose from a similar range of adjectives: *profligate, spendthrift, extravagant,* or *liberal, generous, lavish.*

Project 8-a

(a) List the following words on a separate sheet. Label each as having *positive, negative,* or *neutral* connotations. Underline any that you think could have different connotations, depending on context or tone.

frivolous	pale	limpid	showy	snowy
simulated	black	smooth	neat	stewed
maverick	green	rustic	raunchy	painted
electrifying	yellow	slender	punctual	rich

Do your labels agree with those of others? Has anyone drawn on private associations rather than publicly accepted ones?

(b) For three of those you underlined, compose sentences illustrating their different possible connotations.

> **Caution**: A *thesaurus* can help you find better words to express an idea. It can help you enlarge your vocabulary. It can even help you discover ideas by suggesting new trains of thought through synonyms and antonyms. But there are few exact synonyms; therefore when you are seeking a word, **never depend on a thesaurus by itself. Always use a good dictionary along with it to check on shades of meaning.**

ECONOMY: AVOIDING WORDINESS

$\boxed{w}$

The preceding chapter includes advice on cutting deadwood out of sentences (see pp. 133-36). Here we focus on certain kinds of words and phrases that contribute to wordiness.

Redundant Phrases

$\boxed{red}$

Some phrases that you may accept and even use because you hear them so often are **redundant**: the idea expressed in one part is present in the other. For example, what are *true facts*? A *fact* must be *true,* or it isn't a fact. Why refer to *advance planning*? All *planning* is done in *advance.* Tighten your prose and sharpen your meaning by cutting out such redundancies. Here are a few more examples:

advance warning	necessary prerequisite
basic fundamentals	new innovation
circle around	new record
close scrutiny	other alternatives
consensus of opinion	past history
continue on	personal friend
each and every	precautionary measure
end result	reflect back
exact same	regress back
fellow colleagues	return back
final outcome	revert back
final result	serious crisis
flee away	share in common
general consensus	stereotyped image
mental attitude	surrounded on all sides

Check your **modifiers** for similar redundancy. For example, it's wordy to describe a tyrant as *cruel*. To write that you are *constantly plagued* with something would also be redundant: you could hardly be *occasionally plagued.* Such modifiers don't emphasize meaning; they blur it.

Prefabricated Phrases

Other phrases that produce wordiness are familiar ones that many people use without thinking. You can almost always reduce them. Some examples:

Wordy	**Change to**
along the lines of	like, similar to
at a later date	later
at the present time	now
at the same time that	while
at this point in time	now
by means of	by
despite the fact that	though, although
due to (because of, on account of) the fact that	because
during the course of	during
for the purpose of	for, to
for the reason that	because
in all probability	probably
in connection with	about
in excess of	over, more than
in the event that	if

in the final analysis	finally
in the near (not too distant) future	soon
in the neighbourhood of	about, near
is of the opinion that	thinks
period of time, time period	period, time
previous to, prior to	before
with the exception of	excepting, except for

Another kind of phrase tends to be a mere filler. For example:

DRAFT: Miriam was constantly aggressive *in manner.*

Drop the useless phrase and get a more effective sentence:

REVISED: Miriam was constantly aggressive.

Again:

DRAFT: She always reacted *in* an angry *manner.*

REVISED: She always reacted angrily.

Here are some other such phrases that you can usually either delete or drastically reduce:

in character	in shape
in fact	in size
in nature	the fact that
in number	use of, by the use of

VIGOUR: CHOOSING EFFECTIVE WORDS; AVOIDING WEAK DICTION

Concrete and Specific

ABSTRACT AND CONCRETE

Concrete words refer to objects or qualities you know through your senses: things you see, hear, touch, taste, smell, or feel. **Abstract** words refer to ideas or qualities you know with your mind. For example:

concrete	*abstract*
roommate	companionship
Lake Louise	beauty
Toronto	urbanity
fever	illness
University of Manitoba	education
the Concorde	aviation
Charlie Chaplin	comedy
quiche	gastronomy
battery	power

GENERAL AND SPECIFIC

Related to the distinction between **abstract** and **concrete** is the one between **general** and **specific**. **General** terms refer to classes of things like cats, trucks, and cities. **Specific** terms refer to members of those classes, like Blue-point Siamese, pickups, and Canadian cities. But you can get even more specific: Dodge pickups are members of the class *pickups*, and Fredericton is a member of the class *Canadian cities*.

Usually, abstract words are more general, concrete words more specific. Consider the following range of terms, moving from the most specific to the most general:

Toi-toi —> Blue-point Siamese —> cat —> feline —> animal —> life

The first term refers to a specific object, one of a kind. Each succeeding term is more general, denoting a larger class: there are many Blue-point Siamese, but only one Toi-toi; there are more cats than just Blue-point Siamese; and so on. The terms are all concrete (you can see and touch what they name) until the last one: the word *life* crosses over into the abstract; it refers to a concept, not a thing.

---

conc

STRENGTH FROM CONCRETENESS

When you have a choice, choose the concrete and the more specific. Your writing will be both more precise and more readable. Rather than a vague memo like

DRAFT: It is my belief that we should improve our security arrangements.

try writing

REVISED: I believe the store needs better locks on the front and back doors and an alarm system for the rear ground-floor windows.

Rather than write

DRAFT: My uncle is very wealthy.

get concrete and specific:

REVISED: My uncle is wealthy enough to own three cars and winter in the Caribbean every year.

Of course you will need to use some general and abstract terms. Much thinking and writing depends on them. Writing that was entirely concrete would be tiring and hard to follow. The point is that you can usually improve your writing by making it *more* concrete and specific.

Project 8-b

Starting with each abstract (and general) term below, compose a list of at least five items that are progressively more concrete and specific.

art	science	history	entertainment
industry	hostility	protection	health

Reducing Modifiers

When you increase the concreteness and specificity of your nouns and verbs, you can cut down on modifiers. Substitute precise nouns for adjective-noun combinations and precise verbs for adverb-verb combinations. Especially, don't prop up a general noun or verb with two or three adjectives or adverbs. Suppose you had written a sentence like this:

DRAFT: A big, mean dog came after me and chased me a long way.

Specifics will almost always make it clearer:

REVISED: An Alsatian shot through the gate and nipped at my heels for two blocks.

Project 8-c

(a) Compose a paragraph describing some simple object, perhaps one you can see at the moment (for example a plate of food, a vase of flowers, a stuffed animal, an unmade bed, an ornate paperweight). Do it without adjectives.

(b) Compose a paragraph describing a simple action, some event or movement which you can see happening or which you can remember having seen recently (for example a point during a tennis match, a car pulling away from a curb, a dog rooting in a garbage can, a kid on a bicycle, a sailboat going past, a friend doing a high dive, wind blowing papers off your desk). Do it without adverbs.

Avoiding Weak Modifiers

Look for places where you have used such potentially weak modifiers as these qualifiers and intensifiers:

actually	definitely	rather	totally
certainly	extremely	really	truly
completely	literally	some	very
considerable	quite	somewhat	virtually

You can often sharpen your meaning either by simply omitting such words or by revising your sentences to get rid of them. Look for example at the following sentence:

DRAFT: As long as they keep setting up study panels, there is no *real* sense of *really* tackling the problem.

The attempt at emphasis with *real* and *really* backfires, producing a weak *there is*-clause (see below) and clumsy repetition. Revising sharpens the sense:

> REVISED: As long as they keep setting up study panels, they are not tackling the problem.

Here is another example:

> DRAFT: Unfortunately, his explanation did *very* little to clarify his meaning.

The word *very* is so overused that it has lost most of its ability to emphasize. Delete it:

> REVISED: Unfortunately, his explanation did little to clarify his meaning.

Or change the whole phrase:

> REVISED: Unfortunately, his explanation did almost nothing to clarify his meaning.

Either way, the sentence is now more emphatic, not less. Flabby intensifiers like *very* and *really* may even make readers suspect the words they modify. Especially, avoid the almost automatically weak phrases *very important* and *very significant*. Instead show with specifics just what makes something important or significant. (See also p. 148.)

Potentially Vague or Empty Words

Some general words are useful in speech when a specific word doesn't come to mind. But when you revise your writing, look for vague nouns like these:

thing	occurrence	person	activity	angle
something	concern	quality	case	facet
experience	aspect	field	realm	level
situation	position	mode	concept	area

When hooked to equally general adjectives like *good, bad, nice, pleasant, certain,* such words produce vague or empty phrases like *meaningful experience, certain quality, nice area, interesting field, unpleasant situation.*

Such terms often depend on context and modifiers for their meaning. And often those modifiers turn out to be nouns, producing wordy gobbledygook like *retrenchment mode, thunderstorm activity, power-play situation, playground area.* Such terms also tend to become parts of unnecessary phrases like *in most cases, in many cases, in the case of, the realm of, the field of.* The danger arises when the vague words aren't necessary for the context, when they are merely the vehicles for the modifiers that accompany them.

DRAFT	REVISED
a surprising occurrence	a surprise
in the field of biology	in biology
Her voice had an appealing quality.	Her voice was appealing.
a crisis situation	a crisis

Another danger: To begin a new section or paragraph, inexperienced writers are sometimes tempted to use something like "There were three aspects to the situation." Such a sentence usually indicates that the writer wanted to analyze a topic into three parts but didn't want to write something colloquial like "There are three things I want to say about this." *Aspect* and *situation* come into it because the writer wants to sound more formal and authoritative. In revising such sentences, bring in the more specific, such as "The uprising progressed in three waves. . . ." If you find

DRAFT: Three important *things* resulted from this *occurrence.*

revise it to get rid of the empty words:

REVISED: This unexpected meeting had three important results.

Using Dynamic Verbs

Try to express the main action of a sentence in a dynamic verb. Static verbs like *is, seem,* and *have* rarely express movement or life. If you can, replace them with verbs that suggest some kind of action. Of course all writers need to use static verbs some of the time, but if you let them take over they will sap your prose of vigour.

When you revise look especially for forms of *be* and *have.* Look, for example, at this sentence:

DRAFT: A point that *was* repeatedly emphasized by the mayor *was* the cost of insurance.

The first *be*-verb is part of the passive *was emphasized* (see pp. 140-41), and the second is merely static. To invigorate such a sentence, ask two questions:

1. What is going on here?
2. Who or what is doing it?

In the example, *what* is going on is the act of *emphasizing,* and the *who or what* doing it is the *mayor.* Making these the verb and subject gets rid of the wordiness, the passive voice, and the static verb:

REVISED: The *mayor* repeatedly *emphasized* the cost of insurance.

THERE IS, THERE ARE, IT IS, ETC.

A related weakness comes from overusing these forms:

it is	there is	there are
it was	there was	there were

They can sometimes help you emphasize something, for example by letting you put the real subject of a sentence near the end. But don't overuse them. Look especially for weak topic sentences that begin with them:

DRAFT: *There are* three things we have to do before we can present the resolution for a vote.

REVISED: We must make three changes before we can present the resolution for a vote.

VERBS HIDDEN IN NOUNS

Much writing these days, perhaps influenced by technical writing (see the section on Jargon, pp. 154-55), depends heavily on nouns at the expense of verbs. You can often strengthen your writing by changing an abstract noun into the verb lurking at its heart:

DRAFT: Bertha's *intention* was to become a psychiatrist.

Find the verb in the noun *intention,* and get rid of the *was*:

REVISED: Bertha *intended* to become a psychiatrist.

Project 8-d

For each abstract noun listed below, first write a sentence using the noun; then convert the noun into a verb and revise your original sentence so that it uses an appropriate form of that verb. Try to avoid the passive voice.

communication	definition	investigation
conception	discrimination	mediation
conclusion	divergence	orientation
conversation	establishment	supposition
creation	hope	suspicion

Avoiding Clichés

Clichés (also called "hackneyed" or "trite" expressions) are like prefabricated phrases. Most clichés are metaphors that have been used and used and used until they no longer have any invigorating effect. For example the phrase *toe the line* once called up an image of an obedient group regimented with their toes along a prescribed line. But the phrase has clearly lost its figurative force when some writers now spell it *tow the line,* as if the regimentation consists in pulling something with a rope.

A cliché is a sign that a writer was drowsing, not thinking; and the reader might also drowse. Here's a sentence written by a student:

DRAFT: Most of all we enjoyed the warm and *crystal-clear* waters of the Caribbean.

Now that technology can make glass or even plastic clearer than the older lead-alloyed glass called "crystal," the phrase owes its existence entirely to the cliché. The writer decided that her revision said it better:

REVISED: Most of all we enjoyed the warm, clear waters of the Caribbean.

Another student acknowledged his use of a cliché by enclosing it in quotation marks:

No one can call back "the good old days."

Readers understand the phrase and recognize the nostalgic feeling. But the cliché annoys them by its very familiarity. And the quotation marks, which in effect weakly apologize for the cliché, make it worse by calling attention to it — as if otherwise readers wouldn't be intelligent enough to recognize it.

> Cut out clichés when you can. But if you decide to keep one, DON'T draw attention to it.

Here are some examples of phrases that have become clichés:

acid test	gentle as a lamb	nipped in the bud
as a last resort	hard as nails	par for the course
as the crow flies	last but not least	rears its ugly head
by leaps and bounds	love at first sight	sharp as a tack
down in the dumps	the moment of truth	smart as a whip

You can no doubt think of dozens — hundreds — more. Such phrases are useful in conversation because they allow people to make a point quickly, without pausing to seek fresher and more precise terms. But when revising your writing, you can replace them with more effective words and phrases.

Project 8-e

Make a list of ten phrases you think of as clichés. Then compare your list with those of others. Do you all agree that the phrases are clichés? Perhaps pool your lists and add to them from time to time.

Avoiding Slang

Slang is basically the private language of an in-group, such as a softball team, a sorority, or a club of computer hackers. One of slang's purposes is to keep outsiders out, to make them feel like outsiders.

slang

When a slang term ceases to be part of a private language, it will be replaced with a new term. Therefore slang is continually changing. By the time someone writes it down, it's already out of date.

Most of what teachers and textbooks call slang are bits of a vagrant vocabulary cut off from its in-group but not yet accepted into the general vocabulary of serious discourse. Even when it has been picked up by a wider range of speakers, it is still likely to be dated. And the larger and more diverse your audience, the less likely they are to share the special meanings that slang at its best conveys. You should avoid slang expressions in most academic writing.

When it's still close to its source, however, and when you're *sure* your readers will know it, an occasional slang term is worth risking to invigorate a sentence or a paragraph. But never use much. And, as with clichés, don't draw attention to it.

> DON'T put quotation marks around a slang term, as if to use it and apologize for it at the same time.

Project 8-f

From your own vocabulary and perhaps with the help of a few friends, compile a list of twenty slang words and phrases currently in fashion. Write a sentence using each, and then a sentence saying essentially the same thing without it.

Keep the list among your notes and look at it again in a month or two or six to see how many of the terms have gone out of fashion and perhaps been replaced by others.

---

jarg

Avoiding Jargon

Like slang, **jargon** is the language of special groups, a kind of shop-talk. People in different fields use special words, and familiar words in special ways, to talk and write about their specialties. When they are confined to those specialties, nothing is wrong with such terms; they make communication easier because they let people say more in fewer words.

Trouble begins when specialists or their admirers use such language outside the specialties. It then becomes "jargon" in a broader sense. The frequency of technical terms used in this way is one reason so much writing today is hard to understand. Here for example are a few terms used by those familiar with computers and their operation:

access (verb)	software	byte	parameter	RAM
on-line	interface	baud	modality	modem

Useful as they are among specialists, in other contexts they become jargon. For instance, it may simply annoy a reader — even one who knows what it means — when someone writes in a business memo about "the *interface* between accounting and production." It's usually better to use some other word: *coordination,* or just *communication. Interface* can be even more disconcerting when it turns up as a verb, for example in something like "The chairman has decided to *interface* with the investigating committee" (meaning simply "meet").

It's not surprising that jargon tempts non-specialists, or that specialists like to use it outside their fields. Much of it derives from specialties that are among the most prestigious today. In addition to computer science, there are medicine, psychology, education, law, the military, government, and so on. And, indistinguishable from certain kinds of slang, some jargon derives from sports and entertainment, and even the narcotics underworld — all associated with excitement and big money. Here are a few examples of the kind of terms to guard against:

background (verb)	feedback	interpersonal
bottom line	impact (verb)	replicate
dialogue (verb)	implement	scenario
factor	input, output	target (verb)

Many other terms that aren't specifically technical get overused, become "vogue" words, because they seem to have a scientific or pseudoscientific ring to them; many people would classify them, too, as "jargon." A few examples:

cope	in depth	self-image
evidenced by	life-style	supportive
frame of reference	ongoing	viable
identify with	relate to	time frame

CHECKLIST OF USAGE

US

In conversation many people use *like* as a conjunction, use *hopefully* loosely, use *quote* as a noun, and so on. But many of these same people would take care to keep such usage out of their writing. The following advice pertains to writing — especially writing that has some formality, as most academic writing does. But you may want to apply these principles to all but your most casual speech, as well.

affect, effect *Affect* is a verb; *effect* is a noun: Your headache will **affect** your concentration. The headache tablet may have an unpleasant **effect** on your digestion.

aggravate, annoy These are not synonyms. *Aggravate* means "make worse": Watching television will **aggravate** my headache.

alternate, alternative *Alternate* means by turns, or every other one: The two actors **alternate** playing the lead role. They play the lead on **alternate** days. *Alternative* refers to a choice: The pilot had no **alternative**; she bailed out. There is an **alternative** method which you may find easier.

among, between Use *between* when you write of only two: **between** you and me. Use *among* for more than two: **among** the four committee members.

amount, number Use *amount* to refer to things that are usually measured in bulk: a large **amount** of ice. Use *number* to refer to things counted as individual items: a large **number** of ice cubes. (See *less, fewer*, below.)

and etc. Avoid this redundancy. *Etc.* is an abbreviation of the Latin *et cetera,* which means "*and* others." It's usually best to avoid *etc.* altogether.

and/or Appropriate only in legal contracts and the like. In other writing use *or* along with *or both*: I will confirm the offer by telephone **or** in writing, **or both**.

anyways, anywheres Dialectal. Leave off the final **s**.

as Don't use *as* when it can be taken to mean "because." In this sentence, for example, it's ambiguous: **As** I opened the new book hurriedly, its spine cracked. If you mean *because*, say *because.*

as far as . . . Don't confuse this with *as for*: **As for** (NOT *as far as*) her summer plans, she will have to work. If you decide to use it, be sure you finish the expression: **As far as** her summer plans **are concerned** (or **go**), she will have to work. It is usually wordy.

basis, on the basis of . . . , on a . . . basis A sure sign of wordy jargon in such phrases as *on a monthly basis* (monthly, every month) and *on the basis of* (judging by, according to, based on) *recent data.*

centre around Illogical. A discussion can *centre* **on** something, or it can *revolve around* or *circle around* it.

comprise, compose This checklist **comprises** (contains, takes in, includes) forty-five items. This checklist **is composed of** (is made up of) forty-five items. DON'T use *comprise* in the passive voice *(is comprised of).*

continual, continuous If something is *continual,* there are breaks; it isn't happening all the time: Wilfrid is **continually** quoting Shakespeare. If something is *continuous,* there are no breaks or interruptions: The **continuous** caterwauling kept me awake until three.

different than, different from Use *from* after *different* unless what follows is a clause; then many people will accept *than:* The work was different **than** she expected. But you may want to play safe and use the more formal *from* even then, and even if it does require an extra word: The work was different **from** what she expected.

disinterested, uninterested *Uninterested* means simply "not interested." *Disinterested* means "free from bias, impartial." **Disinterested** referees don't favour one side or the other, but they're **interested** in the game.

due to, owing to Use these only after a *be*-verb: Her victory in the high-jump **was due to** her rigorous training. Otherwise use *because of:* **Because of** her rigorous training, she won the highjump.

enormity Don't use this to mean "largeness"; it has nothing to do with size. *Enormity* means "outrageousness, atrocity": The **enormity** of his behaviour earned him the hatred of his subjects.

equally as Redundant. Drop one or the other: His performance in this game was **as** good as that in last week's game; His performance last week was excellent, and this week it is **equally** good.

first, second, third In this kind of enumeration you don't need to put *ly* after each word. If you want, put *ly* after *second, third,* and so on, but don't use it with *first*: **First . . . . Secondly . . . . Thirdly . . . .**

good, bad, badly, well *Good* and *bad* are adjectives: He looks **good** in that suit; Timmy was punished because he was **bad** yesterday. *Badly* and *well* are adverbs: He behaved **badly**; She played **well** in the semifinals. *Well* can also be an adjective meaning "healthy": Thorsten looks especially **well** after his holiday.

hopefully Don't use this word to modify a whole sentence or clause:

DRAFT: **Hopefully**, Ms. Beyer will bring the contract.

If you mean that you yourself have hope, say so:

REVISED: I hope that Ms. Beyer will bring the contract.

If *I* is not appropriate for the occasion, you can say *One hopes* or *It is to be hoped that.*

individual Not simply a synonym for *person*. Use it only when you intend a contrast of one with many: The theme of the course was The **Individual** and Society.

infer, imply Don't confuse these. *Imply* means "suggest" or "hint"; *infer* means "interpret" or "conclude from the evidence": You **infer** that I am angry because I **imply** it with my silence.

in terms of Often a wordy phrase, like *on the basis of* (see above). You can usually revise to get rid of it, often by changing it to something more specific:

DRAFT: They evaluated the campaign **in terms of** the turnout at the rallies.

REVISED: They evaluated the campaign by measuring the turnout at the rallies.

irregardless No such word. The *ir* is redundant. Use *regardless*.

is where, is when Avoid these when defining. Rather than "an offside is when . . . ," write "an offside occurs when . . . ." Rather than "an oligarchy is where the wealthy families . . . ," say "An oligarchy is a form of government in which the wealthy families . . . ."

its, it's Confusing these is a spelling error. The possessive is spelled without an apostrophe: **its** context, **its** flavour, **its** nocturnal habits. When spelled with an apostrophe, the word is a contraction of **it is**: When **it's** time to go to bed; **It's** never too late. Note that none of the possessive pronouns use an apostrophe: *hers, his, yours, ours, theirs.*

less, fewer Even though supermarket express lanes say "8 items or less," use *less* to refer to things not counted and *fewer* for things that are counted: **less** money, **fewer** dollars; **less** ice, **fewer** ice cubes; **less** weight, **fewer** kilograms. (See *amount, number,* above.)

lie, lay *Lie* does not take an object: Please **lie** still. *Lay* does take an object: Please **lay** the **boards** on the sawhorse. If you confuse these verbs, memorize their **principal parts** (see the Glossary of Terms): **lie, lay, lain,** and **lay, laid, laid.** (A probable cause of confusion is that *lay* is also the past tense of *lie*.)

like, as, as if, as though Use *like* only as a preposition, as part of a phrase: Phil acted *like* a fool. Do not use *like* as if it were a conjunction, to introduce a clause; use an appropriate one of the other terms: Phil acted *as if* *he'd lost his mind*; he was being silly, just *as he had been* the day before.

media This is the plural form of *medium*. The print **media are** (not *is*) newspapers and magazines. The electronic **media are** (not *is*) radio and television. And note that television is **a** powerful **medium**.

momentarily See *presently*.

person, persons, people Just as *thing* is a highly general noun, so *person* is the most general noun for a human being. Use it only when you cannot be more specific (see p. 148). For the plural, use *people* unless you're referring to only a few *persons* (say two or three) or wish to stress that they are *individuals* (see above).

presently Strictly, this word means "in a moment" or "soon," not "at present" or "now": **Presently** the inspector returned with a bloody dagger. In a job application, DON'T write something like "Presently I am employed at Sylvan Landscapes," but "**At present** I am . . . ." In contrast, *momentarily* does not mean "in a moment" but rather "for a moment, for a short time." Because they are often loosely used, you may wish to avoid these words altogether; some of your readers may not know the distinction and will misunderstand you.

quote The word *quote* is a verb: The prosecutor will **quote** from the transcript. The noun is *quotation*: He supplied a **quotation** from the transcript. For "quotation marks," *quotes* is informal.

real, really Don't use *real* as an adverb; the adverb is *really*. A soft drink may be "the **real** thing," but if you happen to like it you might say it tasted **really** good (not *real* good). (But see pp. 149-50.)

reason is because, reason why Each of these phrases is redundant. The word *because* and the word *why* both include the meaning of the word *reason*. DON'T write "The reason I am applying is because . . ."; instead write "The **reason** I am applying is **that** . . ." or just "I am applying **because** . . . ." Not "The reason why he asked was . . ." but "The **reason** he asked was . . . ."

since Because this word can refer to either time or causation, it can be ambiguous: **Since** Clara left, Chester has been irritable. Change it to *because* when you mean to express causation: Chester has been irritable **because** Clara left.

so, and so Use either of these to mean *therefore* only in informal contexts. Usually you can revise like this:

DRAFT: It began to snow, **so** we finished the picnic in the car.

REVISED: **Because** it began to snow, we finished the picnic in the car.

thusly, muchly Drop the *ly*. Write *thus* and *much*.

type, -type The word *type*, when it means "category," often has an air of jargon about it. Avoid it if possible. Consider using the word *kind* instead. If you must use *type*, be sure to follow it with *of*: Change "The new type bearings will need no lubrication" to "The new **type of** bearings will need no lubrication." Often you can simply omit it: The new bearings . . . . And always take out the suffix *type*; it's unnecessary: essay (not *essay-type*) examination.

unique, necessary, perfect, etc. Such terms are absolutes; they should not be part of a comparison. That is, one thing can't be *more unique, more necessary,* or *more perfect* than another. Try *more unusual, more important, more nearly perfect*. Especially avoid *very* with such terms (*very unique, very necessary*).

use, utilize, usage, utilization *Usage* means "customary behaviour": In British **usage** the word *secretary* often has only three syllables; Arabic **usage** is to eat with the right hand only. Use the verb *utilize* only when you mean something like "make use of, turn to practical account": They were able to **utilize** part of an old tire for a temporary drive-belt. Elsewhere the verb *use* will be sufficient. And for a noun, you should almost always replace the pretentious *utilization* with *use*: Careful **use** (not *utilization*) of the map enabled us to find our way back to Kenora. (See also p. 147.)

very A feeble intensifier. You will almost always improve a sentence by either omitting it or changing it and the word it modifies to something more precise: very happy? delighted; very angry? furious. (See also pp. 149-50.)

-wise Unless you're reaching for humour, DON'T use this suffix to make an adverb from a noun:

DRAFT: Energywise, we'll have to rely on petroleum products.

REVISED: For energy, we'll have to rely on petroleum products.

Project 8-g

Here are some draft sentences to practise on. Revise them to get rid of any weaknesses and errors of diction you find.

1. He looked questionably at her.
2. Mr. Bly thought it incumbent on him to extract revenge.
3. Astaire adopted a witty, sophisticated, casual air which belied the enormity of his talent.
4. Properly used, this two-day test will prove to be of use in the classroom.
5. Ultimate decisions concerning project approval lie within the jurisdiction of the provincial government through its utilities commission.
6. The report was centred around the lack of experience of the employees.
7. We must look with suspect at someone who claims to be an authority yet can show us no credentials.
8. They returned the shouting and struggling seaman back to the ship.
9. The youngsters were hooping it up on the public beach.
10. An individual's feelings concerning the future are often motivated by the kinds of life events he has experienced.
11. While the title focusses only on one of the two main characters, I think that it is just as the novel is more his story than hers.
12. Meteorology is not an exacting science.
13. He did his upmost to win the match.
14. They all found it a very worthwhile learning experience.
15. So far four applicants have applied for the new channel.
16. The most important factor in cold-weather camping is choosing the right equipment.
17. Accounting facilitates the informational aspect of the business process.
18. Canadians embraced this new innovation, and in less than ten years most homes were hooked up to cable television.
19. These channels are delivered via satellite directly to each cable company, where their signals are transmitted as discreet audio and video components.
20. As another summer lingers to a close we can again witness the unique, yet still extraordinary, ability of the Council to spend great sums of money in doing so very little.

CHAPTER 9
Revising Punctuation

When you speak you use the sound of your voice (pitch, volume, speed) and physical gestures (facial expressions, arm and hand movements) to help convey meaning. When you write, **punctuation** takes the place of such sounds and gestures. Your punctuation sends signals that tell your readers *how* to read something — in part how to *hear* it.

The Conventions of Punctuation

Punctuation is largely a matter of **conventions** that people have agreed upon in order to communicate more easily. For example, we all accept the convention that a sentence begins with a capital letter and ends with a period (or question mark or exclamation point). If you received a letter that ignored the conventions you have come to count on, it would annoy you because of the extra effort needed to read it.

Here's a passage written by a student. We have removed its punctuation and capitalization. Try reading it:

> the human voice is music itself it rises and falls it pauses it gets louder and softer if this music were not present in our voices we would all speak in monotones and conversation would soon become very tedious our speech pattern is song and it reflects our emotions happiness anger sorrow fatigue and nonchalance all show up in our voices clearly music is our chief way of expressing our inner emotions whether we realize it or not

162

In order to understand the passage you probably had to stop and go back at least once or twice to sort out the meaning and then punctuate it mentally. Now copy it, punctuating it as you think best, and read it again. This time you should be able to "hear" it and understand it easily.

The Goals of Revising Punctuation

Look closely at your punctuation in two ways:

1. Make sure that you haven't used a punctuation mark, or omitted one, in a way that sends the wrong signal.
2. Look for ways you can use it to improve clarity and emphasis.

RULES AND PRINCIPLES OF PUNCTUATION

End-punctuation Marks

Only three marks appear at the ends of sentences: the **period** (.), the **question mark** (?), and the **exclamation point** (!). They indicate whether a given sentence is intended as a **statement**, a **question**, or an **exclamation**.

PERIODS .

Most sentences end with **periods**, for most sentences are statements. But make sure that each group of words you end with a period is a true sentence and not a **fragment** (see pp. 116-17). A period should coincide with the feeling of completeness that comes at the end of a sentence. A period after a fragment may jolt readers because it will contradict what they are experiencing. And omitting a necessary period will disturb them even more: see **Run-on Sentence**, p. 176.

QUESTION MARKS ?

A **question mark** signals the end of a question. If you read your draft aloud, you will usually hear the rise in pitch at the end of a question and not forget to put in the mark. But put question marks only after **direct** questions, not **indirect** ones. Indirect questions are those that aren't being *asked* but merely reported or described:

DIRECT: What did he want?

INDIRECT: I wondered what he wanted.

DIRECT: "Where will the horse go?" Heather asked.

INDIRECT: Heather asked where the horse would go.

EXCLAMATION POINTS !

Exclamation points automatically follow short interjections like *Wow!* and *Good heavens!* But you should minimize or even avoid exclamation points — except in personal letters or when representing dialogue. An exclamation point merely makes a sentence appear emphatic. Sentences will be more effective if words and their order supply the emphasis. For example:

> DRAFT: The other driver denied that he had been speeding! I was astonished!

The exclamation points are feeble. The second seems silly.

> REVISED: Astonishingly, the other driver denied that he had been speeding.

The long introductory word, followed by the comma, sets up and therefore emphasizes the other driver's surprising denial. No exclamation point needed.

Internal Punctuation Marks

COMMAS ,

Commas, the most common marks, have three main uses:

1. *To join **independent clauses** that are already connected by one of these words (called **coordinating conjunctions**): and, but, or, nor, for, yet, so.* For example:

> Her argument sounds convincing, *but* it is based on a false premise.

2. *To separate items (words, phrases, or clauses) in a **series** of three or more:*

> We returned from the hike *hot, dirty,* and *tired.*

or *to separate two or more **parallel** adjectives in a **series** before a noun:*

> Her *graceful, intelligent* prose has won her many readers.

Note: Put a comma between such adjectives only when you could insert the word *and* in its place. For example:

> The Compsons live in the *old red* house down the road.

You wouldn't say "old *and* red house"; it's the *red house* that is *old.* But it would not be odd to speak of "her graceful *and* intelligent prose"; the words *graceful* and *intelligent* are **parallel**, both modifying *prose.*

3. *To set off* **parenthetical** *elements, whether they are beginnings or endings of sentences or interrupters within sentences, and whether they are words, phrases, or clauses:*

> *Indeed,* it was her best performance of the season. (beginning word)

> *With some timely help,* he made it through the week. (beginning phrase)

> *When Alexander died,* his empire was divided into three parts. (beginning clause)

> It was not a good day for their opponents, *however.* (ending word)

> He walked out of the meeting at four, *taking his clique with him.* (ending phrase)

> The suggestion came as a complete surprise, *which made it all the more attractive.* (ending clause)

> It was not, *however,* pleasant news in Jakarta. (interruptive word)

> Teddy Wilson, *pianist with the great Goodman band,* lived until 1985. (interruptive phrase)

> The experiment, *which she performed successfully,* delighted her instructor. (interruptive clause)

Commas also have a few other conventional uses:

After the informal salutation of a letter:

> Dear Jennifer,

After the complimentary close of a letter:

> Yours truly,

To separate the elements of place-names:

> Orillia, Ontario, was the model for Stephen Leacock's Mariposa. (Note the comma *after* the name of the province, as well as before it.)

To set off the year in dates:

> July 30, 1987, was a hot day. (Again, note the comma *after* the year.)

The alternative form of date uses no commas:

> On 30 July 1987 the heat was oppressive.

With only month and year, you can use commas around the year or not; just be consistent.

With a verb of speaking or writing before or after a quotation (see also p. 230):

> And then André said, "I'd be glad to help."
> "Enough questions for now," the general's aide barked.

To indicate a pause where a word or phrase has been omitted:

> To err is human; to forgive, divine.

Unwanted Commas

Check your draft for four common kinds of unwanted commas:

1. Don't put a lone comma between **subject** *and* **verb**:

> DRAFT: Many people in Europe and North America, are being forced to lower their expectations.

Omit the comma. If you want a pause, change the sentence so that a **parenthetical interrupter** comes between subject and verb; it would be set off with a **pair** of commas (or dashes):

> REVISED: Many people, especially those in Europe and North America, are being forced to lower their expectations.

Note: Occasionally you may need to insert a comma after a long or complicated subject in order to prevent misreading:

> How such a nice colour as green ever came to symbolize such nasty human tendencies as envy, greed, and deceit, is a mystery to me.

2. Don't put a lone comma between a **verb** *and its* **object** *or* **complement**:

> DRAFT: After carefully considering all the arguments I decided, that the courses I had originally chosen were best.

The word *that* introduces a noun clause which serves as the object of the verb *decided*. No comma should separate them. The long introductory phrase could well be followed by the pause of a comma — but it should be put in the right place:

> REVISED: After carefully considering all the arguments, I decided that the courses I had originally chosen were best.

3. Don't put a lone comma between the last **adjective of a series** *and the* **noun** *it modifies:*

> DRAFT: It turned out to be an inexpensive, relaxing, enjoyable, and educational, holiday for us all.

Even though each of the other adjectives is followed by a comma, the last one, *educational*, should not be.

4. Generally, don't separate the parts of a **compound structure** *(see the Glossary of Terms)* *unless they are* **independent clauses**. The word *and* is usually enough between **compound words**, **phrases**, and **subordinate clauses**. Use commas between such elements only when you consciously want a pause for emphasis or rhythm. For example:

> DRAFT: Grinding the valve seats in the block, and adjusting the carburetor both require special equipment.

The comma after *block* awkwardly breaks up the two parts of a compound subject; it should be removed.

Project 9-a

Remove unwanted commas from the following sentences.

1. Their early work was not destroyed or ignored, but was built upon.
2. The merchants who came to trade by sea with the Malaysians, were of the Islamic faith and brought their faith with them.
3. Instead, illiterate people from small villages, rushed to Tehran and other major cities, hoping for a job and more security.
4. Maybe some of them will decide, that they are not capable of university work.
5. The configurations that the offensive team will counter with, will change accordingly.
6. Over half the teenagers in a small town, remain for their whole lives in that same town.
7. Educated, industrious, well-groomed, people can usually find a reasonably good job.

SEMICOLONS **;**

Semicolons have only two basic uses:

1. *Use a semicolon to join independent clauses.* This is a semicolon's major function. Use a semicolon when you want to show that the relation between two clauses is closer than a period would suggest. Remember this: *use a semicolon only where you could use a period instead.* For example:

> Riding a motorcycle can be dangerous; one should take every possible safety precaution.

You *could* use a period instead of the semicolon, punctuating it as two separate sentences. A semicolon where a period would *not* be appropriate may confuse a reader:

> DRAFT: In a big city there are always people nearby; hundreds and thousands of them.

A period in place of the semicolon would make what follows a **fragment**. In effect, so does the semicolon. Remember this: after an independent clause,

> A SEMICOLON signals to readers that what comes next is another INDEPENDENT CLAUSE.

But in this example only a **phrase** arrives. To avoid jarring readers, change the semicolon to a comma:

> REVISED: In a big city there are always people nearby, hundreds and thousands of them.

2. *Use a semicolon in place of a comma when you want or need a heavier pause.* This is the only exception to the preceding rule. Occasionally you'll want a heavy pause for emphasis, but not often. Also infrequently, if clauses or the parts of a series have commas or other marks within them, you may need a semicolon just to keep the sense straight, as in this sentence:

> In attempting to explain why religious cults are gaining in vogue, we must consider our increasing inability to accept ourselves as consequential individuals, due largely to the impersonal nature of urban society; for is it not, ultimately, the individual who must bear the herculean burden of existence in a dispassionate universe?

The student writer decided that such a sentence would be much easier to read with a semicolon before *for* rather than just a comma. (See also pp. 171-72.)

Project 9-b
Compose three sentences that use only a semicolon to join two independent clauses. Make sure the relation between the parts of each pair is close enough to justify using a semicolon instead of a period. (See also Ch. 15, #11.)

COLONS :

Like a period or a semicolon, a **colon** stops readers. But colons also push readers toward what follows. When the second part of a sentence explains or elaborates what the first part says, a colon is often the most effective punctuation mark — as, for example, in this sentence from Northrop Frye's "The Motive for Metaphor":

> Many animals and insects have this social form too, but man knows that he has it: he can compare what he does with what he can imagine being done.

This anticipatory quality of colons makes them useful for introducing lists, examples, and quotations.

Project 9-c
Compose three sentences using a colon as a sentence punctuator — not to introduce a list, but to look forward to an explanation or elaboration in the second part. (See also Ch. 15, #11.)

Warning: Don't overuse colons. Their effectiveness would fade if you used, say, more than one or two a page.

And be careful to avoid a common misuse of the colon: use it, like a semicolon between clauses, *only after an independent clause.* For example, DON'T use it to introduce a list after any form of the verb *be*:

DRAFT: The obstacles between us and our goals *were*: poor equipment, too few volunteers, and outmoded procedures.

Since the series completes the verb phrase, it should not be cut off from the verb. If you want to keep the colon, make sure it follows an independent clause:

REVISED: *Three obstacles stood between us and our goals*: poor equipment, too few volunteers, and outmoded procedures.

Similarly, DON'T put a colon between a preposition and its object:

DRAFT: The firm has branches *in*: Alberta, Manitoba, and Quebec.

Either omit the colon or make what precedes it an independent clause:

REVISED: *The firm has branches in three provinces*: Alberta, Manitoba, and Quebec.

Note: Use a colon after the salutation in a formal letter:

Dear Senator Hassenpfeffer:

DASHES ——

Like the colon, the **dash** is a highly effective punctuation mark that you should not use often. Used too often, dashes lose their strength and make prose choppy. DON'T use the dash as a casual substitute for a comma or a semicolon; use it only where it is the most appropriate mark.

Like the colon, the dash sends a specific signal to readers: it calls attention to whatever it sets off. Use it

1. to convey emphasis,
2. to mark a sharp or ironic turn of thought,
3. to set off something that abruptly breaks the structure of a sentence.

Here are some examples:

This is Toronto the Good — smug, solid, respectable.

> (Pierre Berton, introduction to Henry Rossier's *The New City, a Prejudiced View of Toronto*)

Berton chose a dash rather than a colon because it sets off the series more sharply and also conveys a wry tone.

I want to talk about the mainspring of all human affairs, that special mark of humanity by which mankind stands or falls — language.

> (Vincent Massey, "Uncertain Sounds")

The dash is more emphatic than a colon, and more economical than ending with "falls, namely language."

> The chief competitor of modern fiction — of this there can be no doubt — is the great fiction already written.
>
> (Hugh MacLennan, "The Novel as an Art Form")

Dashes add emphasis and also mark the abrupt break with the structure of the sentence; commas would have been too weak.

> Those of us unable to afford a tennis club or a spa membership can be off and running with only a pair of jogging shoes — no white coordinated outfit is necessary.

The student uses a dash to mark the ironic humour of the final clause. A flat semicolon just wouldn't fit the tone.

Note: Use a dash to set off a summing-up clause after a subject consisting of many parts, such as a series; here's an example from the beginning of the next chapter:

> Letters, telegrams, memos, formal essays, lab reports — all these and others have their own forms . . . .

Such clauses usually need to start with *these* or *those* or *all*, referring to or in effect repeating the subject.

Project 9-d

Compose three sentences using dashes in some of the ways illustrated above. (See also Ch. 15, #11.)

PARENTHESES ( )

Dashes emphasize. **Parentheses** de-emphasize, suggesting that something is relatively unimportant, even incidental. Had MacLennan wanted to play down the point in his interruptive clause, he could have written the example above as follows:

> The chief competitor of modern fiction (of this there can be no doubt) is the great fiction already written.

Parentheses are also used to enclose cross-references and numbers or letters that are parts of lists or outlines.

Note: You will find information on **quotations** and **quotation marks**, **ellipses**, and **brackets** in Chapter 12; see pp. 229-31. The **apostrophe** (') and the **hyphen** (-) are matters of spelling, not punctuation. See the next chapter.

Joining Independent Clauses (see Ch. 15, #1, and the
Glossary of Terms)

You can join independent clauses with semicolons, commas, colons, and dashes. You can also join them with coordinating conjunctions. Or you can use both conjunctions and punctuation. You have a good deal of freedom of choice.

JOINING INDEPENDENT CLAUSES WITH SEMICOLONS, COLONS, AND DASHES

To join two separate sentences into a compound sentence, you can use a semicolon:

> Summer is over. The school year begins.
> Summer is over; the school year begins.

Occasionally, for a different effect, use a colon or a dash:

> Summer is over: the school year begins.
> Summer is over — the school year begins.

JOINING INDEPENDENT CLAUSES WITH COMMAS AND COORDINATING CONJUNCTIONS

You can join two independent clauses with a comma and one of the seven **coordinating conjunctions**. Memorize them:

> *and   but   or   nor   for   yet   so*

When you join independent clauses with one of these, you will usually put a comma in front of it:

> Few people consider music to be a real career, *and* even fewer realize the importance of music in education.

But a comma isn't always necessary, especially if the clauses are *short* or *parallel* or *share the same subject:*

> He went one way and she went the other.

(A comma after *way* would lightly emphasize what follows.) Sometimes a comma is needed before *and* in order to keep readers from mistaking the subject of the second clause for another object of the verb of the first clause:

> Music 320 includes a lot of listening to recordings, and the study of the basic forms is its main component.

But and *yet* will almost always need a comma, since they mark a contrast or other sharp turn in thought. With the conjunction *for*, a comma is essential to keep readers from mistaking it for the preposition *for*:

DRAFT: I decided to take two courses in the summer *for* the extra credits would look good on my record.

REVISED: I decided to take two courses in the summer, *for* the extra credits would look good on my record.

Project 9-e
Insert commas where necessary in the following sentences.

1. His presence does not deter her and she participates in the initiation.
2. We don't often have to go into Toronto for all the commodities are available nearby.
3. A vague feeling of nostalgia assailed her when someone mentioned Devon but it soon vanished.
4. Concepts are dandy but programs need people and students who are lucky enough to have free time are usually filling it with part-time jobs.
5. There must be no exceptions for any drug may be abused in some way.
6. The 3-D effect doesn't make the movie any better, just different and in order to get the 3-D effect, you have to sit in the centre section.
7. He had no opportunity to discover love for he had been leading a nomadic life.

Comma Splice

CS

If you join two independent clauses with ONLY a comma, you commit a **comma splice**. A comma splice is a serious error because it misleads readers. After an independent clause, a comma without a coordinating conjunction signals readers that some kind of **subordinate** element is coming next. When another **independent clause** arrives instead, they will be surprised — and annoyed. Consider the following sentence:

COMMA SPLICE: We were able to complete the project, many of us worked overtime.

The comma wrongly splices together two clauses that are **independent**; each could stand as a separate sentence:

We were able to complete the project. Many of us worked overtime.

Written thus, the relation between the two sentences or clauses is only implied by their being side by side. To show that the two are more closely related than the period suggests, use a semicolon:

We were able to complete the project; many of us worked overtime.

If you want to be explicit about the causality, you can use a **subordinator**, such as *because:*

We were able to complete the project *because* many of us worked overtime.

The second clause is no longer independent; the subordinator makes it a **subordinate** clause (see p. 116 and Ch. 15, #2). You could also put the *because*-clause first:

> *Because many of us worked overtime,* we were able to complete the project.

EXCEPTIONS

Occasionally a comma can effectively join two independent clauses. If readers can take in both clauses in a single glance, a comma won't disturb them. Therefore don't risk using a comma alone unless the two clauses are *short,* are *parallel in structure,* and preferably *have the same subject:*

> I worked all day, I slept all night.

And if there are more than two clauses — that is, if they are part of a **series** of three or more — commas are sufficient:

> I worked all day, I read all evening, I slept all night, and I woke next morning refreshed and ready.

CONJUNCTIVE ADVERBS

Check to see if you have joined independent clauses with any of the following words — called **conjunctive adverbs**:

accordingly	finally	likewise	particularly
afterward	furthermore	meanwhile	similarly
also	hence	moreover	still
besides	however	namely	subsequently
certainly	indeed	nevertheless	then
consequently	instead	next	therefore
conversely	later	otherwise	thus

Look also for such connecting phrases as these:

as a result	in addition	on the other hand
for example	in fact	that is

Because they sometimes "feel" like conjunctions or subordinators, these connectors can tempt you to splice two independent clauses with a comma.

> Whenever you use one of these to connect two independent clauses, PUT A **SEMICOLON** IN FRONT OF IT.

The words *therefore* and *however* are the most frequent offenders. Here's an example from a student's paper:

> DRAFT: My teddy bear is covered with a layer of white fur, *however,* in some places the fur is worn away.

The comma before *however* must be changed to a semicolon:

REVISED: My teddy bear is covered with a layer of white fur; *however*, in some places the fur is worn away.

This diagram will help you see how to join independent clauses. Think of the independent clauses as bricks and the items listed between the dotted lines as mortar. *A comma alone is not enough mortar to hold the bricks together.*

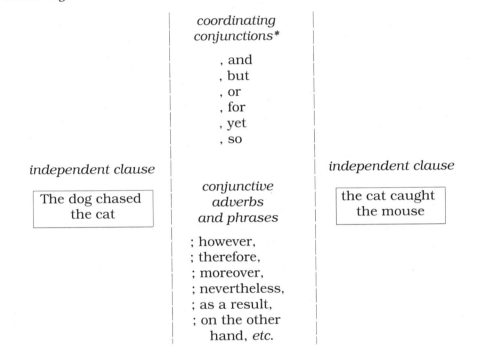

*We omit *nor* because it doesn't work in the example. It requires a negative and a change in the word order: "The dog did not chase the cat, *nor did* the cat catch the mouse."

Note that you can place the **coordinating conjunctions** only between the two clauses. But you can place the **adverbs** in several different spots: between the clauses, after the word *cat*, and even at the end of the sentence:

The dog chased the cat; nevertheless, the cat caught the mouse.
The dog chased the cat; the cat, nevertheless, caught the mouse.
The dog chased the cat; the cat caught the mouse, nevertheless.

You can often improve the rhythm of a sentence by tucking such terms a little way in. Especially, don't begin a sentence or clause with the word *however* unless you want it to sound heavily emphatic; it is usually better delayed:

> The cat, however, caught the mouse.

Another advantage of delaying such a connector is that you will be less likely to commit a comma splice.

Note: Don't use the conjunction *so* except on informal occasions. (See **so** in the Checklist of Usage, Ch. 8.)

Project 9-f

(a) Compose three sentences using a comma and a coordinating conjunction to join two independent clauses.

(b) Compose three sentences using a semicolon and a conjunctive adverb to join two independent clauses.

Project 9-g

Correct the unacceptable comma splices in the following sentences. Consider other kinds of revision besides the obvious changing of the faulty comma to a semicolon.

1. The term *lauds* is found only in the quarto edition of 1605, other editions use *tunes.*
2. The first wave ashore was successful in establishing a beachhead, nevertheless fierce fighting lay ahead.
3. We were successful with this defence, in fact, we went to the provincial finals.
4. No one bustles, all is tranquil.
5. The village is not far from the city, therefore the few winter residents can easily travel back and forth.
6. This park used to be surrounded by cedars and firs, now it is just a weed-grown field.
7. I decided not to comment on their marriage, however, in turning down the invitation I suppose I was making my feelings clear.
8. They led us into the house, it was still furnished in Afro-American style.
9. My sister was merely ignorant, she didn't know how to behave in those circumstances.
10. Such an attitude is destructive, it taints all those who come in contact with it.
11. My uncle was pessimistic, for him most of life was pointless.
12. The most common reaction to change is fear, thus the government shouldn't be surprised at all this criticism.

Run-on Sentence (Fused Sentence)

A **run-on** or **fused** sentence results from a failure to put any punctuation whatsoever between two independent clauses:

> DRAFT: I had to be careful to keep away from the tent wall otherwise I would get wet from the condensation.

The student was misled by the word *otherwise*, a **conjunctive adverb** (see above). It is not a conjunction like *or; therefore* not even a comma would be enough mortar between the independent-clause bricks. If the clauses are part of one sentence, they need a semicolon between them, or a comma and the coordinating conjunction *for:*

> REVISED: I had to be careful to keep away from the tent wall; otherwise I would get wet from the condensation.

> REVISED: I had to be careful to keep away from the tent wall, *for* otherwise I would get wet from the condensation.

Project 9-h

Correct the run-on sentences below. You may wish to separate a pair of independent clauses, to join them in one way or another, or to subordinate one of them.

1. Serve it with any dish of meat or fish it is a pleasant substitute for potatoes.
2. On the whole, I don't like buses nevertheless they are the only practical way for me to get here.
3. It is hard to find a full-time job therefore some of my friends are going back to school to get a more specialized education.
4. She is tense and distracted she doesn't really want to speak to her daughter.
5. In June 1836 the British and the Dutch wiped out the pirates' base at Galang even so the British suspected that the Dutch participated only to expand their own political influence.

Punctuating Subordinate Elements

Subordinate elements are words, phrases, and clauses that function as modifiers. Some kinds should never be set off; others should always be set off; but with many you have a choice. When you set off such elements you usually use commas, though sometimes you will use dashes or parentheses.

CONNECTORS AND SENTENCE-MODIFIERS

Generally, set off a conjunctive adverb or other short transitional element. The word *however* with the meaning "nevertheless" or "yet" MUST be set off to keep it from being mistaken for *however* meaning "in whatever way" or "to whatever degree" ("However much it cost, it was worth it"). *Nevertheless, moreover, furthermore, that is, besides,* and *similarly* almost always need setting off, as do sentence adverbs like *unfortunately, luckily, interestingly, obviously,* and *evidently.* But such terms don't always need setting off. If you don't want a pause, don't use a comma. Here are some examples of such words; all of these sound acceptable without commas:

> It began to rain; *therefore* we decided to stay home.
>
> *Accordingly* she moved on to the next stage of the analysis.
>
> They were well trained; *indeed* they performed like professionals.
>
> *Finally* the answer came to him.

Commas are optional. In the last example, a comma would be appropriate if you wanted to emphasize *finally.*

Caution: Especially do not set off an opening *But* or *Perhaps* with a comma, even though they are often spoken with a pause. If a following phrase needs to be set off with a **pair** of commas, the first one will follow the opener; but they will set off the phrase, not the *But* or *Perhaps.*

INTRODUCTORY PHRASES AND CLAUSES

Adverbial Phrases

You don't usually need to set off a short phrase:

> *In a year* he was back at work.
> *From there* they moved to Halifax.

Even longer phrases will sometimes not need commas:

> *At the beginning of their terms* elected officials enjoy a good deal of freedom.
>
> *While writing her second draft* she discovered what she really wanted to say.

But set off long phrases to keep your readers oriented:

> *In a period of higher prices and lower real income,* financial security becomes difficult to maintain.

Adverbial Clauses

Generally, treat opening adverbial clauses the same as phrases. Set off long ones, but not short ones:

> *When the heroine returns from Europe with a foreign husband in tow,* her family is at first flabbergasted.

> *When they left* I went back to painting the fence.

But when you want to, you can set off even a short clause for a desired emphasis or rhythm. And note that a sentence like the following demands a comma to prevent misreading:

> DRAFT: Although sales are increasing profits in the textile industry are declining.

> REVISED: Although sales are increasing, profits in the textile industry are declining.

> Whenever you're not sure whether to put a comma after an introductory element, PUT ONE IN: it will never be wrong, even though it may strike some readers as unnecessary.

Project 9-i

Punctuate the introductory elements in the following sentences as you think necessary.

1. With a good deal of help from the government the company continued to show a profit.
2. Of course if you punch in the numbers wrong the answer will be wrong but that's not the computer's fault.
3. Without publicity people would have no way of finding out about the place.
4. When Godzilla walked all over Tokyo causing widespread destruction you could tell the buildings were fake.
5. But when I opened the door there was no one there.
6. If you follow three simple steps you should experience almost no trouble.
7. Because grass is so sparse in the area the cattle ranches are enormous.
8. As a rule when you play one-on-one defence you stay about an arm's length away from the player you are guarding.
9. When people come in the door they are greeted effusively.

SETTING OFF NONRESTRICTIVE ELEMENTS

With **restrictives** and **nonrestrictives** you have no choice.

1. A **restrictive** modifier **restricts** — that is, in some way *identifies, defines, limits* — what it modifies; omitting it would significantly change the sense of the sentence. When an element is **restrictive** — essential to the meaning of the sentence — it MUST NOT be set off.

2. A **nonrestrictive** modifier adds incidental information; omitting it would not seriously affect meaning. When an element is **nonrestrictive** — not essential to the meaning of the sentence — it MUST be set off.

Relative Clauses (see Ch. 15, #4, and the Glossary of Terms)

Adjective clauses (beginning with the relative pronouns *who, whom, which,* or *that* or the relative adverbs *where* or *when*) are either **restrictive** or **nonrestrictive**. Consider the difference in meaning between the following examples:

RESTRICTIVE: The order *which you have already paid for* will be delivered on Friday.

With no commas, the *which*-clause **restricts** the meaning of *the order* to the one *you have already paid for.* THAT'S the order that will be delivered on Friday.

However, if you want your readers to understand the sentence as saying something like this — "The order will be delivered on Friday. (By the way, you have already paid for it, as you probably remember.)" — then set it off with commas to mark it as incidental, parenthetical:

NONRESTRICTIVE: The order, *which you have already paid for,* will be delivered on Friday.

Now the *which*-clause does NOT restrict the meaning of *the order.* Only one order is under discussion. Again:

RESTRICTIVE: The teacher *who came from a small town* was kind to me.

NONRESTRICTIVE: The teacher, *who came from a small town,* was kind to me.

The first sentence specifies which teacher was kind: the one from a small town, as opposed to others who were not from small towns. The relative clause is marked as essential. In the second sentence, only one teacher is being discussed; the information that the teacher was from a small town is therefore incidental; it could be omitted without destroying the sense of the sentence.

If you aren't sure about a particular clause, try substituting *that* for *who* or *which*. If the sentence still says what you want, the clause is restrictive, since *that* cannot begin a nonrestrictive clause:

The order *that* you have already paid for will be delivered on Friday.

The teacher *that* came from a small town was kind to me.

Appositives (see Ch. 15, #5, and the Glossary of Terms)
Most appositives are **nonrestrictive** and need to be set off:

Ms. McGillivray, *my grade ten teacher*, had been an actress.

You can test whether an appositive is nonrestrictive, parenthetical, by trying actual parentheses around it:

Ms. McGillivray *(my grade ten teacher)* had been an actress.

Another example:

Einstein, *the great physicist*, was born in 1879.

The phrase *the great physicist* cannot further restrict the meaning of the name *Einstein*, which clearly identifies the man being discussed. The phrase is therefore **nonrestrictive** and set off with punctuation. But try reversing the two:

The great physicist *Einstein* was born in 1879.

Now the appositive, the name *Einstein*, is necessary to the meaning; the phrase *the great physicist*, now the subject of the sentence, does not sufficiently identify the man, since there are other great physicists. The appositive is therefore **restrictive** and not set off with commas.

If you want to de-emphasize an appositive, you can set it off with **parentheses**, for example when using it as a way of defining (see pp. 73-74). If you want to emphasize one, you can set it off with **dashes**. And if an appositive consists of more than one noun, you almost have to set it off with dashes in order to avoid confusing readers; for example:

DRAFT: Three students, *Alice, Nicole*, and *Bruce*, raised their hands.

Even with the comma after *Bruce*, readers could think that the sentence referred to six people. Setting the appositive off with dashes removes the ambiguity:

REVISED: Three students — *Alice, Nicole, and Bruce* — raised their hands.

An appositive as part of a name is **restrictive**, not set off:

William the Conqueror   Ethelred the Unready

Absolute Phrases (see Ch. 15, #10, and the Glossary of Terms)
An **absolute phrase**, usually a noun with a participle, in effect modifies all the rest of the sentence. Since they never modify any particular

element in the sentence, they are always **nonrestrictive** and must be set off:

> The ship, *all its flags flying,* triumphantly entered the harbour.

> *The device securely installed,* we took the car onto the test track.

ADVERBIAL CLAUSES AND PREPOSITIONAL PHRASES IN THE MIDDLE OR AT THE END

Adverbial clauses and prepositional phrases at the beginnings of sentences are seldom a problem (see above). But when they come elsewhere, it isn't always easy to decide how to punctuate them. Sometimes you can think of them as similar or analogous to restrictive and nonrestrictive elements; sometimes you have to consider the meaning and emphasis you want or even the rhythm of the sentence.

Adverbial Clauses at the End

Generally, don't set off clauses of time, place, manner, and causation when they occupy their natural place at the end of a sentence; they will in effect be restrictive:

> Archimbault studied oceanography *while she was in Tahiti.*

> Peron found himself welcomed as a hero *when he returned to Buenos Aires.*

> The company hired him on the spot *because he had the kind of experience they were looking for.*

If you move such clauses to the beginning of a sentence, however, they become introductory elements and may or may not need setting off. Of the above examples, the first and second could be followed by a comma; the third, because of its length, would almost have to be.

But sometimes a comma before a closing adverbial clause is necessary to clarify or emphasize your meaning. For example, clauses beginning with *though* or *although* are usually like nonrestrictive elements:

> The minister had no authority to order the hearing, *though he was not aware of it at the time.*

When a *because*-clause (or phrase) follows a negative, you usually need to set it off:

> He was not given the job, *because he lacked experience.*

Without the comma, that sentence would be ambiguous: it would seem to say that he *was* hired, but for some reason other than his lack of experience. The comma prevents the ambiguity by separating the two clauses, in effect saying "He was not given the job. Why? Because he lacked experience." (Note that changing the negative verb to a positive one also removes the ambiguity: "He *was denied* the job because he lacked experience." No comma needed.)

Adverbial Clauses As Interrupters

As interrupters, such clauses usually need to be set off because they amount to a heavy break in the main clause (in these examples, between subject and verb):

> Archimbault, *while she was in Tahiti* , studied oceanography.

> Peron, *when he returned to Buenos Aires,* found himself welcomed as a hero.

Prepositional Phrases (see Ch.15, #3, and the Glossary of Terms)

Prepositional phrases, whether adverbial or adjectival, may or may not need setting off. Often you can think of them as restrictive or non-restrictive. That is, if you consider a phrase essential to the meaning of your sentence, don't set it off; if it's incidental, parenthetical, set it off:

> Studying *with the radio on* is difficult.

> Studying, *with your face in a book and your pencil going constantly,* is tiring.

> The boat *with the red sail* won easily; the others hardly seemed in the same race.

> The consortium's boat, *with its red sail flapping in the light breeze,* slowly pulled ahead of its competitors.

(Note that if you drop *with* from the second and fourth sentences, the phrases become absolutes — nonrestrictive.)

Here are some prepositional phrases that we used earlier as examples of introductory phrases; none of these would need setting off within or at the end of the sentence; they can be thought of as restrictive, since omitting them would significantly alter the meaning:

> Elected officials *at the beginning of their terms* enjoy a good deal of freedom.

> Elected officials enjoy a good deal of freedom *at the beginning of their terms*.

> They moved *from there* to Halifax.

> He was back at work *in a year.*

When you're not sure, read the sentence aloud. You may feel a slight pause when commas are needed or possible. In the first of the four examples above, the phrase could even be set off with dashes; it's a matter of tone.

PARTICIPLES AND PARTICIPIAL PHRASES (see Ch. 15, #7, and the Glossary of Terms)

As Sentence Openers When a participial modifier *begins a sentence and modifies its subject,* you have no choice. Set it off with a comma:

> *Writing the second draft,* she discovered what she really wanted to say.

> *Altering the proportions in the formula,* I began to think the experiment might work after all.

> *Disappointed,* the committee adjourned early.

Within and at the Ends of Sentences Usually, set off such modifiers in the middle or at the end, as well:

> She discovered, *writing the second draft,* what she really wanted to say.

> The committee, *disappointed and tired,* adjourned early.

> The committee adjourned early, *disappointed by the results.*

But some participial modifiers will in effect be restrictive and thus not set off, even in the middle of a sentence:

> She pointed to the man *sitting in the front row.*

> The player *having the lowest score* begins the new hand.

> Those *most disappointed by the results* were the subcommittee members.

The phrases are essential to the meaning; removing them would destroy or significantly alter the sense.

Project 9-j

Set off with punctuation any nonrestrictive elements in the following sentences, as well as any other elements, such as absolutes and participial phrases, that need to be set off. If a word, phrase, or clause is an *interrupter* in a sentence, be sure to set it off at both ends.

1. Children who move many times when they are young learn to adapt to new environments.
2. The most important influence was my father who early on drilled certain principles into me.
3. Yeats's poem "The Second Coming" makes a strong impact on the reader.
4. The author illustrates how selfishness in the guise of "good" or moral behaviour can be damaging to others.
5. In Regina and its vicinity, barley, rye, and the main crop wheat are grown under the ideal conditions of the prairies.
6. Walking my dog after dark one night last week I stumbled onto a potentially violent scene.

7. The hinges perform the same function as a door hinge allowing the ear-pieces to lie flat against the front part of the frame.
8. These unwritten laws of conduct such as those of politeness and honesty will be severely enforced by society.
9. We might expect them to be in love, but in fact they demonstrate only affinity which is not the same.
10. The first step introducing children to the water is designed to give them confidence.
11. The prosecutor sometimes dominated, but others during the trial in particular the defence lawyer, his client, and the major character witness made a stronger impression on the jury.
12. Stephen Huan when he travels to the Far East always flies first class.
13. The term *simple* hardly seems accurate to describe either character considering their general ability and their capacity for learning.
14. They can see how according to the advertiser it will improve their lives.

Punctuating Series

All you need to remember is to separate the items in a series with punctuation, usually commas:

Dogs, cats, birds, and fish are the most common household pets.

But be careful not to put one after the last item *(fish).*

COMMA BEFORE THE *AND* OR THE *OR*

In the example above, note the comma after *birds.* Some people treat such a comma as optional, but if you include it you will not risk confusing your readers. For example:

For breakfast we could choose from ham, bacon, eggs, toast, hot cereal and bran muffins.

This may make sense, but most readers would feel some ambiguity: do the cereal and the muffins go together as one item? Are the muffins *hot,* like the cereal? It's impossible to be sure. A comma before *and* clearly separates the two items (it also improves the rhythm of the sentence):

For breakfast we could choose from ham, bacon, eggs, toast, hot cereal, and bran muffins.

USING SEMICOLONS TO SEPARATE ITEMS IN A SERIES

Sometimes the elements of a series will themselves contain commas. To keep things clear for your readers, use semicolons rather than more commas to separate them:

The firm has branches in Lethbridge, Alberta; Brandon, Manitoba; and Hull, Quebec.

Occasionally you may want to use semicolons because the elements are unusually long, or because you want heavier pauses for emphasis, as in this sentence by a student:

> Honesty; trust; patience; love — these are the qualities of an ideal marriage.

Project 9-k

Here is the way the student punctuated the paragraph we quoted — without punctuation — at the beginning of the chapter. Compare it with your version.

> The human voice is music itself. It rises and falls, it pauses, it gets louder and softer. If this music were not present in our voices, we would all speak in monotones, and conversation would soon become very tedious. Our speech pattern is song, and it reflects our emotions: happiness, anger, sorrow, fatigue, and nonchalance all show up in our voices. Clearly music is our chief way of expressing our inner emotions — whether we realize it or not.

Here is another passage you can try punctuating:

> Abroadening
>
> travel can be broadening as almost everyone who has travelled much will agree experiencing a foreign culture stretches the mind it can so to speak enrich one's soul further we need to learn about other people how they live and think foreign countries being increasingly important to us in today's rapidly shrinking world and how better to learn about foreign countries than by actually visiting them what one can learn from books won't stick so well in the mind it tends to evaporate soon after but the sensation of eating foreign food of hearing foreign voices of seeing foreign buildings of walking about in foreign streets these experiences will last in one's memory become a vital part of one's inner self even though many details may be forgotten the essence will remain onc can perhaps get along without travelling nevertheless one would then be missing the considerable enrichment that it can bring

Project 9-l

Here are some poorly punctuated sentences from students' drafts and elsewhere. You will discover other problems in them as well. Practise your revising techniques.

1. Therefore, it is much more beneficial to the reader, because they can better understand the story.
2. Every mature adult possesses a vocabulary of several thousand words; but, how many of us really know the meaning of these words?
3. No matter how well perfectionists do something they always ask themselves "Could I have done better."

4. It would seem that for politicians the issues aren't what's really important, it's the argument that counts.
5. When you are unable to see your senses become highly tuned and your imagination will react to any message received by the senses.
6. It has been hypothesized that the new brain, or cerebral cortex controls reason and intuition, and allows cognitive thought processes.
7. But, I decided to go ahead with the project.
8. The network's new, family adventure series starts later this month.
9. The weather is a force we will never control and it is a good thing.
10. Her character, throughout the early part of the novel is most definitely flat.
11. The plain omelette is a simple quick meal of eggs mixed with water, salt, pepper and herbs such as dill, chives or marjoram.
12. Harmony, as opposed to melody, is the vertical structure of a musical composition; the melody being the horizontal structure.
13. It is good for one to get out of the city now and then and enjoy the world of nature; specifically the forests and mountains.
14. By the early 70's the author observes, people's habits had changed.
15. Professor Blank is considered one of Canada's best, young virologists.
16. The classes last only fifty minutes which is considerably shorter than the eighty-minute classes I was used to.
17. Teenagers, who skip meals regularly, should discipline themselves to follow a proper diet.
18. On a larger scale however, I would like to discuss athletic scholarships at universities.
19. He flew back from a Caribbean vacation, to make sure the committee held on to the documents.
20. Don't overexert yourself because it is hazardous to your health.
21. We never really believed we could get away with it, instead we were merely trying to put up a brave front.
22. This helplessness; this feeling of being overpowered, brought out something in my character that I didn't know was there.
23. The old cliché, which says that a dog is a man's best friend, acquired a new meaning for me last summer.
24. In Joseph Conrad's, *Heart of Darkness*, the principal setting is the African jungle.
25. She makes no bid for sympathy she is too honest.

Project 9-m

Punctuate the following sentences as you think necessary. Some may need no punctuation. Be prepared to defend your choices.

1. The flowers in the garden were predominantly roses daffodils and camellias.
2. Having received his degree after four long hard years Sean felt that he deserved a decent job.
3. The salesman was no doubt eager for the sale was an important one.

4. The clerk carefully explained to me that no interest would be charged.
5. The next day however Dorothy changed her mind.
6. She was born in Halifax Nova Scotia on December 15 1911 of immigrant parents.
7. The mayor made a long statement describing the issue then council began to debate it.
8. While parking the car he suddenly remembered that he had left his wallet at home.
9. Winding the clock I thought once again of the work awaiting me the next morning.
10. It promised to be an unusually warm day but we decided to go on the hike anyway.
11. High winds were forecast for the afternoon therefore the regatta had to be postponed again.
12. She started for the door as soon as the whistle sounded.
13. The book they sent me interesting as it was was not the one I had ordered.
14. In the introduction to her book Campbell argues that a vegetable diet is essential for good health.
15. Three years have passed since they moved to the country and they find that they no longer miss busy city life.
16. He was assured it would not be a difficult task however he still did not look forward to it.
17. Disturbed by the event she tried hard to remember when it had all begun.
18. Clearly it was time to call Mr. Bannerjee our plumber.
19. The gardener told me that my roses my lilacs my hydrangeas and my geraniums all needed fertilizer.
20. Diana didn't like the look of the house at all in fact she couldn't imagine why her friends had bought it.
21. Jonathan slept until almost noon and then fixed himself a large and leisurely breakfast it being a holiday that he was determined to enjoy in his own way.
22. Otherwise the child will be taken as rude and therefore made an outcast.
23. Three major thinkers whose influence on our century we need to understand are Darwin Marx and Freud.
24. Finally Magda looked up and said I refuse to be intimidated.
25. During lunch my supervisor asked what I planned to do on my holiday.
26. After carefully slitting each banana use your fingers to widen the slits a little.
27. Another favourite method of advertising is to compare two brands of a product for example laundry detergents.
28. There are three things wrong with that theory it is based on unsound premises it fails to account for some important exceptions and frankly it seems to me to contradict common sense.
29. Her lawyers no doubt will seek to settle out of court.

30. I don't think this law is unjust in fact it seems designed to protect society.

CHAPTER 10
The Last Step: Preparing and Proofreading Your Final Draft

When you are through revising you are ready for the final step in the process of writing: preparing your final draft, the finished product.

The *occasion* for a piece of writing determines the *form* in which you present it. Letters, telegrams, memos, formal essays, lab reports — all these and others have their own forms, and each form has its own restrictions and demands.

As a student, you will present most of your written work in the standard format for academic papers.

MANUSCRIPT CONVENTIONS

Follow these standard cnventions for format unless you have good reason to depart from them — for example, if an instructor wants something done differently:

Neatness Be neat. Nothing puts readers off faster than a sloppy or illegible piece of writing.

Type if possible. Use a good black ribbon. If you write by hand, write *legibly*, and use black or dark blue ink. If you use a word-processor with a dot-matrix printer, make sure your instructor will accept its output.

ms

189

Corrections Make any corrections or other changes *in ink.* If you make more than two or three on a page, redo it. Don't make big black blots; delete by drawing one line through the rejected parts; they should remain legible.

Paper Use standard size (21 x 28 cm or 8.5 x 11 inches) white paper of good quality, plain for typed work, ruled for handwritten work. Do not submit work on "erasable" paper or paper torn from a spiral notebook.

Margins Leave generous margins on *all four* sides: approximately 2.5-3.5 cm (1-1.5 inches) at the left, 2.5 cm (1 inch) at top, bottom, and right.

Spacing If you type, double-space. If you write by hand, write on every other line. Use only one side of each sheet. Don't leave extra space between paragraphs except to indicate a break between major sections.

Endorsement Endorse each paper with your name, your instructor's name, the course number, and the date. For papers folded vertically, put the endorsement in the upper right-hand section of the back of the last page. For papers handed in flat, put the endorsement in the upper left-hand corner of the first page, or below the title on a separate title page.

Your own title Except when you use a separate title page, centre your title about a quarter of the way down the first page, and quadruple-space below it. Don't underline or put quotation marks around your own title; don't write it all in capital letters; and don't put a period after it, even if it is a sentence (a question mark or exclamation point is all right).

Page numbers Number all pages, with unadorned Arabic numerals, in the upper right-hand corner. As a precaution, you may want to put your name, or just your surname, in front of the page number (except of course on an already endorsed first page).

Indention Indent each paragraph five spaces. Indent block quotations eight or ten spaces (see Chapter 12).

Punctuation marks Don't begin a new line with a punctuation mark (except the first of a pair of parentheses, opening quotation marks, a dash, or the dots of an ellipsis).

Always leave *two spaces* after the period or other mark at the end of a sentence.

In a title or an item of documentation, a colon is followed by one space; elsewhere, a colon may have either one or two spaces after it — but be consistent.

For a dash, type *two* unspaced hyphens WITHOUT a space before or after them.

Except in the following instances, do not put two punctuation marks together: Obviously, an opening or closing quotation mark may have another punctuation mark next to it. A pair of parentheses may be *followed* by another punctuation mark, but never put a comma in front of a pair of parentheses. The period of an abbreviation may be followed by any other mark except another period; for example, if you end a sentence with *etc.*, do not put a second period after it.

Word division As much as possible, avoid dividing words at the end of a line; better an uneven right-hand margin than a lot of divided words. When you must divide a word, do so only between syllables — and don't guess: use your dictionary. Never break off a syllable of only one or two letters. Indicate the break with a hyphen at the end of the line, and always try to divide a word so that the next line begins with a consonant rather than a vowel: *con-tinuation* or *continua-tion* rather than *contin-uation* or *continu-ation*.

div *syl*

Abbreviations Use only standard abbreviations: Mr., Mrs., Jr., M.D., B.A., A.D., a.m., Ltd., and so on. Some are not followed by periods: NASA, CBC, CDC, ABM, and so on. Some can be written either way, for example Ms or Ms., RCMP or R.C.M.P., SPCA or S.P.C.A. (Check your dictionary.) Otherwise, avoid abbreviations when possible, unless they are appropriate, as for example in a technical report. In formal writing, write out "that is," "for example," and "and so forth" or "and so on" rather than use *i.e.*, *e.g.*, and *etc.*

abbr

Numerals Except in technical reports and the like, use numerals only in the following instances: when it would take more than two words to spell out a number; when you are citing two or more numbers for comparison or as statistics; for time of day with *a.m.* and *p.m.*; for dates; for addresses; for page and chapter numbers and the like. Never begin a sentence with a numeral.

num

Capitalization Capitalize the beginnings of sentences, the pronoun *I*, proper nouns and their abbreviations, titles when part of a name (Sir, Judge, Princess, Premier, Admiral), months and days (but not seasons), languages (English, French), derivations of proper names (Shakespearean, Haligonian), the first and last and all other important words of titles of written or other works (but not

cap *lc*

prepositions and conjunctions unless five or more letters long). (If your tone and the occasion of a particular piece of writing permit it, you may even want to capitalize a whole word, phrase, or sentence for graphic emphasis.)

Titles of other works When you refer to other works by their titles, enclose in *quotation marks* those of short works or parts of works (stories, essays, short poems, chapters, songs); *italicize* (underline) those of long works or works published as units (books, plays, long poems, operas, movies, magazines, newspapers, paintings, sculptures).

Italics Use italics (underlining in typed or handwritten work) for titles of long works (see above); names of ships, planes, and the like; words, letters, or numerals referred to as such ("The word *italics* refers to slanted type"); French and foreign terms not yet fully accepted into English (check your dictionary); and perhaps occasionally — not often — for emphasis.

ital

THE MECHANICS OF OUTLINES

If you submit an outline as part of an assignment, use the conventional format, as illustrated by the topic and sentence outlines in Chapter 3 (pp. 59-60) and the research paper outline in Chapter 12 (p. 238). Indicate main headings by Roman numerals, subheadings under them by capital letters; if you need to subdivide further, use Arabic numerals, then lower-case letters, then numbers and letters in parentheses. But you should seldom need to go beyond one or two levels of subdivision. And be sure to *indent* sufficiently to make the relationship of headings and subheadings graphically clear.

Thesis statement Whatever form you use, *always begin your outline with a full thesis statement*. It is an essential part. Its relation to the rest is similar to that of the main headings to the subheadings that come under them.

Parallel headings In a good outline, the main headings will in effect be subheadings under the thesis statement, and they will be *parallel* in meaning, importance, and even in form. Similarly, the subheadings under each main heading will also be parallel; and so on with any successive levels of subheading. Note also that you cannot "divide" a heading into only one subheading: if you have an *A*, you must have at least a *B*, and so on. If you find yourself with a single subheading, find a way of integrating it with the heading; to leave it as a single subheading could lead to distortion of the material when you develop it.

Beginnings and endings Note also that *beginnings* and *endings* (or "introductions" and "conclusions") are not integral parts of the body of an outline; don't number them.

PROOFREADING

Proofreading is your last chance to exercise any control over the effect a piece of writing will have on your readers. Do it carefully.

When you revise your drafts, you of course correct any errors you see, of whatever kind. And when you proofread, you may find more, perhaps even enough to make you rewrite the final draft. But when the final draft is done, go through it slowly at least once or twice more. Look especially for **typographical errors** and **spelling errors**.

READ BACKWARD
You will probably want to go through the final draft from beginning to end, just to see how it reads. But when you are looking for typographical errors and misspellings, start at the end and work toward the beginning, ONE WORD AT A TIME.

Spelling

Don't take spelling lightly. Poor spelling is one of the first things readers will notice. If you misspell words, your readers will likely conclude that if you are careless about spelling, you are probably careless about ideas as well. If you want your readers to respect your writing, you must show respect for it yourself.

Two practical hints to help you improve your spelling:

sp

---

1. KEEP YOUR OWN SPELLING LIST. Include on it all the words that you have misspelled or that you know you have trouble with. Work on the list regularly. Practise the correct spellings until you know them. Have someone test you on it periodically. You can also use it as a checklist when proofreading.
2. Whenever you are not SURE of the correct spelling of a word, LOOK IT UP IN YOUR DICTIONARY.

BASIC SPELLING RULES AND COMMON PROBLEMS

There is no substitute for memorizing your problem-words and using a dictionary. But reviewing a few basic rules will help you avoid some of the more common errors. And if you know the common trouble spots, you will know when to be especially careful.

ie, ei Memorize the old jingle: "Use *i* before *e* except after *c*, or when sounded like *a* as in *neighbour* and *weigh* ." Errors of this kind almost always occur after *c*; just remember to use *ei*: *receive*, *perceive*, *conceive*. But there are a few oddities and exceptions to this rule; therefore if you aren't sure, LOOK IT UP.

-cede, -ceed, -sede Memorize *supersede*, the only word that ends in *sede*. And only three end in *ceed*: *exceed*, *proceed*, *succeed*. All the rest with this final sound end in *cede* (excluding, of course, compounds ending with the word *seed*, such as *cottonseed*).

Final *e* before a suffix If the suffix begins with a consonant, keep the *e*: *merely*, *tasteful*, *hopeless*, *awesome*. If the suffix begins with a vowel, drop the *e*: *arguing*, *desirable*. But there are some common exceptions, such as *argument*, *truly*, *outrageous*. Whenever you're not sure, LOOK IT UP.

Final *y*, after a consonant, before a suffix Before *ing*, keep the *y*: *trying*, *carrying*. Otherwise change it to *i*: *trial*, *happiness*, *angrily*. But again there are exceptions, such as *shyly* and *dryness*. If you aren't sure, LOOK IT UP.

Final consonant before a suffix Double the final consonant
    (a) if it is preceded by a single vowel,
    (b) if the root is either one syllable or has the accent on its last syllable, and
    (c) if the suffix begins with a vowel.
For example: *shopping*, *admitted*, *occurred*, *hitter*, *referred*, *referring*. But if adding the suffix shifts the accent, don't double the final consonant: *reference*.

-able, -ible The *able* ending predominates, but *ible* ends many common words: *audible*, *eligible*, *irresistible*. Don't guess; whenever you're not sure, LOOK IT UP. For this and other problems for which there are no rules, your dictionary is indispensable.

-ent, -ence; -ant, -ance Again, there's no rule. Since the two endings often sound the same, you have to LOOK IT UP if you're not certain which is right.

Plurals Plurals of most nouns are formed by adding either *s* or *es*. Add *es* if forming the plural adds a syllable: *church — churches*, *box — boxes*. Add only *s* if the plural doesn't form a new syllable: *girls*, *cedars*. If the noun ends in *ce*, *ge*, *se*, or *ze*, adding the *s* will make a new syllable anyway: *fireplaces*, *cages*, *bases*, *mazes*.

Whenever you're uncertain about a plural, LOOK IT UP. Quite a few nouns have irregular plurals, which your dictionary should list (for example *child — children, goose — geese, deer — deer*). Words ending in *o* or *f* don't always follow the usual patterns. And words from other languages sometimes follow English rules and sometimes don't (for example *bureau — bureaus, antenna — antennas* or *antennae, criterion — criteria*).

Plurals of nouns ending in *y* If the *y* is preceded by a consonant, change the *y* to *i* and add *es: cities, tries.* Otherwise just add *s: bays, valleys.*

Homophones Don't confuse words that sound alike but are spelled differently. Errors with such words can distract readers even more than other spelling errors, since they may see them as errors in diction (see p. 144). Here are some that are often confused:

boarder — border	led — lead
born — borne	passed — past
capital — capitol	pedal — peddle
compliment — complement	phase — faze
counsel — council	principal — principle
coarse — course	ring — wring
discreet — discrete	sight — site — cite
fair — fare	sole — soul
forgo — forego	stationary — stationery
holy — wholly	there — their — they're
incidence — incidents	to — too — two
its — it's	vein — vain — vane

If you are unaware of or not certain about the meanings of any of these words, LOOK THEM UP. Perhaps add them to your own spelling list.

Other often-confused words Some pairs of words are easily confused even though they aren't pronounced exactly alike. Careful pronunciation will help you avoid errors of spelling or diction with words like these:

accept — except	device — devise
access — excess	diffuse — defuse
adapt — adopt	elicit — illicit
advice — advise	insight — incite
allude — elude	loose — lose
allusion — illusion	persecute — prosecute
bizarre — bazaar	quite — quiet
choose — chose	then — than
climactic — climatic	whine — wine

If you are unsure of the meanings or pronunciations of any of these, LOOK THEM UP.

Separate words If you find that you've carelessly run any of these terms together, separate them again:

a lot	even though	in fact	in other words
all right	every time	in front	in spite of
at least	in between	in order to	up to

One word or two? Here are some terms whose meanings or functions differ, depending on whether they are spelled as one word or two. Be careful to distinguish between them or you will confuse your readers.

altogether — all together	awhile — a while
anybody — any body	everyday — every day
anyone — any one	maybe — may be
anyway — any way	someday — some day
apart — a part	sometime — some time

$\boxed{apos}$ ## APOSTROPHES '

Apostrophes have three uses:

1. *To form the possessive case of nouns.* Usually, add an apostrophe and an *s* to show possession:

Einstein's theory	Ralph's car	women's rights
society's structure	a week's wages	a day's work

If the noun is a *plural* that already ends in *s*, add only an apostrophe. Note that often only the position of the apostrophe tells readers whether a word is singular or plural (*boy's, boys'; province's, provinces'*). A second's carelessness could seriously mislead them.

boys' club	the Joneses' house
two days' work	the provinces' wealth

When a *singular* noun — usually a proper noun — ends in *s* or an *s*-sound, it is usually best to add both an apostrophe and another *s*, for most people pronounce such words with an extra syllable:

Yeats's poetry	Tom Jones's voice
Dickens's novels	the bus's brakes

If this produces an awkward pronunciation, for example because of other *s*-sounds in the word, avoid the problem by using an *of*-phrase to show possession:

Moses's leadership —> the leadership of Moses
Camus's philosophy —> the philosophy of Camus
carelessness's cost —> the cost of carelessness

Caution: Do NOT use apostrophes to form the possessive of pronouns: *its, theirs, hers, yours, ours.*

2. *To form contractions.* Apostrophes take the place of omitted letters; for example:

isn't (is not)	don't (do not)	they're (they are)
she's (she is)	it's (it is)	aren't (are not)
I've (I have)	he'd (he had)	we'll (we will)

3. *To form the plurals of numerals, symbols, and words referred to as words.* Some writers prefer to add only an *s* to form such plurals, but we think the apostrophe helps avoid confusion:

the 1930's	two &'s	the ABC's
three *9*'s	mind your p's and q's	too many *is*'s

Such instances are the *only* times apostrophes can be used to form plurals.

HYPHENS -

Whenever you aren't sure whether to use a hyphen, an up-to-date dictionary may solve the problem for you, for practice is always changing. But some basic uses of the hyphen are clear:

1. *With numbers.* Use hyphens in compound numbers from *twenty-one* to *ninety-nine*, with fractions used as adjectives (a *two-thirds* majority), with compounds indicating time (*eight-fifteen*), and to indicate a range of numbers (pages *12-17*).

2. *With prefixes.* Use hyphens with prefixes before proper nouns:

pre-Cambrian	pan-Slavic	all-Canadian	un-American

and with compounds beginning with the prefix *self:*

self-sufficient	self-made	self-esteem

and usually with the prefixes *vice* and *by:*

vice-president	vice-consul	by-election
(but *viceroy, bylaw, bygone*)		

3. *In words for relatives.* Use hyphens with *great* and *in-law:*

great-grandmother	great-uncle	brother-in-law

4. *For clarity.* Use a hyphen to prevent a word's being mistaken for another:

re-cover	re-count	re-dress

5. *In compound adjectives.* Hyphenate a compound adjective when it precedes a noun, but not when it follows:

a well-done steak (but "The steak was *well done*")

but do not join an *ly* adverb to an adjective:

cleverly contrived plan	loudly proclaimed belief

6. *As suspension hyphens.* When two or more prefixes are used with a single root, use what is called a "suspension hyphen," as in this sentence from Donald Creighton's *The Story of Canada*:

> Montcalm signalled the advance, and the whole array of white- and blue-clad soldiers edged forward.

Otherwise, consult your dictionary to find out whether to hyphenate compound modifiers, nouns, and verbs.

LIST OF FREQUENTLY MISSPELLED WORDS

Here is a short list of words that students misspell particularly often. Have someone test you on these; any that you don't know should go on your own spelling list.

accessible	dining	leisure	sacrilegious
accommodate	dissatisfied	luxury	separate
adorable	divide	majestic	servant
affidavit	drunkenness	mandatory	shepherd
aging	ecstasy	medieval	sheriff
a lot	elegiac	minuscule	shining
among	embarrass	mischievous	significance
apparent	equipment	myriad	similar
argument	exalt	mementos	simile
article	excerpt	miniature	skiing
authoritative	existence	necessary	solely
auxiliary	exorbitant	negotiations	soliloquy
beneficial	expatriate	obstacle	speech
bulwark	feasible	occasion	sponsor
calendar	forgettable	occurred	strategy
category	forty	opinion	stupefying
cemetery	fulfill	optimistic	symbolic
challenge	further	opulent	synonymous
changeable	gauge	parliament	temperament
coherent	genealogy	perceive	tendency
coincide	germane	perseverance	tragedy
committee	goddess	persuade	transcendent
commitment	guard	playwright	tries
competitive	harass	preceded	tyranny
congratulate	height	predominantly	undoubtedly
conqueror	homogeneous	prejudice	unkempt
consensus	hypocrisy	profession	unnoticeable
convenience	hypocrite	pronunciation	until
create	imagery	psychology	usage
cries	incidentally	putrefy	variegated
criticism	inconsistent	receive	vicious
customs	indefinite	religious	vilified
decrepit	independent	remembrance	villain
definitely	indispensable	reminisce	warrant
descendants	inevitable	resurrection	whether
description	inoculate	rhythm	whisk
develop	intimate	ridiculous	wondrous
dilemma	lackadaisical	sacrifice	writing

Special Purposes and Forms

CHAPTER 11
Composing an Argument

WHAT IS AN ARGUMENT?

The word *argument* may make you think of two people disagreeing, perhaps heatedly, about some issue. In that sense an argument is a dispute, even a fight. But for the purposes of *written* arguments, we have to define the word differently: *an argument is a piece of writing intended to change the way readers think or feel about something, to change their minds or their behaviour.*

Persuasion and Other Purposes

Factual reports, memos, and analyses are not likely to be arguments. But much writing intended primarily to inform will include some argument, some intention to persuade. For example, a report that includes recommendations is in effect an argument. A set of instructions may not be an argument, but it may implicitly be trying to persuade readers both that something is worth doing and that this is the right way to do it. Though our primary purpose in this chapter is to inform you, we also use some argumentative techniques to help persuade you that our advice is worth following.

THE PROCESS OF WRITING AN ARGUMENT

Drafting, revising, and preparing the final copy of an argument are much the same as for other kinds of writing. **Planning** an argument, however, requires some different strategies. This chapter, then, focusses on the first three steps.

Step 1: Determining Topic, Readers, and Purpose

ESTABLISHING YOUR TOPIC

If you are not assigned a topic, here are some suggestions to help you choose one:

1. Argue matters of opinion. You cannot *argue* about matters of taste; you can only make assertions about your preferences. And there is no point in arguing about easily verifiable facts or generally accepted assumptions. Arguments centre on disagreements about *what facts mean, how they should be interpreted.* For example, a set of statistics could mean quite different things to different political parties.

2. Choose with yourself in mind. Debaters sometimes have to be prepared to argue either side of a question, and doing so is no doubt good practice. But when you choose a topic for yourself, choose one that you know about and care about, and argue for what you believe. Sincerity should add strength.

3. Choose with your readers in mind. Try to choose a topic that is or will be of genuine concern to your readers.

NARROWING YOUR TOPIC

Consider the scope of your project. How much room do you have? How much time? If you're tempted by some vast and earth-shaking topic, do some drastic narrowing. Even seemingly small topics can require unexpected amounts of development when you're composing an argument for or against them. Think of your readers and your specific purpose, and limit your topic to something you can treat adequately in the time and space you have. (Some notoriously controversial topics are best avoided because they are too big, and also because they are highly emotional issues — for example abortion, capital punishment, religious belief.)

Project 11-a

Try to identify each of the following as a matter of *fact, opinion,* or *taste.* Imagine yourself taking a *pro* or *con* position on each. Which ones could be topics for formal arguments? Could some of them be in more than one category, depending on how they were handled? If so, explain.

1. It is better to live in the country than in the city.
2. The voting age should be lowered.
3. Big cars consume more fuel than small cars.
4. Margaret Atwood is a better writer than Jane Austen.
5. Higher insurance rates for drivers under 25 are justified.
6. B.C. is a more beautiful province than Ontario.
7. Hitch-hiking should be made illegal.
8. Violence in hockey hurts the game.
9. Canada's parliamentary system adequately represents the population.
10. Winnipeg is the crossroads of the continent.

DETERMINING YOUR READERS AND YOUR PURPOSE

1. Identifying your readers. When you write an argument, your sense of your readers is even more important than for most other kinds of writing. By the nature of argument, many of your readers will likely be against you, or at least skeptical (and of course there's little point in even trying to convince readers whose minds aren't open). Go carefully through the questions about readers and the list of variables (pp. 18-20). Construct as detailed a profile of your readers as you can. Pay particular attention to their value systems. If you know what they think and feel about your topic, what they believe and disbelieve, their likes and dislikes, you will know how to handle your material: what points to downplay, what points to emphasize, what points require the most arguing.

2. Identifying your purpose. You know your purpose: to persuade; but refine it further. Do you want to change your readers' minds, or their behaviour? Of course thinking is a kind of behaviour; but if people are persuaded strongly enough, they will not only change their thinking but will also act. If you primarily want to correct their thinking, your argument will rely on logic. If you want them to *do* something — to buy, to vote, to sign a petition — you'll probably appeal also to their loyalties, desires, and other feelings. Students are usually expected to write the former kind of argument, but don't forget that readers have hearts as well as heads. Some appeal to the feelings can help an argument addressed mainly to the reason.

FORMULATING A THESIS QUESTION OR THESIS STATEMENT

When you're planning an argument, you should go beyond a thesis question to a thesis statement. You may well refine it further as you go through the next steps, but try to come up with one here, for two reasons:

1. Putting your ideas about the topic into a thesis *statement* at this point will help you make sure you have narrowed your topic sufficiently.

2. Having a *statement* will be more helpful when you are generating material (see below).

Here are some examples of how you might progress from topic to thesis statement:

LARGE TOPIC	Women's rights
NARROWER TOPIC	Rights of women in the military
NARROWED TOPIC	Women in military combat roles
THESIS QUESTION	Should the military distinguish between men and women in combat roles?
THESIS STATEMENT	The military should not distinguish between men and women in combat roles.
LARGE TOPIC	Jobs
NARROWER TOPIC	Job security
NARROWED TOPIC	Strikes over job security
THESIS QUESTION	Should labour law allow workers to strike over the issue of job security?
THESIS STATEMENT	Labour law should not allow workers to strike over the issue of job security.
LARGE TOPIC	Rock music
NARROWER TOPIC	Rock music's effects on youth
NARROWED TOPIC	Rock music and the morals of youth in the sixties
THESIS QUESTION	Did rock music corrupt the morals of youth in the sixties?
THESIS STATEMENT	Rock music did not corrupt the morals of youth in the sixties.

Step 2: Finding Material

For an argument, use the strategies in Chapter 2 just as you would for any other topic. For the above examples, already formulated into thesis statements, you could run through the questions with several key terms — *women, women's rights, combat, job, work, job security, labour laws, music, rock music, young people, the sixties* — and generate a great deal of material to help you argue. Look especially for material that you can use as **evidence***;* that's what you need in order to argue convincingly. Look for facts, concrete details, statistics, a common experience your readers will know about, an authority you can quote. But make sure that the evidence you gather is both **reliable** and **relevant**.

THE THESIS STATEMENT

With argument, there is also another way to generate material. In an argument, your thesis is a **proposition** like that read out at a debate ("Resolved, tuition must be increased"). You then set out to prove or defend that proposition. That is, you argue not so much a topic as a statement of opinion about that topic. You don't argue about "farm price supports" but about whether the government should subsidize farm prices. Put it as a proposition:

> The government should continue subsidizing farm prices.

That is something you can *argue* about, partly because it is something someone can *disagree* with you about. (You'll find that many propositions include *should* or *must*.)

The Reporter's Standard Questions

To frame your thesis in as helpful a way as possible, try to word it so that someone is doing something. That is, try to put it in such a way that a human or natural **agent** appears as the **subject** and a specific **action** appears as the **predicate**. In the above example, suppose you first decided merely that you were in favour of "farm price supports." But "farm price supports" is just a noun phrase; no verb. But the word *support* is primarily a verb, so you try it again:

> Somebody should support farm prices.

The *What?* of the reporter's questions is taken care of in the predicate. Now asking *Who?* will enable you to identify the "somebody" in the subject:

> The government should continue supporting farm prices.

Then you try asking *Where?* and *When?* and think about the implications of the term "government" and decide that you can make your thesis even more specific:

> Parliament should defeat the bill currently before the House proposing changes in farm-price-support policies.

As you keep clarifying your thesis, it begins to provide a context. And as you pursue such questions you will also be finding support for the thesis. Asking *Why?* could lead you to a useful argument for a related proposition about the importance of the independent family farm in the Canadian economy and social structure. Asking *How?* might suggest a look at the possible value of indirect rather than direct support; perhaps the government should merely continue to subsidize the shipment of grain to deep-water ports.

And so on. As your thesis-proposition becomes more and more specific, you sound more and more authoritative. It's easier to convince readers if they can see that you know what you're talking about.

LOGIC

When you try to convince readers, you appeal primarily to their intelligence, their reason. And appeals to reason depend on logic. The purpose of the conventions of logic is to test statements for truth and validity. As you focus on your topic and define the issues it raises, and as you gather evidence to support your major proposition and its subsidiary propositions, you will necessarily be engaging in reasoning processes.

There are two basic kinds of reasoning: **inductive** and **deductive**. Using induction, you move from particular facts to a generalization. Using deduction, you move from general truths or assumptions to a particular statement. You need to understand these processes so that you can make sure you are using them correctly.

Induction

Inductive reasoning moves from a group of statements about *some* events to a generalization about *all* such events. It is through induction that you have learned to be careful about walking on ice or handling electrical wires. Or suppose you've noticed that a number of your friends (Jan, Ken, Eddie, Audrey, and Carl) are all college students and that none of them has much money. You would probably be right to conclude, by inductive reasoning, that college students generally don't have much money.

That is, you would have made an "inductive leap" from *some* specific instances to *all* or (if you're being cautious) *most* such instances. Induction always leaps beyond the evidence at hand. That is why inductive reasoning cannot *prove* something; it cannot establish certainty, only probability — but high probability, if you're careful about the reasoning process. Science depends upon it.

Induction is common in our everyday thinking:

"That's the third police car that's passed us in ten minutes. Something must have happened up ahead."

"That's the sixth time Harold's number has been busy this afternoon. He must always be on the phone. Or else there's something wrong with the line."

This last example illustrates another principle of induction that is common both to everyday conversation and to scientific thinking: for many sets of observations, more than one conclusion or generalization is possible. People often have to decide among competing inductive conclusions, known as **hypotheses**. The very business of some arguments is to sort through several possible hypotheses to find the most probable one for a particular set of observations.

Obviously the *number* of specific observations affects the degree of probability of the conclusion. The more the better. A hypothesis becomes a **law** ("the law of gravity," "the law of diminishing returns") when it has been verified by so many observations that it is assumed to be invariably true. In everyday life such truths are known as "common sense" (which is why sensible people stay off thin ice). But in a written argument you wouldn't want to cite hundreds of specific examples; you could point to their number (statistics), but you'd settle for describing a few *representative* or *typical* examples. And you can certainly appeal to common sense.

You must also be careful to explain away any *exceptions* among your examples. If your readers know about exceptions that you don't mention, you'll have lost their confidence, and with it any chance of convincing them.

Conclusions or generalizations are only as good as the support or evidence behind them. How much support your generalizations need depends, again, on how much your readers need. Sympathetic friends might be willing to take your word; skeptical strangers may require a lot. Ask yourself:

> How much evidence do I need to supply for *these* readers on *this* occasion?

Deduction

This is a traditional example of deductive reasoning:

1. All men are mortal.
2. Socrates is a man.
3. Therefore Socrates is mortal.

The two general statements, 1 and 2 — called the **premises** — provide the proof for the **conclusion**, 3. This form, two premises followed by a conclusion, is called a **syllogism**. The first premise is called the **major premise**, not because it is more important but because it is more general. The second premise, less general, is called the **minor premise**. For the conclusion to be valid, its subject must be the subject of the minor premise (*Socrates*), and its predicate the predicate of the major premise (*is mortal*). If both the premises are true, the conclusion is true.

The truth of the premises is tested by other means, often by inductive reasoning. For a particular argument, in fact, you may have to focus on a minor premise. In an argument about violence in sport, for example, you may decide to show that basketball has become a contact sport in order to argue that what applies to hockey and football should also apply to basketball. Put into a syllogism, such an argument might look like this:

1. Athletes injured in violent sports can sue.
2. Basketball is a violent sport.
3. Therefore athletes injured in basketball should be able to sue.

Stated explicitly, the relationships are fairly obvious. Usually your wording won't be so formulaic, but more like this:

> Injured basketball players, like others injured in violent sports, should be able to sue.

You would have to decide whether your readers would accept the assumption that basketball is a violent sport or whether you would have to argue for that minor premise first.

Unlike induction, deduction can lead to proof, to certainty, but only if the generalizations in the premises are true or accepted as true by your readers. And for the conclusion to be a certainty, there must also be an "absolute," an *all* or *every* or *none* or some other such word, either explicit or implicit in one of the premises.

Most of the time you will not be able to be so sweeping. You will have to qualify premises with words like *most, many, usually, few*. But even if you aren't able to establish absolute proof or certainty, you may still have a persuasive argument.

Project 11-b

Examine the following premises and conclusions and revise them as you think necessary. What is being *assumed* in each set? What needs qualifying?

A. 1. People go to hockey games to see violence.
   2. Owners want to increase gate receipts.
   3. Therefore the owners encourage violence.
B. 1. Women are not as physically strong as men.
   2. Police work calls for physical strength.
   3. Therefore women shouldn't be hired to do police work.
C. 1. Welfare leads to idleness.
   2. Idle people are not productive.
   3. Therefore welfare should not be part of a society, like ours, that needs to increase its productivity.

THE OPPOSITION

An important part of finding material for arguments is to think of as many opposing arguments as you can. If you present only your own side, you're not arguing but merely asserting. Readers who don't agree with you can accuse you of being unfair. Worse, they will continually be calling to mind the objections that could be raised.

You not only have to acknowledge the counter-arguments; you also have to deal with them effectively. Look for ways to dispose of them. Here are some possible techniques for attacking an opposition point:

- Demolish it logically. For example, look for its hidden assumptions; point out flaws in evidence or reasoning.
- Dismiss it as essentially trivial or irrelevant — if it is.
- Acknowledge its force, but provide a better alternative.
- Acknowledge its immediate advantages, but show that its long-term results will be bad.
- Acknowledge its validity, but point out that it covers only part of the issue.
- Point out that it is valid only part of the time.

If there's no way to dispose of it, and if it's too obvious to ignore, readers will appreciate your candour if you admit its truth. Then of course you must try to counter it with several forceful points of your own.

Step 3: Organizing Your Material: Planning Development and Constructing an Outline

When you have gathered all or most of your material, think about how you're going to handle it. The following are points to consider:

INDUCTION OR DEDUCTION?

Most often you will use both induction and deduction, for they work together. But try to decide if one or the other will be your basic method. Then you can make other decisions about organization and development more easily.

METHODS OF DEVELOPMENT

Consider the methods of development (see Chapter 3) and try to decide which ones will work best for your argument. They can all be useful, even description and narration. You may end up using a combination of several of them. But a few are especially useful:

Example and Illustration

If you use inductive reasoning you will use examples and illustrations to support your generalizations. They will constitute the evidence for the assertions you make as you proceed with your argument.

Definition and Classification

Definition can be invaluable in argument, since terms must be clearly understood. Classifying and defining your topic or its parts can help establish the *common ground* between writer and reader that is essential before an argument can proceed effectively.

Cause and Effect

Many arguments depend on cause and effect. You argue for or against something because of what it *causes,* because of what happens or will happen as a result of it.

Comparison and Contrast

These can be powerful in argument. For example, you may get readers to see something in a new way by showing them what it is like or unlike. But be careful of **analogy** (see p. 76). If you are tempted to use it, use it only to clarify a point; never depend on it alone as a device for argument. It can never lead to certainty, usually not even to strong probability. It is weak because usually opponents can easily come up with significant differences to counter whatever similarities you point out.

ORGANIZATION: THE STRUCTURE OF ARGUMENT

Climactic Order

Arrange the issues or major points in the most effective way. A common order is that of relative importance: begin with your weakest point and end with your strongest. Or, since the beginning is also an emphatic position, you might want to begin with your second or third strongest point and then put the rest in climactic order.

The Rhythm of *pro* and *con*

As you deal with a series of opposition points, refuting each and making your counter-points, you can establish a strong back-and-forth momentum. Here is a sample of the kind of organization that works well for many arguments:

1. Statement of the problem, ending with your thesis-proposition
2. Background of the problem; setting out the facts; restatement of thesis toward end of this part
3. a. First issue
   b. Opposition argument
   c. Refutation, and establishment of your point

4. a. Second issue
   b. Opposition argument
   c. Refutation, and establishment of your point
5. a. Third issue
   b. Opposition argument
   c. Refutation, and establishment of your point
6. If possible, a marshalling of two or three of your strongest points
7. An ending that draws it all together, perhaps re-emphasizing the thesis and making a recommendation about attitude or action

THE OUTLINE

Because structure and proportion are so important in an argument, take extra pains with your outline. Don't rely on a rough sketch; draw up a detailed sentence outline. It will make writing the first draft much easier, and it will save you a lot of time during revising. Or, if you are using drafting as part of your planning, try a quick draft to see if it can help you come up with a workable development or arrangement. If it does, construct a careful outline before you go on to further drafts. If it doesn't . . . back to the drawing board.

Project 11-c

Find some good arguments in books, magazines, or newspapers. Analyze them to see how they work. Perhaps draw up an outline for each in order to reveal their structure.

Project 11-d

Examine half-a-dozen full-page advertisements from one or two popular magazines. What methods of persuasion do they use? Do appeals to the head predominate, or appeals to the heart? Can you find any flaws in their logic?

Project 11-e

Find a *small* local issue that is controversial. Write a short piece (about 300 words) presenting one side of the issue, then another presenting the other side. Then look at both pieces, decide which side you're on, and write a balanced argument for it; represent the opposition fairly.

Project 11-f

Investigate the attitudes of your fellow students toward one of the following:

the athletic program	the grading system
food services	student government
required courses	tuition policies
provision for the handicapped	counselling
vocational training	class sizes

When you have enough data, compose an inductive argument that arrives at a generalization about the topic and makes a recommendation based on the evidence.

Project 11-g
Write a formal report analyzing some place you've worked or some job you've had, with recommendations for improving it.

Project 11-h
Choose one term from each of the three columns, in 1-2-3 order. Use the resulting sentence as your thesis or proposition, and develop an argument of 500-700 words. Don't be afraid to be funny if that's how your thesis strikes you.

1	2	3
Automobiles		abolished.
Educators	can be	categorized.
Food	cannot be	deplored.
Government	could be	forgiven.
Landladies	must be	ignored.
Marriage	must not be	improved
Poetry	should be	investigated.
Science	should not be	recycled.
Snow		tolerated.
Unions		welcomed.

CHAPTER 12
Writing a Research Paper

Writing a library research paper follows the same process as other kinds of writing, from planning through drafting and revising. But to find material for a research paper, you must use external sources. During writing and revising, a research paper requires careful handling and documenting of sources. And scrupulous proofreading is essential.

STEP 1: DETERMINING TOPIC, READERS, AND PURPOSE

Choosing Your Topic

Select a topic that interests you. Instructors usually offer a range of topics so that you can explore some of a course's issues in more depth. As you work through a course, you probably grow curious about some matters that aren't fully resolved in class or in the texts. You need such curiosity to keep up your interest over several weeks of work on a topic. A similar curiosity will help you choose a topic on your own.

But since a topic for a research paper by definition needs to be *researchable,* and since you need to be able to manage it, keep in mind these additional points:

1. Make sure (a) that there is sufficient material on the topic, and (b) that your library has enough of it. Many topics haven't had much written on them, and even big libraries can't afford to buy everything published.

212

2. Avoid nine-day wonders, topics that are only briefly popular, like a fad in music, a recent flood or volcanic eruption, a short-lived political scandal. You probably could find material only in newspapers and popular magazines. Such events provide excellent hooks for beginnings, but they won't support sustained research.

3. Choose a topic you can handle. Don't get in over your head by attempting something too specialized or technical. You probably won't be able to assimilate the material and still complete your project in time. If you embark on a seemingly simple topic like "the meaning of the Bible" or "modern trends in economics," you may find yourself in a thicket of incomprehensible language about scriptural hermeneutics or the abstract calculus of micro-economics. Get out while you can.

4. Consider the scope of your project. *Narrow* it as much as necessary for the length assigned. A short paper can't encompass the full sweep of World War I or the Napoleonic Wars, but you could assemble and present material on Gallipoli or the battle of Trafalgar. The material available on Michelangelo or Elizabeth I is immense, overwhelming except for experts. But you could work up a paper on one episode in their lives, or on someone like Käthe Kollwitz or Jomo Kenyatta.

Determining Your Readers

Even though your instructor may be your only reader, think of your potential audience as your fellow students — all those taking the course, those who took it in recent years, and those who will take it in the next few. Then you can count on a certain amount of shared knowledge. For a course in modern European history, for example, such readers won't need to be told that the English defeated the French and Spanish at Trafalgar. For a survey course in literature, you won't needlessly inform your readers that Shakespeare was a well-known Elizabethan playwright or that John Milton wrote *Paradise Lost* in the seventeenth century. Think of your readers — including your instructor — as interested colleagues: they want to see how you reach your conclusions and what evidence you use to support them.

Determining Your Purpose

Most library research papers fall somewhere on a spectrum between these two extremes:

1. *Providing information on the topic.* You report facts. You mainly inform your readers about what others (your sources) have written about the topic.

2. *Evaluating what others have written on the topic.* You explore a topic and arrive at your own conclusions about it. You may need to evaluate what others have written in order to persuade your readers that one position or one interpretation of the evidence is better than others.

Where the purpose for your essay falls on this spectrum will often be clear from the assignment. For example, in "Compare and contrast the main proposals for dealing with the problem of acid rain in Canada," the words *compare and contrast* direct you to evaluate the principal methods science and government have proposed. Another assignment might ask you only to report, to provide a sampling of published opinion about a topic. For example, a paper for a commerce course might ask you to explain the sorts of bonds, public and private, that are currently available to investors and the ways they are discounted. But sometimes the assignment won't be so clear. Suppose a topic in anthropology invites you to "discuss the kinship structure of the Micmac people in the nineteenth century." Presumably you can either report or evaluate, or perhaps do some of each. In such instances, check with your instructor before you decide.

STEP 2: FINDING MATERIAL

Use Questions

By definition, a library research paper depends heavily on material you gather from external sources. But before you go to the library, *do what you can on your own.* Use the questions in Chapter 2. To begin with, by framing specific questions you can find out if you are genuinely interested in a topic. Perhaps you can frame a thesis question that will help you narrow your topic and focus your research.

A student in a history course chose the topic "Science and Technology Before the Industrial Revolution." It looked interesting, and the library had plenty of material on it. But she needed to narrow the topic somehow. She made up questions to throw at it (What were the principal scientific discoveries in the early 18th century? When did the terms "science" and "technology" appear? Are they entirely "modern" ideas? Were there any major inventions in the 1600's?). Then she realized she had chosen the topic partly because she had once written a report on Sir Isaac Newton and was still curious about him and his period. She soon had a tentative thesis question: *What was going on in science around 1700?* She had at least a preliminary focus for her first forays of research.

Try Brainstorming

Quickly write down all the facts and ideas you already have about your topic. Include any other ideas or associations that come to mind. You may be surprised at how much you already know about the topic or the contexts in which you can discuss it. And your random associations can lead you to questions that will help you direct your research.

Research Strategy

Think of your research as comprising three stages:

1. *Locate:* First you locate the most promising sources.

2. *Evaluate:* Then you evaluate them to determine which ones look genuinely useful, eliminating those that are out of date, unreliable, or that lead away from the topic.

3. *Assimilate:* Finally, you take notes, assimilating the material from the remaining sources.

1. LOCATING SOURCES

Collect titles of works that look as though they will help you start answering the questions you have framed. Begin with the **subject catalogue** and the **reference section.**

The Subject Catalogue

Here you will find the titles of books on your topic. You may also find related topics listed as cross-references, some of which you may want to pursue. If you can't find anything under your topic, don't give up. For example, under "mental telepathy" you may not find anything; but the helpful *Library of Congress Subject Headings* will direct you to Thought-transference, a heading that might not occur to you. Under it you will find other possibly useful related headings, such as Clairvoyance, Crystal-gazing, Hypnotism.

For the sake of efficiency, when you write down a promising title that you've found in the catalogue, write down its library **call number** beside it.

The Reference Section

Here you will find such useful resources as dictionaries, encyclopedias, bibliographies, and indexes. An article in an **encyclopedia** is only a beginning, but it will help you develop some background for your topic; and many articles include a short bibliography, a list of books for those who want to pursue the topic further. Look not only at general encyclopedias, such as the *Encyclopaedia Britannica* and *Collier's Encyclopedia,* but also at specialized ones having to do with the field you're researching, such as the *African Encyclopedia, The Canadian Encyclopaedia, The Cambridge Encyclopaedia of Astronomy,* the *Encyclopedia of Educational Research,* and the *Encyclopedia of Religion and Ethics.* There are hundreds of such specialized encyclopedias.

For listings of articles in magazines and journals, consult one or more **indexes**, such as the *Readers' Guide to Periodical Literature* or the *Canadian Periodical Index.* There are also newspaper indexes, such as *The New York Times Index.* For essays in books, try the *Essay and General Literature Index.* There are also specialized indexes, such as the *Book Review Index,* the *Biological and Agricultural Index,* the *Canadian Business Index,* and the *Art Index.*

Look for useful specialized **bibliographies**, such as the *Arctic Bibliography,* the *Bibliography of Current Computing Literature,* and the *Bibliographic Guide to Theatre Arts.* To help you find them, there are such aids as the *Bibliographic Index: A Cumulative Bibliography of Bibliographies* and the *Bibliography of Canadian Bibliographies.*

An **abstract**, a brief summary of an article, can help you decide whether it's worth hunting up the article itself. Again, there are many sources, such as *Ecology Abstracts, Economic Abstracts, Abstracts of English Studies,* and *Peace Research Abstracts Journal.*

You may want to consult some sources of **facts**. Besides atlases, gazetteers, and yearbooks, there are such useful collections as *Facts on File: A Weekly World News Digest, Canadian News Facts,* and the *Gallup Opinion Index.*

Explore the reference section of your library. You may be astonished at the number and kinds of helpful resources it contains. And here and elsewhere in the library, never hesitate to ask a librarian for help if you need it.

The Preliminary Bibliography

Without having consulted the actual works, except perhaps an encyclopedia article or two, you now have a **preliminary bibliography,** a list of works that look promising. For titles you found in reference books, check the catalogue to see which ones are available, and record their call numbers.

How many works you list will depend on a number of variables, but try to locate at least two sources for each page of your projected paper. For a ten-page paper (about 2500 words), you'd want at least twenty potential sources on your list. You'll eliminate some — but you'll add others.

2. EVALUATING

Find the books and journals on your list and have a look at them. At this point you need evaluate them only briefly. When you are simply trying to determine what an article or book is about, you can skim it. Glance at its organization, its vocabulary, and its main points of argument. Check the index to see how much attention it devotes to points you think might be central to your paper. Your purpose is to sample in order to decide what to read more carefully.

As you look over the items on your list, you will be learning more about your topic, a process that will help you sharpen your thesis question and also see where you might find answers. If you take notes at this stage, confine them to the broad kind that will help you focus your topic and draw up an outline. Don't begin taking detailed notes yet.

Cross off the titles that don't look useful. (DON'T blot them out, or discard them. You may unexpectedly shift your focus later and find them promising once more.) As you browse the shelves and the journals, you'll probably come across promising items to *add* to your list, as well.

Bibliography Cards

For each item you decide is worth further attention, make out a **bibliography card** (7.5 x 12.5 cm or 3 x 5 inches). Do so while you have the actual work in your hand. Carefully and legibly copy the *author's name* (last name first) as it appears on the title page or with the article; the *title* (underlined for a book, in quotation marks for an article, with the journal's title underlined), and the *publication data.* This information is for the bibliography of your paper. Here are sample cards for a book and an article:

Schneer, Cecil J.

Mind and Matter: Man's Changing
Concepts of the Material World

New York: Grove Press, 1969

QD11
S29   [history of chemistry]
1969

MacLulich, T.D.

"Colloquial Style and the Tory Mode"

Canadian Literature, 89 (Summer 1981),
pp. 7-21

PR 8900   [uses Davies as example of
C27   "Tory style"]

In addition, put the item's call number on the card (the lower left corner is a good place, as illustrated). And if possible write yourself a brief note — a few words recording your impression of the work, highlighting its apparent strength (or weakness), as a reminder when you return to it

3. ASSIMILATING: TAKING NOTES

Two major principles that you must keep constantly in mind:

> 1. TAKE EVERY PRECAUTION TO
> AVOID PLAGIARISM.

Every word, phrase, or idea that you get from a source must be fully and accurately acknowledged and documented. **Plagiarism** is literary burglary. A plagiarist is a writer who filches something that belongs to someone else and presents it to readers as his or her own. In the world of professional writing, plagiarism is a crime. In the academic world, the penalties for plagiarism are customarily severe, ranging from loss of credit for the guilty paper to dismissal from the course or even from the institution. Don't be a plagiarist, either intentionally or accidentally.

ack
doc

---

2. STAY IN CONTROL OF YOUR
SOURCES.

Don't just copy a bunch of quotations from sources and then try to stitch them together with a few bits of your own prose. In the resulting patchwork the sources would dominate. Remind yourself constantly: YOU are the boss. YOUR purpose and thesis should determine all decisions about what to use and where to use it. Keep refining your thesis question so that you can take notes selectively. If you allow yourself to become merely a passive recorder, you will be under the control of your sources.

Stay in the saddle:
don't let your sources ride you.

Use Cards

Take your notes on cards so that your material will be manageable. Use the same size you use for your bibliography cards or the 10 x 15 cm (4 x 6 inch) size.

In the upper left corner, record the name of the author and the page number for the source of the note. If you're using more than one work by an author, include a short version of the title. You'll need this information for documentation in your paper. If you quote or paraphrase something that occurs on more than one page of a source, mark the page break; you may decide to use only part of the material, and you need to know which page it comes from.

In the upper right corner you may want to label the note in some way, for example by indicating what part of your outline you think it will pertain to.

One Note per Card Record only one point on each card. Then you can arrange points according to your own needs rather than according to their order in a source. If you get several points from one paragraph of a source, you may want to use them in different parts of your paper. If you use small cards, you'll be less tempted to write too much on one card. Be brief.

Minimize Quotation Another way to guard against letting sources take over is to minimize quotation. Genuinely ASSIMILATE the material. Try to make the material your own at the note stage; that will make it much easier to work with later. Take notes in your own words as much as possible. Use **paraphrase** and **summary**. Even if you find it convenient to photocopy source material, remember that you still have to assimilate it: take notes.

Paraphrase and Summary To **paraphrase**, restate a point in *your own words* and *your own sentence structure.* Merely substituting synonyms here and there does not constitute paraphrase. Most paraphrases are about the length of the original, or a bit shorter.

To **summarize**, again use your own words, but condense the original to its essential points. Perhaps use only a sentence or two for a whole chapter or article.

If you decide to include a few striking or significant words from the original, *enclose them in quotation marks.*

The only times you should need to quote a source at any length is when it cites specific figures or statistics, or when it is particularly striking or well-expressed.

Mark Material Clearly: Avoid PLAGIARISM If you decide you must quote something — whether a word, a phrase, a sentence, or a whole paragraph — enclose it in prominent, clearly visible **quotation marks.** If you are careful to put quotation marks around ANYTHING you copy verbatim onto a card, you will know what to enclose in quotation marks in your paper. Failure to acknowledge direct quotation *as quotation* is one form of **plagiarism.**

Quote Accurately

Double-check each quotation as you copy it. If you add anything to a quotation, enclose the addition in square brackets **[ ]**; if you omit anything, indicate the omission with the three spaced dots (. . .) of an ellipsis (see pp. 230-31). Do not quote unfairly out of context, or in any other way distort the meaning of what you quote.

Further, when you *paraphrase* or *summarize*, make it clear that the ideas are the source's, not your own. Perhaps use the author's name: "Jones thinks that . . . ." Another way to guard against slip-ups is to put heavy double brackets or parentheses around anything that is entirely your own — for example your comment on an author's ideas; anything not so marked is then clearly from a source. **All such material, even though not quoted, must be acknowledged and documented in your paper; otherwise, it's plagiarism.**

As you work with your notes, good ideas may occur to you. Record them too on separate cards — and mark them clearly so that later you'll know they're your own.

Here are two sample note cards, one with a quoted note and one with a paraphrased note:

Burke, Connections, 177   Priestley's "eudiometer"

"Two wires were introduced into a glass vessel, each connected at the other end to an electrostatic generator. Inside the glass, the wires were brought almost within touching distance; then the gas to be tested was pumped in, and a charge sent down the wires, causing a spark."

Burke, 177   Priestley and gases

In order to test gases, Priestley devised what came to be called a "eudiometer," a device consisting of a glass tube in which he made a spark jump a gap between two wires to see if the gas in the tube would ignite.

STEP 3: ORGANIZING YOUR MATERIAL

As you get well into your research and note-taking, you may be already sorting your cards into groups and putting labels on them. By the time you're about through, a fairly clear organization may have emerged from these groups. If so, you can write a preliminary outline to guide your drafting. But don't stop at the first arrangement that suggests itself. Try others. You might find a better one — and it could, in turn, suggest other and better methods of development.

Decide on Your Main Methods of Development

Stay in control of your material. Don't simply echo your sources; consider several methods of development. For example, if your sources use a chronological development, that doesn't mean you have to. Instead, you might begin with an effect, analyzing it in detail, and then consider causes. Presumably each of your sources has its own purpose; but don't let that force you into making one of them your purpose as well. Be independent and tough-minded. Let your own thinking and your own purpose guide you.

Look over the various methods of development we discuss in Chapter 3, and try to decide which ones will best organize your note cards. Since a research paper will probably be longer than other papers you write, you may want to develop different parts in different ways.

Formulate a Thesis Statement and Arrange Your Material

Stay in control of your material by refining your thesis question as you go through the early steps. Then try to formulate a thesis statement that reflects your decisions about what you've read and recorded. One student, for example, first wrote his thesis question as follows:

> How did the education of women in early Victorian England compare with that of men?

Reformulating it as a guide for organizing his notes, he first tried this:

> Women in mid-Victorian England generally received a poorer education than men.

But such a statement did little to help; it invited only random or arbitrary organization. As he arranged and rearranged his groups of note cards, he found himself looking for reasons, and reformulated his thesis:

> In Victorian England, women's education was inferior to that of men because . . . .

He finished the sentence with his three major points. Such a statement helped because it better reflected his thinking; it provided a cause-effect scheme for his organization.

Construct a Preliminary Outline

A research paper will likely require a more detailed outline than the rough sorts you can often use elsewhere. Before you begin your first draft, draw up a *preliminary outline*, complete with tentative thesis statement or thesis question.

As an example, here is the preliminary outline the history student drew up for her paper on eighteenth-century science (see pp. 238-52). Note that the act of writing it all down prompted several questions and other notes to herself — which she also jotted down, in order to keep them in mind as she wrote her draft:

Newton and His Contemporaries

<u>Thesis Question</u>: What was going on in science around 1700?
<u>Possible beginning</u>: Look at science field by field. Newton was not alone; many scientists were busy. Mention names (surely familiar to most people): Newton, Boyle, Halley, Fahrenheit, Newcomen.

I. Astronomy
       observatories (why?)
       Flamsteed
       Newton and Halley and his comet
       Halley and Ptolemy's star chart

II. Mathematics
       Newton again
       Calculus: Newton vs. Leibnitz

III. Physics
       Newton yet again; "the greatest" (use as transition) <u>Opticks</u>, <u>Principia</u> and "Queries"
       Fahrenheit (what about Celsius?)

IV. Chemistry
       the phlogiston caper

V. Medicine (try to organize my grab-bag of material)

VI. Biology
       Linnaeus's taxonomy (too late?)
       on to Darwin (off my chronological map?)
       (reverse V and VI? Can biology lead to medicine?)

VII. The steam engine — Savery or Newcomen?

VIII. Science vs. Religion
       Darwin and evolution
       Voltaire on Newton

<u>Ending</u>: Much in present-day science was prepared for earlier: Newton and others set the stage for later discoveries and advances. (sounds rather tame)

(<u>Queries</u>: Too many parts? Can IV be part of III? Can VIII be part of VI, via Darwin? See if Newton works as a frame.)

Such an outline is clearly tentative, preliminary. At this point the student hadn't even formulated a thesis statement; she was still using her preliminary question — much less serviceable to head an outline. As you can see from her queries and notes, it was going to take her a draft or two to get enough of a grip on her material to be able to formulate a thesis statement and construct a firmer outline.

Compare this preliminary outline with the final outline and the essay that it accompanies (see p. 238). Note that during drafting and revising the student not only answered her queries but also changed her mind about other points. For example she reduced the number of parts to six by moving her discussion of the steam engine and by using biology as lead-in to Science and Religion, a strategy that also gave her a context for introducing Darwin and enabled her to build toward an effective ending. She moved Chemistry to take advantage of the transition provided by Stahl, who also appears at the end of Medicine. And she changed her thesis and title to reflect her decision to de-emphasize Newton and broaden the focus of interest of her paper.

An outline is not a straitjacket. Be prepared, even eager, to alter your preliminary outline. Don't be trapped into sticking with something just because you've written it down. As you draft and revise, you'll also revise and refine your outline until eventually you'll have a polished outline that conforms to the finished paper. (For this final version, we recommend a *sentence* outline, for both its clarity and its formality.) This outline, as it takes shape, will serve as a constant guide and safeguard for you as you write and revise, and in its final form it will serve as a guide for your reader.

STEP 4: WRITING THE FIRST DRAFT

With a good set of note cards and a preliminary outline that reflects your decisions thus far about development and arrangement, you're ready to begin drafting. Follow the advice in Chapter 4. For example, write rapidly, and don't bog yourself down in an elaborate introduction.

Integrating Quotations

To avoid sounding like your sources, blend quotations into the flow of your own writing — for example as the history student does with a quotation of part of a sentence:

> Even though his studies were not conclusive, they approached the discovery of electrostatic induction, but unfortunately he was not able "to grasp the connection between electricity and the luminous phenomena observed."

It is *her* sentence, *her* sentence structure: the quoted material occurs in it, but doesn't control it. Try to avoid quoting entire sentences — or if you do, try to include even them *within* your own. Above all, use long "block" quotations only when they will be preferable to paraphrase, genuinely effective for your purpose — for example when their language is especially memorable, as in Newton's striking statement of scientific modesty that the student sets off as a block quotation — the only one in her paper (see p. 243).

Don't let your anxiety about filling up a page tempt you to use long quotations for their own sake. Rather, as another way of maintaining *your* control over *your* paper, try to make your comments on any quotation or paraphrase at least as long as what you have quoted or paraphrased.

Keeping Track of Sources

As you write successive drafts, be scrupulously careful with material that you got from your sources. Remember that you must acknowledge these items *in your text.* Merely listing a source in a bibliography at the end is not enough. Doing so may absolve you of dishonesty, but you will still be guilty of extreme carelessness — and a form of plagiarism.

After each citation, whether quotation, paraphrase, summary, or direct reference, put in parentheses the last name of the author — and the title if necessary — along with the page number(s). This information will enable you to provide documentation as you prepare your final draft.

What to Acknowledge and Document; "Common Knowledge"

ack

When told to acknowledge everything that comes from a source other than their own heads, students sometimes feel that they have to put a note after nearly every sentence. But if you've made good use of the strategies for finding material, and if you've made it a point to comment on the material as you took notes, a good deal of the content of your draft will be your own and will not need documenting.

Nor do you have to document what is called "common knowledge" — for instance that Charles Dickens wrote *Great Expectations*, that Bern is the capital of Switzerland, that Newton formulated the law of gravity, or that Daniel appears in the Old Testament. But other kinds of facts or ideas are harder to assess. Ask yourself, "*Common* to whom?" Many facts in a journal on nuclear physics are common knowledge to nuclear physicists, and many facts in a specialized book on linguistics will be common knowledge to most linguists. It depends on your assessment of your readers.

English teachers know that the lines "Let me not to the marriage of true minds / Admit impediments" come from a Shakespeare sonnet; but that wouldn't be common knowledge for most students in grade twelve: for them you would need to identify the source. But for readers who had been studying that and several other Elizabethan sonnets, no such acknowledgment would be necessary. If you think of yourself as writing for the students and instructors of the course you're preparing the paper for, you should have little difficulty deciding what to acknowledge and document. But whenever you're not certain, play safe and acknowledge the source. And if something is new to *you*, however "common" it may be in the world outside, it's probably safer to assume that it will be new to your readers as well.

STEP 5:   REVISING THE RESEARCH PAPER

Because research papers are longer and more complex, careful revising is even more important for them than it is for other kinds of writing. Go through your drafts several times, each time focussing on only one or two things. As always, use Chapters 6 through 10 as your guide; but a research paper requires additional, special attention.

Making the Paper Your Own

Because so much of a research paper depends on sources, it's almost inevitable that some of their orientation and language have crept in. While revising, you can reclaim your writing. This is your last chance to make sure the paper is under *your* control and not that of your sources.

THESIS STATEMENT AND INTRODUCTION

Begin by scrutinizing your thesis. After working through a draft or two, you may be able to refine your thesis statement, focus it further. Then, because you know where the whole paper is going, you can write your beginning paragraph — and perhaps also the ending. Use your opening to prepare your readers: provide any necessary background, indicate the purpose and scope of your paper, and probably at least indicate the main lines you will develop.

Checklist for Revising the Research Paper

Here are some questions and suggestions to help you revise the various elements of your paper. Treat these conscientiously; they are designed to alert you to common potential weaknesses of research papers.

THE WHOLE PAPER

1. Are all the developed points genuinely relevant to *your* purpose and not just that of one or more of your sources?

2. Can you substantially reduce the first third or even the first half of your draft? (Often, in getting going, writers include much more background or history or other facts and quotations than purpose and thesis require.)

3. Have you left anything out? Recheck your outline. Ask yourself what your reader needs to know for each section. Do you need to make any underlying assumptions clear?

4. Are the various sections and subsections in the best order? If your purpose is even partly to persuade, have you kept your strongest arguments for near the end? Does your newly focussed thesis suggest a better order?

5. Are main ideas emphasized? While drafting, you may have been so engrossed in facts, quotations, and paraphrases that you let some of your points become obscured.

6. Recheck your beginning paragraph to make sure that it accords with how you now see your thesis and purpose, and that it establishes your own tone, not that of a source.

7. Does your ending reflect and re-emphasize the thesis? Does it harmonize with the tone of your new beginning?

PARAGRAPHS

1. Do any paragraphs end with a quotation — especially a long one? If so, add a comment or observation indicating how you want your readers to take what you have quoted. Keep the paragraph in your control right to its end.

2. Can you divide any longer paragraphs into shorter ones for sharper emphasis and easier reading?

3. Think how your paragraphs will look when typed. Is there a string of short paragraphs that might distract readers from the progress of your explanation or argument?

4. Consider using a transitional paragraph between major sections. It can also help emphasize important ideas.

5. Would a particularly complicated batch of data in a paragraph be clearer if put into point form or a chart?

6. Check the first sentence of each paragraph to see that it (a) refers in some way to your overall topic or guiding purpose; (b) provides a smooth transition from the preceding paragraph; (c) clearly introduces the topic of the paragraph. Then make sure each paragraph is *unified*.

SENTENCES

1. Have you cut out as much deadwood as you can?

2. Can you break up some of a series of long, complicated sentences into shorter ones, for contrast and clarity?

3. If you begin a sentence with *There is* or *There are*, try to eliminate the phrase by finding an effective verb.

4. Check to see that you have provided all necessary explicit transitions between sentences to help your readers keep track of where you're taking them. Don't rely on the word *also* or on such often vague transitions as the pronoun *This* and phrases such as *Another factor was*.

5. Have you put main ideas into independent clauses — and made these clauses parts of *your* sentence structure rather than that of your sources?

WORDS AND PHRASES

1. Have you maintained a reasonably consistent style and tone? Don't be lured off by the diction of your sources.

2. Have you looked up any words you're not sure of?

3. Check your diction against the Checklist of Usage in Chapter 8. You may have followed a source into error.

4. Have you preferred shorter words to longer ones, and avoided prefabricated and other deadwood phrases?

5. Can you improve your paper by substituting concrete for abstract terms (not *youth* but *young people*; not *transportation* but *cars, ships, airplanes*)? For example, have you taken from your sources any abstract concepts that can be made clearer by being put in concrete terms, or illustrated with concrete examples? Can you

substitute the specific for the general (not *scientific experts* but *marine biologists*)?

6. Have you avoided technical jargon — especially if your audience is different from that of your sources?

7. Can you substitute active verbs for abstract nouns (not "the board's decision was to . . . ." but "the board decided to . . . .")?

8. Have you used a series of nouns as modifiers? If so, make it a phrase. (Not "voter distribution reorganization" but "reorganizing the distribution of voters.)

PUNCTUATION: USING QUOTATIONS AND QUOTATION MARKS

Check your drafts according to the principles of punctuation discussed and illustrated in Chapter 9. In addition, check your handling of quotations and related matters pertaining to research papers according to the following principles.

Quotation Marks

Quotation marks have three main uses:

1. around the titles of short works (see Chapter 10),
2. around pieces of dialogue or other direct speech, and
3. around verbatim quotation from any printed or other source — even just one or two significant words — run into your own text. Omitting them is **plagiarism.**

Use *double* quotation marks (". . .") except around a quotation within a quotation. If a quotation has another quotation inside it, enclose the inner one in *single* quotation marks:

> In 1972 David Suzuki wrote that "In the past 20 years, the science of 'molecular genetics' has dazzled the world with its insights into living organisms."

Quotation marks, whether double or single, come in *pairs*. If you open with one, don't leave off the closing one.

Block Quotations

Generally, avoid long quotations. But if your purpose requires a quotation that takes up four or more lines,

1. indent it eight or ten spaces (not just the usual five),
2. single-space it, and
3. leave an extra line before and after it.

DON'T ADD QUOTATION MARKS around such "block" quotations; indenting and single-spacing *is* quoting.

Note: You may put quotation marks around a term you want to qualify or use in a special sense (as we do with *block* just above). But DO NOT put them around slang or clichés; to do so only calls attention to them and apologizes for them (see pp. 153-54).

Other Marks with Quotation Marks

1. Generally, use a comma before or after a quotation with a word that has to do with speaking or writing:

    > Cinderella whispered, "It's nearly midnight."

    > "I guess I should have stayed in bed this morning," muttered John, picking himself up out of the mud.

    > "Nothing," wrote Goethe, "is more frightful than ignorance in action."

2. To introduce a longer or more formal quotation, one consisting of a full sentence or more (especially if it is a block quotation), a colon is appropriate:

    > In his essay "Teaching the Humanities Today," Northrop Frye writes: "Everything we know is formed out of words and numbers, and literature and mathematics are the only subjects of knowledge which are also means of knowing."

    But if a quotation — even a block quotation — is part of the structure of your own sentence, for example after a *that,* put neither a comma nor a colon in front of it:

    > Northrop Frye claims **that** "Everything . . . ."

    When you run **parts** of sentences into your own sentence structure, similarly do not use punctuation for them:

    > Frye claims that these two studies are at the same time "subjects of knowledge" and "means of knowing."

    (unless your own sentence needs internal punctuation).

3. *Periods and commas* go **inside** the closing quotation mark; *colons and semicolons* go **after** it. *Question marks and exclamation points* go **inside** the quotation mark when part of the quotation, **outside** when part of your own sentence:

    > Matilda asked, **"When can we stop for a meal?"**
    > **Did she say**, "I want to stop for a meal"**?**

    Note that when a question mark (or an exclamation point) ends a quotation, no other mark is needed after it:

    > "When can we stop for a meal?" she asked.

Indicating Omissions: Using Ellipses • • •

You can cut down on what you quote by leaving out whatever isn't necessary. But when you omit something, you must indicate the omission with three *spaced* dots (. . .), called an **ellipsis**. If the omitted material includes the end of a sentence, add a fourth dot, the period:

> Northrop Frye observes that ". . . literature and mathematics . . . are also means of knowing."

> Northrop Frye claims that "Everything we know is formed out of words and numbers . . . ."

Indicate omissions at the beginning or end only when you want to make sure your reader won't mistake what's left for the actual beginning or end of the original sentence — for example if the part you're quoting begins with a capital. If you omit a sentence or more, use four dots (the first, the period for the preceding sentence, with no space before it). Indicate the omission of a paragraph or more, or of a line or more of poetry, with a whole line of spaced dots.

Indicating Additions: Using Square Brackets [ ]

If you insert a clarifying word or phrase in something you're quoting, or if you make a slight change in order to make a quotation fit your own sentence structure, enclose the added word or words in square brackets. For example:

> Mathematics, as Frye points out, is not only one of the "subjects of knowledge" but one "which **[is]** also **[a]** means of knowing."

You can also put the word *sic* (Latin for "thus") in brackets after an error in the material you're quoting, so that your readers won't think you made the error yourself.

DOCUMENTING YOUR SOURCES

A major feature that makes a research paper different from other writing is the acknowledgment of sources. You must do this acknowledging formally, following one or another *system* of *documentation*. Documentation has three purposes:

1. It lets you acknowledge your debts to sources.
2. It helps you support your points with authority.
3. It enables your readers to follow up on your discussion — just as you do during your research.

The Different Systems of Documentation

Basically there are three different forms for documenting sources.

1. the **parenthetical** method,
2. the **note** method, and
3. the **number** method.

doc

You should know about all of them, since you may encounter them in your studies. And for any particular research project, you must decide or find out which method you need to use.

1. THE PARENTHETICAL METHOD

This is the predominant method in the humanities and social sciences. After a citation of a source, you insert, in parentheses, a brief identification of that source. Since this is how you keep track of sources in your drafts, you won't need to change much when you prepare your final copy. At the end of the paper, provide a detailed bibliography — an alphabetical list of "Works Cited" or "References."

The parenthetical method appears in two forms:

a. The Name-Page Method

Many English courses and other courses in the humanities use the **name-page** method. In the parentheses after a citation, put the surname(s) of the author(s) and the relevant page or pages in the source. Here are some examples for different kinds of citation and different kinds of works; following each example of a reference in the text of a paper is the way that work would appear in the list of Works Cited.

A book by a single author:

```
It is easy to agree with one authority that "The
crossword is the most popular and widespread word game in
the world . . ." (Augarde 52).
```
```
Augarde, Tony.  The Oxford Book of Word Games.  Oxford:
     Oxford UP, 1984.
```

```
Zinsser (158-76) offers good advice on writing humour.
```
```
Zinsser, William.  On Writing Well: An Informal Guide to
     Writing Nonfiction.  2nd ed.  New York: Harper, 1980.
```

Note that if you use the author's name in your sentence, you put only the page number in parentheses — a technique that is less distracting for the reader.

A reference to a whole work, mentioning the author's name, is enough; no parenthetical note is needed:

```
Atwood's novel is set in the future.
```
```
Atwood, Margaret.  The Handmaid's Tale.  Toronto: McClelland
     and Stewart, 1985.
```

A book by more than one author:

```
Wells had "astonishing prescience" about the sort of
international organization of nations that came out of each
world war (MacKenzie and MacKenzie 316).
```

MacKenzie, Norman, and Jeanne MacKenzie. <u>H. G. Wells</u>. New
York: Simon and Schuster, 1973.

If a work has more than three authors, give only the first and add *et
al.* (abbreviated Latin *et alia*, "and others").

A reprint of an earlier edition:

<u>The Land of Green Ginger</u> is one of Holtby's more successful
novels.

Holtby, Winifred. <u>The Land of Green Ginger</u>. 1927. London:
Virago, 1983.

A work in an anthology:

Northrop Frye calls "literature and mathematics"
both "subjects of knowledge" and "means of knowing" (99).

Frye, Northrop. "Teaching the Humanities Today." <u>Divisions
on a Ground: Essays on Canadian Culture</u>. Ed. James
Polk. Toronto: Anansi, 1982. 91-101.

An article in a journal using continuous pagination throughout the several issues of a volume, as most do, rather than for each individual issue:

"Although Solecki concedes that <u>Fifth Business</u> is Davies's
masterpiece, he finds it somehow predictable in its
thematic preoccupations and its manner of presentation"
(Mulvihill 182).

Mulvihill, James. "<u>The Rebel Angels</u>: Robertson Davies and
the Novel of Ideas." <u>English Studies in Canada</u> 13
(1987): 182-94.

An article in a monthly magazine; an unsigned article:

More and more people are having to deal with a lower
standard of living ("Life at the Edge" 375).

"Life at the Edge." <u>Consumer Reports</u> June 1987: 375-78.

Part of a work of more than one volume:

Schopenhauer's remarks on rhetoric are severely limited (2:
305-06), unlike his remarks on many other topics.

Schopenhauer, Arthur. <u>The World as Will and Idea</u>. Trans.
R. B. Haldane and J. Kemp. 3 vols. New York:
Scribner's, 1883.

Behaviourism is probably the major influence on modern
psychology (Zangwill 174).

Zangwill, O. L. "Psychology." <u>1918-1945</u>. Vol. 2 of <u>The
Twentieth-Century Mind</u>. Ed. C. B. Cox and A. E. Dyson.
3 vols. London: Oxford UP, 1972.

More than one work by the same author; include the title of the work being cited (if the title is long, a short but clear version is enough):

```
Craven calls Van Gogh's face "gruesome and holy" (Modern
Art 92).
Craven, Thomas.  Men of Art.  New York: Simon and Schuster,
     1931.
---.  Modern Art: The Men the Movements the Meaning.  New
     York: Simon and Schuster, 1935.
```

Note that in all the parenthetical references, the period (or other punctuation) follows the parentheses. With a block quotation, the reference comes *after* the period and two spaces (see p. 5 of the sample paper).

If you need a note including comment of some kind, or if you need to list several sources in one note, you may, to avoid disruption, use a raised numeral referring to a footnote or an endnote (see p. 3 of the sample paper).

The sample paper (pp. 239-52) illustrates the **name-page** method. For further discussion and examples, see the latest edition of the *MLA Handbook for Writers of Research Papers,* published by the Modern Language Association of America.

B. The Name-Date Method

Many of the social sciences use the **name-date** method. There are variations of format among different versions of this method; here we briefly illustrate that prescribed by the *Publication Manual of the American Psychological Association* (1983 edition). In the parentheses after a citation, put the author's surname (if more than one, use an ampersand [**&**] between the last two), the date of the work, and the relevant page number(s), separated by commas. For example:

```
Appropriate assertiveness promotes effective and satisfying
communications in which "resentment and suspicion [are]
decreased" (Galassi & Galassi, 1975, p. 352).

Galassi, J. P., & Galassi, M. D. (1975). Relationship
     between assertiveness and aggressiveness. Psychological
     Reports, 36, 352-354.
```

Note the following features: in the entry for the bibliography (called "References") both names are in reverse order; only initials are used, not authors' first names; the date, in parentheses, follows the authors' names; only the first word and any proper nouns of the title (and subtitle, if any) are capitalized, but normal capitalization is used in the journal's title; there are no quotation marks around the title of the article; the volume number is underlined (or italicized); the reverse indention is only three spaces; and there is only one space between elements.

Here are a few more examples, using again some of the items above:

```
Zinsser (1980, chap. 18) offers good advice on writing
humour.
Zinsser, W. (1980). On writing well: An informal guide to
    writing nonfiction. 2nd ed. New York: Harper.
```

```
Atwood's novel (1985) is set in the future.
Atwood, M. (1985). The handmaid's tale. Toronto: McClelland
    and Stewart.
```

```
Northrop Frye calls "literature and mathematics" both
"subjects of knowledge" and "means of knowing" (1982, p.
99).
Frye, N. (1982). Teaching the humanities today. In J. Polk
    (Ed.), Divisions on a ground: Essays on Canadian culture
    (pp. 91-101). Toronto: Anansi.
```

```
"Although Solecki concedes that Fifth Business is Davies's
masterpiece, he finds it somehow predictable in its
thematic preoccupations and its manner of presentation"
(Mulvihill, 1987, p. 182).
Mulvihill, J. (1987). The Rebel Angels: Robertson Davies and
    the novel of ideas. English Studies in Canada, 3, 182-194
```

```
More and more people are having to deal with a lower
standard of living ("Life at the Edge," 1987, p. 375).
Life at the edge. (1987, June). Consumer Reports, pp. 375-
    378.
```

```
According to Zangwill (1972), behaviourism is probably the
major influence on modern psychology (p. 174).
Zangwill, O. L. (1972). Psychology. In C. B. Cox & A. E.
    Dyson (Eds.), The twentieth-century mind: Vol. 2: 1914-
    1945. London: Oxford.
```

Note that putting the date of the work in parentheses is enough to show which of Craven's two works is being cited:

```
Craven calls Van Gogh's face "gruesome and holy" (1935, p.
92).
```

If you use two works by the same author published in the same year, distinguish them with *a* and *b* after their dates.

2. THE NOTE METHOD

This was formerly the standard method in many disciplines, and one you will likely encounter often in your reading. After a citation, a raised numeral directs readers to a footnote or endnote identifying the source. Most instructors will permit or even prefer notes at the end (starting on a new page) rather than footnotes. Further, since a bibliography would mainly duplicate the information in the notes, you may not need to include one. If you do, the form will be the same as for the name-page method. Here are sample notes referring to some of the sources above:

[1] Tony Augarde, <u>The Oxford Book of Word Games</u> (Oxford: Oxford UP, 1984) 52.

[2] "Teaching the Humanities Today," <u>Divisions on a Ground: Essays on Canadian Culture</u>, ed. James Polk (Toronto: Anansi, 1982) 99.

[3] William Zinsser, <u>On Writing Well: An Informal Guide to Writing Nonfiction</u>, 2nd ed. (New York: Harper, 1980) 158-76.

(Since the text used only his surname, the full name is needed in the note.)

[4] James Mulvihill, "<u>The Rebel Angels</u>: Robertson Davies and the Novel of Ideas," <u>English Studies in Canada</u> 13 (1987): 182.

[5] "Life at the Edge," <u>Consumer Reports</u> June 1987: 375.

[6] Arthur Schopenhauer, <u>The World as Will and Idea</u>, trans. R. B. Haldane and J. Kemp, 3 vols. (New York: Scribner's, 1883) 2: 305-06.

The *MLA Handbook* also discusses this method.

3. THE NUMBER METHOD

This method is most commonly used in the physical sciences, and sometimes in the social sciences as well. After a citation of a source, you put, in parentheses, a numeral referring to a numerical (not alphabetical) list of sources at the end of the paper; for a quotation — as opposed to a reference to an entire work — a page number may accompany an underlined reference number in parentheses. Since there are several variations within this method, you may need to consult a style manual for your particular discipline.

THE LAST STEP: PREPARING AND PROOFREADING THE FINAL DRAFT

Always type a research paper, or have it typed. If you use a word-processor, make sure your instructor will accept the hard copy it produces. In addition to the manuscript conventions in Chapter 10, carefully follow the pattern for the system of documentation you use. If a formal outline is part of the assignment, lay it out clearly and correctly. If you use a title page, don't repeat the title on page 1.

Spacing: Single or Double

The *MLA Handbook* calls for double-spacing everything, including block quotations, notes (if any), and bibliography. In the sample paper which follows, however, we single-space the outline, the block quotation (with an extra space above and below it), the single footnote, and the list of Works Cited (but double-space *between* entries), since this is the way many instructors prefer it (it makes the paper more closely resemble printed work). Before you prepare your final copy, check with your instructor.

Proofreading

Because of the greater complexity of a research paper, be exaggeratedly careful when you check it. Proofread slowly, and more than once. Check all the usual things, and in addition scrupulously recheck each note and each item in the bibliography, for it is extremely easy for errors to creep in. Double-check all spellings of names and all page numbers and dates against your bibliography cards and note cards; if you made the cards out carefully, you won't have to return to the sources to check for accuracy. Check all documentation to make sure it follows the right form in spacing, punctuation, indention, and underlining. For example, does each bibliographical entry end with a period?

SAMPLE RESEARCH PAPER

The following research paper is intended less as a model than as an illustration of various techniques discussed in this chapter. Note for example how the writer handles quotations. The paper also provides further examples of the forms for the name-page system of documentation.

Scientific Endeavour in the Early Eighteenth Century

Thesis Statement (Beginning): It is interesting and instructive to see how much happened in science before our own time, for example in the pivotal period of the early eighteenth century.

   I. Interest in astronomy was growing.
     A. Observatories were being built throughout Europe.
     B. Flamsteed and Halley worked on the first modern star catalogues.
     C. Newtonian theory was bolstered by the return of Halley's comet.

  II. Mathematics was an active field.
     A. Newton refined his earlier work on calculus, and won out in his dispute with Leibnitz.
     B. Other mathematical discoveries were also important.
       1. William Jones introduced the concept of π.
       2. Jacob van 's Gravesande did influential work on geometrical perspective.

 III. There was progress in both theoretical and practical physics.
     A. Newton left physics a double heritage.
       1. He made significant discoveries in dynamics and in theories of light and colour.
       2. His "Queries" stimulated further investigation.
     B. Fahrenheit established his temperature scale.
     C. Haulksbee worked on luminescence in rarefied gases.
     D. Savery and Newcomen invented the steam engine.

  IV. In medicine, work was done on diseases and physiology.
     A. Several discoveries helped fight common diseases.
       1. Citrus juices were used against scurvy.
       2. Epidemics were first studied systematically.
       3. Inoculation against smallpox was developed.
     B. In physiology, there were disputing theories about how the brain controls the body.
       1. Boerhaave and Hoffmann favoured a "mechanistic" theory.
       2. Stahl's "spiritual" theories, however wrong, led to later studies in neurology.

   V. Chemistry was held back by the theory of "Phlogiston."

  VI. In biology there were disputes about science and religion.
     A. Basic identification of plants and animals led to Linnaean taxonomy and eventually to Darwin's theory.
     B. Scientists believed that their findings supported Christian teachings.
       1. Newton studied theology and biblical chronology.
       2. Voltaire later claimed that Newton's work "undermined" scriptural authority.

Ending: The dispute between science and religion is still with us. But in general the achievements of early eighteenth-century science provided many beginnings for today's world of science.

1

Scientific Endeavour in the Early Eighteenth Century

Most of us think of the twentieth century as the great age of science, of astonishing discoveries and dazzling technological advances. There is no denying the achievements of our age, but there is a danger that we will be so impressed by them that we will tend to forget about how much was done, or at least begun, long before. For example, look at what was going on in scientific fields during the early eighteenth century. Not only are some of the scientific activities during this short period interesting in themselves, but more important, a brief look at them should help us see our own age in a clearer perspective.

By the early eighteenth century in Europe, the religious revolution of the seventeenth century had only recently begun to recede, and the thoughts of many Europeans were turning to science. In Dartmouth, England, Thomas Newcomen and Thomas Savery were working--quite separately--on the steam engine; Edmund Halley was beginning to study the stars and planets visible from the northern hemisphere; Bartolomeo Christofori was working on his new invention, the piano; and Isaac Newton was busy revising some of his earlier works. Several different sectors of the scientific world were undergoing change, and all

2

were beginning to realize the advantages of the modern approach
to science as set out by Sir Francis Bacon and as practised by
such important seventeenth-century figures as Robert Boyle.

Because of the rising interest in astronomy, mainly as an
aid to navigation, new observatories were popping up all over
Europe: in 1706 an observatory was built on the Great Gate at
Trinity College, Cambridge; between 1706 and 1711 a larger one
was built at Berlin; and in 1712 a third major observatory was
constructed on top of the University building in Bologna
(Donnelly 19, 21). In 1709, John Flamsteed, England's first
Astronomer Royal, was hard at the laborious task of compiling a
star catalogue. He published his partial results in 1712, at
Newton's insistence, but his main work, the <u>Historia Coelestis
Britannica</u>, was not published until 1725, several years after his
death. According to a French historian, it was the first modern
star catalogue and showed "the right ascensions and polar
distances, as well as the longitudes and latitudes, of nearly
3,000 stars . . ." (Lévy 451). Edmund Halley, during the same
period, was studying Ptolemy's catalogue of the stars. After
many careful observations of approximately three hundred stars
that had been mentioned by Ptolemy, Halley inferred that the
stars had significantly changed position since Ptolemy had
written his catalogue in A.D. 150, while others seemed not to
have moved at all. Halley decided that different stars were at
different distances from the earth, and that those that appeared
to have remained in the same places must be so far away that it

3

would be impossible to detect their movements over 1,500 years (Ronan 70).

By the beginning of the eighteenth century, "the Copernican revolution was virtually won," and astronomy was beginning to be based securely on Newtonian physics.[1] One of Newton's theories has to do with the attraction of objects to one another (his well-known law of gravity). Using this theory, he made several calculations that led him to predict that the orbit of a comet has the shape of a flattened ellipse, but he had not yet proved his hypothesis. Then, in 1705, Halley published in the Philosophical Transactions of the Royal Society his deduction that the three comets observed in 1507, 1631, and 1682 were one and the same (Ronan 69). He held that this comet had a period of revolution of seventy-six years and went so far as to predict its return in 1758. Newton was proved right when the comet actually "did return in 1759--having been delayed by the pull of Jupiter and Saturn--[and] the Newtonian theory scored one of its greatest triumphs" (Lévy 444). The work of these men was crucial to the future of astronomy: present-day studies of the movements of the planets, the sun, and the stars depend heavily upon star catalogues such as Flamsteed's and upon Newton's theory and Halley's proof of it.

In the early years of the century, mathematicians were

[1] For this fact and for part of the phrasing, I am indebted to Professor H. J. Metcalf, in his lecture in History 155, University of British Columbia, 11 Feb. 1986.

4

consolidating old ideas and introducing new ones. Newton was
revising several of his earlier works on differential and
integral calculus. He had by this time realized the importance
of accuracy in studying convergence and stated firmly that "the
very smallest Errors in mathematical Matters are not to be
neglected" (Cohen, DSB 51). Two Swiss brothers, Jacques and
Johann (Jean) Bernoulli, as well as Gottfried Wilhelm von
Leibnitz, the eminent German philosopher and mathematician, had
also developed theories of calculus and practical uses for it.
A. Rupert Hall tells how in 1710 one of Newton's pupils, John
Keill, accused Leibnitz of plagiarizing Newton's work on
fluxions, the calculus of velocities. A similar accusation had
been made at least twice before, but this time the quarrel was so
bitter that the influential Royal Society, of which Newton was
president, was asked to arbitrate. The Society concluded that
Leibnitz was in the wrong, and from then on Leibnitz and Newton
were set against each other (145).

In 1706 William Jones, a teacher of mathematics who briefly
collaborated with Newton, introduced a new symbol, π, and
contributed to work on proving its value as an algebraic
notation. A Dutch professor, Jacob van 's Gravesande, in 1711
published a book on geometrical perspective, a book whose
importance was not to be realized until almost a hundred years
later (Baron, DSB; see also Taton, "Rise" 419).

Isaac Newton was undoubtedly "the greatest figure of the
period" ("Science"), the most influential scientist active during

5

the late seventeenth and early eighteenth centuries. He made
major contributions to mathematics and astronomy, but by far his
greatest discoveries dealt with physics: Newton defined the three
basic laws of motion, wrote a book on the nature of light and
colours (Opticks, 1704), and discussed dynamics in his Principia,
the second edition of which appeared in 1713. Yet he was a
modest man when it came to his own achievements. Shortly before
his death, he wrote:

> I do not know what I may appear to the world, but to
> myself, I seem to have been only like a boy playing on
> the seashore, and diverting myself in now and then
> finding a smoother pebble or a prettier shell than
> ordinary, whilst the great ocean of truth lay all
> undiscovered before me. (qtd. in Cohen, WBE)

By 1710, Newton was busy working on the set of sixteen "Queries"
that he planned to add to his Opticks; these consisted of
questions that had occurred to him throughout his career but that
he himself did not wish to research (Cohen, DSB 59). As
Newtonian ideology spread through Britain and the continent in
the first quarter of the eighteenth century, his queries proved
to be important, for they spurred other scientists to further
investigation. Newton therefore left science a double heritage:
the benefits of his own discoveries, and ideas to stimulate
further study.

But Newton was not the only eminent physicist of these
years. In his survey, Georges Allard tells of Fahrenheit
experimenting with heat and ways to measure it, and of how he

6

defined his temperature scale in 1719 (467)--and Celsius was working during this period too. Edmond Bauer tells of Francis Haulksbee making observations on electrical discharges in rarefied gases. Even though his studies were not conclusive, they approached the discovery of electrostatic induction, but unfortunately he was not able "to grasp the connection between electricity and the luminous phenomena he had observed" (472).

Science in the early eighteenth century was not only theoretical, but practical as well. Probably the most important practical application of physics at the time was the steam engine. Thomas Newcomen has officially been credited with its invention in 1712, but another Englishman, Thomas Savery, had designed a simpler engine ten years before. According to Robert Henry Thurston, Savery's engine was "the first really practicable and commercially viable steam engine," and therefore "Savery is entitled to the credit of having been the first to introduce a machine in which the power of heat, acting through the medium of steam, was rendered generally useful" (38). Unfortunately, Savery's engine could not stand high pressures and his machine once blew up, with fatal results to an attendant. Thurston points out that Newcomen remedied this problem by proposing an engine that would incorporate a steam cylinder with a safety valve. This new device was successful enough for Newcomen and John Galley, his assistant, to take out a patent for it in 1705 and to begin adapting it for use in pumping water out of the mines. By a lucky accident, they discovered that cold water condensed the steam much more efficiently when applied directly to the inside of the cylinder than when sprayed on the outside. This modification made Newcomen's steam engine especially useful in mine work and is the development that earned him his reputation as the inventor of the steam engine (39, 58).

In the field of medicine in the early eighteenth century, progress was less spectacular than in physics, but interesting things were going on even so, as shown by an almost random dipping into what various contributors to René Taton's <u>The Beginnings of Modern Science</u> describe. For example, eighteenth-century rationalism went to work: ". . . the considerable body of anatomical knowledge handed down by the Renaissance and the 17th century was put into some sort of order" (Dulieu 540). But individuals were active as well. For example, in 1720 an obscure Austrian doctor named Kramer suggested using lime or orange juice to treat scurvy (Dulieu 547). Kramer's small discovery must have been particularly important, because it enabled ships' crews (the "Limeys") to remain healthy on long voyages of exploration later in the century, such as those of Cook and Vancouver.

A Viennese surgeon named Planciz "suggested that all diseases are caused by micro-organisms"--but he "provided no evidence" (Dulieu 541); perhaps he was too far ahead of his time. But specific diseases were causing concern, not least bubonic plague, which was still a serious threat in Europe. This period saw the beginnings of the systematic study of epidemics, and as

8

Louis Dulieu tells us, such diseases as malaria, diphtheria, typhoid, rabies, influenza, and yellow fever--"the new scourge"-- were the subjects of epidemiologists' attention; they even studied whooping cough (547). And experiments with vaccination were giving preventive medicine greater credibility. In a crude form, known as "variolation," inoculation against smallpox, for example, was performed by "prick[ing] the skin in three places with a needle that had previously been pushed into a fresh smallpox pustule." In 1717 Lady Mary Wortley Montagu had her son inoculated (I suppose successfully)--a courageous act which along with others helped gain wide approval for the new technique (Dulieu 548). Only recently has smallpox been virtually eradicated from the earth; we can only guess how much we owe to the early experimenters and people like Lady Mary, who pioneered so many things that we now take for granted.

In physiology, less dramatically perhaps, but nonetheless interestingly, contending theories were surfacing. The Dutch professor Hermann Boerhaave and others were beginning to make connections between specific bodily movements and different parts of the brain. But toward the end of the first decade of the century, a German scientist, Georg Ernst Stahl, published three books arguing against the theories of Boerhaave and Friedrich Hoffmann (Dulieu 542, 544). They believed that "Biology could be reduced to simple mathematical, chemical or mechanical laws," and that it was blood and nerves within the muscles that produced muscular activity; but Stahl held out for a spiritual component in which "the soul's action" played a part. Ironically, by their attempts to combat mechanistic explanations of the movements of the muscles, Stahl and others opened the door to such later studies as Galvani's on the electrical characteristics of the nervous system and Lavoisier's proof of the chemical nature of respiration (Canguilhem 534-36). It seems clear that the early eighteenth century was a period not only of some exciting advances and discoveries but also of considerable systematizing of previous and current discoveries, all refining the scientific method in ways that would eventually make it possible for medicine to become a true science.

Chemistry, which in the seventeenth century was only just emerging from the centuries-old domination of alchemy, accelerated more slowly than physics because it was retarded by the erroneous theory of "phlogiston." Stahl had given that name to a substance first hypothesized by Johann J. Becher, who had argued that fire can be explained by the idea that "all combustibles contain a subtle material that is given off from them when they burn" (White 31). The notion of a combustible substance within the burning material was eagerly taken up by most of the advanced scientists in Europe, and the strength of its apparent simplicity and explanatory power set chemistry back for nearly a century. The theory of phlogiston seemed to be confirmed by the common observation that many combustible materials, like wood, lose weight when they are burned; the weight loss was explained by the hypothesis that the original material contained phlogiston which it lost during the process of combustion. The observed fact, however, that several metals actually gain weight when they are burned was explained by an ingenious--but totally wrong--notion that "phlogiston had negative weight, or levity rather than gravity" (Schneer 85). Despite the skepticism of some well-known scientists, like Boerhaave, who wrote the most important chemistry textbook to appear in the first half of the century, most of the English chemists, especially Henry Cavendish and Joseph Priestley, took up the theory because it seemed to explain so much. It was not until nearly the end of the eighteenth century that the Frenchman Antoine Laurent Lavoisier (who provided chemistry with a new terminology that included such words as <u>oxygen</u> and <u>hydrogen</u>) finally discredited the phlogiston theory by exposing its confusions and contradictions (Williams 2; White 117).

Finally we turn to biology and the growing conflict between science and religion. Most educated people today know of the Linnaean classification for plants and animals. Its inventor, the Swedish botanist and taxonomist Carl von Linné (Latinized to <u>Carolus Linnaeus</u>), was not born until 1707, but much of the work of basic identification was accomplished in the early years of the eighteenth century, preparing the way for him. Sir Hans Sloane studied Caribbean flora and made drawings of eight hundred plants (Virville 554, 562). In 1709 Johann Jacob Scheuchzer of Switzerland published the <u>Herbarium diluvianum</u>, in which he described many European fossils. His work also convinced him

"that the Flood must have taken place in the month of May!" Such
an idea sounds odd now, but it was not unusual in the early
1700's, when science was still trying to support the authority of
the Bible. In 1716 Scheuchzer published a catalogue of fifteen
hundred fossils (Furon 566-67). These and other studies were the
beginning of a collection of data that helped Linnaeus with his
classification and helped lead Charles Darwin to the theory of
evolution almost a century and a half later.

Of course Darwin's theory caused great controversy between
those who accepted the idea of evolution and those who believed
in the biblical story of creation. But in the early years of the
eighteenth century, the majority of scientists still felt that
their discoveries strongly supported scripture. For instance,
according to his recent biographer, Newton spent a great deal of
his time on questions of theology and biblical chronology
(Westfall 589-94), and most of his contemporaries saw no conflict
between science and religion. As early as 1750, however,
"Voltaire held that Newton's discoveries undermined much orthodox
Christian dogma and the authority of the scriptures" (Cowie 33).
Voltaire was responding to the statement by P. L. M. de
Maupertuis in 1744 that it "cannot be doubted that all things are
governed by a supreme Being who has impressed on matter forces
that reflect His power, and has destined them to produce effects
that reveal His wisdom." Maupertuis had come to this conclusion
by trying to prove that nature does not follow the shortest path,
but the path requiring the least energy. He believed that this

12

principle of the "economy of energy" was the final proof of the
existence of God (Dugas and Costabel 428).

The early eighteenth century, then, witnessed the beginning
of the struggle to find a harmonic co-existence between science
and religion, a struggle that is in part still with us today.
Newton's discoveries in mathematics, dynamics, celestial
mechanics, and natural philosophy spurred younger scientists to
investigate the complexities of the material world. His
"Queries" have been seen by some as his greatest contribution to
the furthering of scientific discovery (Cohen, DSB 59). When
Halley's predictions of his comet's return were fulfilled in
1759, the science of astronomy gained greatly in both progress
and prestige. Halley's and Flamsteed's studies of the stars then
got much more notice than when they were first published.
Although the preoccupation with the theory of phlogiston retarded
the development of chemistry, its refutation showed how closely
scientific theory and experimental method must work together.
Botany was advanced by the several plant catalogues compiled in
the first quarter of the century. Further, scientists of that
period were among the first to unite theoretical science with
technology: Newcomen's steam engine greatly eased the
difficulties of mine work and has become the identifying symbol
of the industrial revolution. The methods of early eighteenth-
century scientists and their sometimes ingenious approaches to
the problems they faced have set high standards for the
scientists of today.

13

Works Cited

Allard, Georges. "Heat in the 17th and 18th Centuries." Taton 467-70.

Baron, M. E. "William Jones." Gillispie.

Bauer, Edmond. "Electricity and Magnetism in the 18th Century." Taton 471-88.

Canguilhem, Georges. "Animal Physiology." Taton 527-39.

Cohen, I. Bernard. "Isaac Newton." Gillispie.

---. "Isaac Newton." World Book Encyclopedia. 1964 ed.

Cowie, Leonard W. Eighteenth-Century Europe. London: Bell, 1963.

Donnelly, M. C. Astronomical Observatories in the 17th and 18th Centuries. Brussels: Académie Royale de Belgique, 1964.

Dugas, René, and Pierre Costabel. "The Organization of the Principles of Classical Mechanics." Taton 425-36.

Dulieu, Louis. "Medicine." Taton 540-53.

Furon, Raymond. "Earth Sciences." Taton 565-77.

Gillispie, Charles Coulston, ed. Dictionary of Scientific Biography. 16 vols. New York: Scribner's, 1970-80.

Hall, A. Rupert. Philosophers at War: The Quarrel Between Newton and Leibnitz. Cambridge: Cambridge UP, 1980.

Lévy, Jacques. "The Solar System." Taton 437-54.

Ronan, Colin A. "Edmond Halley." Gillispie.

Schneer, Cecil J. Mind and Matter: Man's Changing Concepts of the Material World. New York: Grove, 1969.

"Science." The New Columbia Encyclopedia. 1975 ed.

Taton, René, ed. The Beginnings of Modern Science: From 1450 to 1800. Vol. 2 of History of Science. Trans. A. J. Pomerans. 4 vols. New York: Basic, 1964.

---, "The Rise of Analysis." Taton 397-424.

14

Thurston, Robert Henry. <u>A History of the Growth of the Steam Engine</u>. 1939. New York: Kennikat, 1972.

Virville, Adrien Davy de. "Botany." Taton 554-64.

Westfall, Richard S. <u>Never at Rest: A Biography of Isaac Newton</u>. Cambridge: Cambridge UP, 1980.

White, J. H. <u>The History of the Phlogiston Theory</u>. London: Arnold, 1932.

Williams, Trevor I. "Hermann Boerhaave, 1688-1738." <u>Endeavour</u> 28 (1969): 2-6.

Project 12-a

By consulting reference books only, come up with five potentially useful facts about some of the following. Cast each fact in the form of a sentence, in your own words.

Babylon	Paul Bunyan	Tamerlaine	Socrates
Rembrandt	Walt Whitman	the Gulf Stream	Mars
Wimbledon	the Galapagos	Garibaldi	the Yukon
Charlemagne	Giordano Bruno	the Pyramids	Swedenborg
Louis Riel	The War of 1812	Beau Brummel	Henry VIII
Rasputin	Sarah Bernhardt	Joan of Arc	Lucretius
Krakatoa	Sitting Bull	Jim Thorpe	Pisarro
Vivaldi	Marie Curie	Charles Dickens	Erasmus
alchemy	Rocket Richard	Margaret Laurence	Akhenaten

Project 12-b

One way to approach a large research project is to survey the subject and draw up a concise report setting out basic facts, relationships, chronologies, structures — whatever is appropriate to the topic. Here is a list of historical events of various times, kinds, scope, and complexity. Choose one and do enough preliminary research on it to present a summary report of no more than 1000 words. Include full documentation of your sources.

putting the first men on the moon	the Boer War
the Charge of the Light Brigade	the Industrial Revolution
the coming to power of the P.Q.	cleaning up Lake Erie
the defeat of the Spanish Armada	the discovery of insulin
Newfoundland joins Confederation	the 1837 rebellion
the Vikings in North America	the battle of El Alamein
the mutiny on the *Bounty*	building the Aswan Dam

These are large topics. Most have had books written about them. In your report, you will have to either.

(a) present a broad overview of the whole subject, or

(b) sketch in the whole event, but focus on a small part.

Project 12-c

Choose a three-year period from 1750 to 1900 and prepare a report (1000-1200 words) on what was happening in one of the following areas of interest or activity. Narrow your topic as necessary; don't present a mere list. OR write a full-length research paper on the topic (2500-5000 words).

advertising	fashion	penology	agriculture	music
agriculture	religion	medicine	architecture	drama
police work	marriage	literature	psychology	sports
banking/finance	commerce	education	philosophy	science
travel/exploring	painting	geography	transportation	law

Project 12-d

(a) Choose a year from recent history, but before your own time — perhaps the year of your parents' or grandparents' marriage, or the year one of them was born, or the year an ancestor arrived in Canada. Research it thoroughly and present a "portrait" of it. You may decide to focus on one or two kinds of events, but give a sense of the year as a whole.

(b) Do the same thing for the *day* of your own birth. How does your research differ from what you did for (a)? Is it harder, or easier? Why?

CHAPTER 13
Writing Essay Examinations and In-Class Essays

When you write an essay examination or an in-class essay, you will spend most of your time planning and drafting; you won't have time for the thorough attention demanded by several sweeps of revising. Even more than for other projects, then, answering an examination question requires careful planning. This chapter offers specific advice for such occasions.

STEP 1: DETERMINING TOPIC, READERS, AND PURPOSE

Think About Your Readers

Even more than at other times, you will seem to be writing only for your instructor or some other individual marker. The occasion, therefore, is difficult: your overall purpose is to inform, but you will be informing someone who knows more about the topic than you do.

Think of yourself as writing not for your instructor only, but for other members of the class as well, as if you were giving a report. Writing for them may keep you from feeling that you are telling readers what they already know.

Think of your instructors less as primary readers than as "overhearers." Their purpose in reading is not to be newly informed but rather to see how well you go about informing your fellow students. You can best persuade your instructors that you know what you're talking about by doing a good job of explaining the material to your classmates.

Establish and Narrow Your Topic

ESTABLISHING PRIORITIES

Examinations often have more than one part. When you have to answer several questions, READ THROUGH ALL OF THEM CAREFULLY before deciding which ones to answer and in what order. An examination may offer several questions with different weights. For example, a three-hour examination might have five questions weighted as follows:

Question	Time (minutes)	%
A	35	20
B	20	10
C	20	10
D	70	40
E	35	20

You see that question *D* is worth twice as much as any other. You might well decide to answer it first in order to make sure you have time to finish it. And you might decide to write on *B* and *C* last because they carry the least weight. Or you might decide to deal first with the question you feel most confident about, even if it isn't the most heavily weighted. You can answer it fully and receive maximum credit for what you know best. If you save your best for last, you might run out of time before you can finish. Generally, budget your time according to the relative values of the questions.

NARROWING TOPICS

Essay questions often give you a choice of ways to narrow a topic. For instance in a philosophy course you might get this:

> Discuss the role of the senses in the epistemology of one of the following: Hobbes, Locke, Hume.

Part of the topic is clear ("the role of the senses"), but you are told to narrow it by discussing the theories of only one of the philosophers named. You would probably choose the one you know most about.

Another way to narrow a topic is to think about the examples you feel most confident about discussing. In an hour, you can't hope to cover all Hume had to say about the senses. You will have to summarize his main ideas and illustrate them with the examples you know best.

STEP 2: FINDING MATERIAL: DECIDE WHAT TO SAY ABOUT THE TOPIC

Staying on Track

Your memory of the course material and the studying you do for an examination will supply most of what you need. And here lies an important danger: in your eagerness to get everything down, to impress your instructor, you may unconsciously stray from the stated topic. That's why you should narrow the topic first: it will help you decide what to include and what to leave out.

Therefore *take time to plan.* DON'T start writing out sentences immediately, for that might confine you to the first thing that comes to your mind. Instead try jotting ideas on a scratch page, and begin not at the top but in the middle, so that you can write related ideas above and around as well as below.

Or try a more orderly strategy: set up a table of six columns, one for each of the reporter's standard questions:

What (happened)	*Who*	*When*	*Where*	*How*	*Why*

Suppose that a political-science test asks you about the main processes of decision-making in the Chinese government. A moment spent filling in the first four columns might provide you with a context in which to deal with the *How* column, toward which the question directs you.

STEP 3: ORGANIZING YOUR MATERIAL

Choose Your Method Of Development

The question will usually suggest how to develop your answer. Often an imperative verb or other word will explicitly or implicitly indicate the desired method:

   A. **Compare** the kinship systems of the Navajo and the Hopi.
   B. **Define** the term *baroque.*
   C. **Describe how** the vocal apparatus produces fricative consonants.
   D. **Why** was the Assyrian empire able to conquer Samaria so easily?
   E. **Summarize** the main features of Darwin's argument in *The Descent of Man.*
   F. **Identify** Abraham Maslow's principal contribution to clinical theory.
   G. **Explain** the relationship between the social assumptions of Bentham and Fourier.

The verb in question *A* is actually instructing you to *compare and contrast*. Rather than describe all of the Navajo system before turning to the Hopi, deal with the two systems feature by feature (see pp. 51-52). That way your reader can more easily see that you are aware of how kinship systems differ. You will also have a less lopsided answer in the event that you can't finish.

Question *B* asks for a *definition*; you can decide which of the several methods of defining will be most useful (see pp. 72-74). And remember the powerful strategy of supplying concrete examples.

Obviously question *C* asks you to analyze a *process*.

As for question *D*, on the Assyrian empire and Samaria, you are to sort out the competing *causes*.

The verb *summarize* in question *E* does little more than direct you to do what most essay questions require: be succinct. Examination time-limits allow no more than a summary of Darwin's arguments. In effect, then, question *E* is asking you pretty much what *F* asks: to *identify* the main points. Both questions could as easily have begun with the word *discuss*, a favourite of examiners.

The word *discuss* could also have been used instead of *explain* in question *G*. Such questions usually want you to show *how* X and Y are related, and they mean for you to develop your answer either by comparing and contrasting or by analyzing causes and effects.

Formulate a Thesis Statement

A good thesis statement is both a goal and a commitment. It keeps you on track, and it lets your reader know what to expect.

USE THE WORDING OF THE QUESTION

Frequently you can turn the question into the framework for a thesis statement. Question *A* in the above samples could become

> The kinship system of the Hopi has gradually come to resemble that of their neighbours, the Navajo.

The process isn't automatic: you still have to know what you're writing about. But try to use the wording of the question as a springboard for your answer; it may help ensure that you stay on track. Consider question *C* above: "Describe how the vocal apparatus produces fricative consonants." You can begin your thesis statement by using much of the wording of the question:

> The vocal apparatus produces fricative consonants . . .

and then go on to indicate the main steps in the process:

> . . . by controlling the pulse of air from the diaphragm through the larynx and into the mouth where it is pushed through a restricted opening to produce a continuous hissing sound.

BE SPECIFIC

Because you will have to work fairly quickly in an examination, *begin* with as specific a thesis as your planning allows. An answer to question *D* above, for example, should start more efficiently than this:

> There were many reasons for the Assyrians' being able to conquer Samaria.

Even though this thesis turns the question into a statement, the word *many* won't help you decide how to organize your answer, nor will it give your reader more than a vague sense of what's coming. A more helpful thesis is more specific:

> The Assyrians were able to conquer Samaria for four main reasons: Samaria had depended too much on Egypt; Assyria could draw its military resources from . . . .

And so on until you list the four. There may have been "many" reasons, but you could handle only a few in an examination answer (though you could mention that there were "other," less important reasons).

Construct an Outline

Whether or not the wording of the question helps you choose a method of development, decide on an arrangement for your answer. Look at the material in your jottings and draw up at least a rough outline for it. Include the major headings and the kinds of support you have for each. Try to include not only the *ideas* but also an indication of the *relations* between them and at least some of the *specifics* you intend to use to support or explain each one: that will make it easier when you begin writing.

STEP 4: WRITING

You should

    (a) know what your instructor wants or will tolerate,

    (b) know your own strengths and weaknesses,

    (c) consider the immediate circumstances (importance of the event, degree of time pressure, difficulty of the material, how you're feeling),

and then decide how to handle the immediate occasion:

Writing fast

If you can draft quickly and if you know you won't feel rushed, you can leave time at the end for revising and perhaps even making a clean copy. But even with a clear outline, you're still likely to use your draft to clarify your ideas and prompt your memory for evidence, reasons, or examples. So it's better not to count on having much time for revising, let alone for recopying.

Writing slow

Paradoxically, during an examination or an in-class essay, when time is short, you are usually better off writing like a tortoise than like a hare (see pp. 62-64). Most instructors will accept relatively scratchy copy, with deletions and insertions here and there. Therefore your "draft" and your final copy will have to be one and the same. With a good outline, you won't have to worry about going astray; you can keep your attention partly on smaller matters of style as you go along. And you won't have to leave that large chunk of time at the end for recopying your whole essay.

But whether you go fast or slow, *write legibly*. Your draft, or part of it, may well end up being what your reader sees. And as always, write on every other line and on one side of the page only. Then what you write will be easier to read, and you will have room to make corrections and changes, whether as you go along or as you go over it afterward.

STEP 5:   REVISING: DO AS MUCH AS POSSIBLE

If you plan carefully, you should be able to leave yourself enough time at the end to check through your essay at least once. Check your main points to make sure they're clearly accessible to your reader. Ask yourself questions like these:

- Have I put in anything that doesn't belong?
- Have I inadvertently left out anything important?
- Do I need another piece of evidence anywhere?
- Do I need to rearrange any large parts?
- Have I emphasized the most important points?
- Do I begin and end briefly and tidily?

Make whatever improvements you have time for. If you have enough time to copy out rough parts, or even the whole thing, by all means do so; but consider whether the time would be better spent revising and proofreading. Again, write legibly, even if you feel rushed — or especially if you feel rushed. If markers can't follow what you've written because a word is unrecognizable or because a punctuation mark is missing, they will be distracted and annoyed — not a state of mind you want to create or sustain.

THE LAST STEP: PROOFREADING

This final check is essential. Even if you can't *revise* in any thorough way, make sure you leave yourself a few minutes to check for slips of the pen, omissions of letters and even words, and other such matters that are usually due to haste rather than ignorance.

> **Some final advice:** Read each question slowly and carefully, so that you end up writing on the assigned topic, not on one you have only imagined. You can't expect to get full credit unless you stay close to the question as asked. Whatever you do, DON'T keep writing on and on, hoping desperately that your marker will find something among all those words to give you credit for.

Special Exercises

CHAPTER 14
Idioms

Idioms are expressions peculiar to a given language. Idioms are often metaphorical, proverbial, or colloquial or slangy, and often they are clichés as well: *mind your p's and q's, know your onions, spill the beans, lay an egg, in the soup, on the carpet, behind the eight-ball, bolt from the blue, fly-by-night, put your foot in it,* and so on. These idioms cause little difficulty — except in requiring you to be on guard against clichés.

But another meaning of the term *idiom* or *idiomatic* refers to the customary way words work in a given language. For example, no one familiar with English should have any difficulty understanding *put in an appearance* or *behind the times* or *not cut out for,* though such expressions would likely not make sense if translated literally into another language.

Clearly, people who learn English as a second language will have some trouble with such idioms, but native speakers sometimes also find them troublesome. For example, a student failed to use the word *long* idiomatically:

DRAFT: I have *long* come to realize how precious time is.

Different revisions are possible to make it idiomatic:

REVISED: I have *long since* come to realize how precious time is.

REVISED: I *long ago* came to realize how precious time is.

Another example:

DRAFT: The circumstances *demand* you *to pay* close attention.

To someone whose native language isn't English, the words *demand* and *require* may look synonymous in such a context; but English idiom won't allow *demand* followed by an infinitive like *to pay.* Again, different revisions are possible:

REVISED: The circumstances *demand that* you *pay* close attention.

REVISED: The circumstances *require* you *to pay* close attention.

In the following sentence, a student didn't understand how the verb *lavish* works:

DRAFT: She obviously enjoys *lavishing* herself in colourful clothes and jewellery.

The verb *lavish* won't work with the receiving person as direct object; it requires a phrase with the preposition *on:*

REVISED: She obviously enjoys *lavishing* colourful clothes and jewellery *on* herself.

Most problems with idioms result from using the wrong preposition after a particular verb, adjective, or noun. For example, it is idiomatic to say "the enemy *encroached on* (or *upon*) our territory"; but to say "the enemy *encroached against* (or *into*) our territory," however logical it may sound, is not idiomatic. (Nor would it be correct to omit the preposition and say "the enemy *encroached* our territory.")

Idiom Exercises

Here are some exercises to help you find out how comfortable you are with some common idioms that consist of a word and a preposition. For convenience, we have divided them into nine small groups. To increase your command of idiom and also to strengthen your vocabulary, compose at least one sentence for each verb, adjective, or noun listed, following it with the appropriate preposition. The first three groups include the prepositions; after that, you have to supply them yourself. (For extra practice, try composing sentences using the words *without* any accompanying preposition: many of them can be used idiomatically that way, as well.)

If you can't figure out how to use a particular word, get some help. "College" or "desk" dictionaries (see p. 143) sometimes include information about which prepositions are appropriate with certain words, but unabridged dictionaries are usually more informative. One smaller dictionary that is helpful with idioms (and with other matters that cause difficulty for those whose native language is not English) is A. S. Hornby's *Oxford Advanced Learner's Dictionary of Current English* (1985); and Theodore M. Bernstein's *The Careful Writer* (1977) lists many words that require particular prepositions.

The first three groups list words that can be followed by different prepositions to fit different meanings or contexts. Compose at least one sentence for each verb + preposition. Use whatever number (singular or plural) or tense you need for your sentences. For example:

confide in: He pretended to *confide in* her, but he related only a heavily edited version of his past.

confide to: She *confided* her deepest secrets *to* her diary, and kept it under lock and key.

plunge in: Eric just sat there, silent, motionless, *plunged in* despair.

plunge into: When Fat Albert *plunged into* the pool he created a minor tidal wave.

GROUP 1

accountable to	assist at	compare to
accountable for	assist in	compare with
admit of	astonished at	concur with
admit to	astonished by	concur in
afraid of	careless with	consist of
afraid for	careless of (in, about)	consist in

GROUP 2

contrast to	healed of	liable for
contrast with	healed by	liable to
differ from	intervene in	mastery of
differ with	intervene between	mastery over
grateful to	introduce to	responsible for
grateful for	introduce into	responsible to

GROUP 3

adapt to	agree with	decide on (upon)
adapt for	agree to	decide for
adapt from	agree on	decide against
prevail on (upon, with)	pronounce on (upon)	treat of
prevail against	pronounce against	treat with

In the next two groups, the words are all **verbs**. In seeking the idiomatic preposition for each of these, remember that you want one that normally or automatically goes with the verb. For example, one could take the verb *collide* and say that two cars collided *at the corner,* or *in the street*, or *on the bridge*. The *at*, *in*, and *on* here are not a matter of idiom; they simply introduce "where" phrases modifying the verb. The preposition that idiomatically accompanies *collide* is *with*, as in "The car *collided with* the oncoming bus." The unidiomatic error that sometimes occurs is the use of *against* instead of *with*.

GROUP 4

accede	arrive	coincide	culminate	deviate
accuse	assent	conform	cure	discourage
acquiesce	border	consent	debar	dissent
acquit	calculate	convict	deprive	dissociate
adhere	chide	credit	derive	divest

GROUP 5

divorce	frown	infuse	obtrude	strive
emigrate	grapple	liken	prohibit	substitute
enlighten	hint	meddle	rid	theorize
exonerate	immigrate	minister	rob	trust
forbid	impose	object	saturate	vie

In the next three groups, the words are all **adjectives** (including some participles, when that seems a likely form to be used). Again, find an idiomatic preposition for each, and use each phrase in a sentence.

GROUP 6

addicted	amenable	averse	characteristic	consequent
adept	analogous	based	clear	consistent
adjacent	angry	bent	compatible	consonant
alien	appended	bereaved	conducive	contemptuous
aloof	approximate	blasé	confident	deficient

GROUP 7

destitute	exclusive	ignorant	indigenous	lacking
disengaged	faced	impenetrable	inimical	obedient
dissimilar	fascinated	incongruous	innate	obliged
enamoured	fond	inconsistent	inseparable	observant
estranged	grateful	independent	jealous	paranoid

GROUP 8

partial	prejudiced	receptive	superior	void
peculiar	prejudicial	redolent	sympathetic	vulnerable
pertinent	preparatory	scared	tired	wanting
piqued	propitious	separate	unmindful	wary
precluded	punishable	solicitous	vested	worthy

In the next group, the words are all **nouns** which will take a preposition. Use each noun + preposition in a sentence.

GROUP 9

analogy	fondness	insight	prerequisite	resemblance
confidence	friend	martyr	pride	respect
distaste	hindrance	motive	pursuit	solution
equivalent	incentive	opposition	regret	tendency
fascination	influence	precedence	repugnance	want

Finally, here are some sentences that contain unidiomatic usage. Most of the errors are with prepositions like those you've been using in the exercises above. You may find other problems as well. Practise your revising skills.

1. He credited his wife, Christine, for the idea.
2. She weighed in the order of one hundred kilograms.
3. If we are paranoid of flying, we may not remember of being scared by something when we were small.
4. The winner of the downhill credited his good time with improved equipment.
5. The reporter had a lot of questions of the minister.
6. He came here to lend his support for the association in its fight.
7. The narrator makes this point very clear in the beginning of the novel.
8. He is woefully ignorant to the fundamental reasons for the decision.
9. He wrote an essay along a similar theme.
10. Khan pirates a ship and sets out after the *Enterprise*, hell-bent not only for revenge, but also for the secrets to the Genesis Effect, a new invention with the capacity both to destroy and create life.
11. We are so confident in our quality that we can offer this amazing guarantee.
12. Novels are able to enlighten readers to some part of human character.
13. There was an attempt, but only at the last moment, of avoiding hostilities.
14. It was during his pursuit for a better education that he discovered the value of what he had left behind.
15. She has pride of her social class and prejudice of his.
16. He makes no secret of his resentment for the newcomers.
17. Pastor Pat Dickerson officiated the service.
18. I was frustrated after being waylaid from my desired course.
19. I still had doubts in my untried ability.
20. The tragic hero is doomed for failure and destruction.
21. Her last wish is that her estranged husband reconcile with their twelve-year-old son.
22. The two are different, however, in their outlook at human nature and potential.

23. If people don't succeed to realize their aspirations, they feel cheated.
24. The committee's proposals may sound good, but they are lacking of any substance.
25. One should be wary to adopt a one-sided view.

CHAPTER 15
Sentence-Combining

These exercises in **sentence-combining** will help you gain strength and flexibility in your writing. The strength will come in part from your increased confidence as you learn how to control your sentences. The flexibility will come as you grow more familiar with the variety of ways to write what you want to write.

You begin with simple, familiar patterns and build up to more complicated ones. By the end you should be able to choose among alternatives to find the best form for communicating your meaning. The point, however, is not simply to learn to write longer and more complicated sentences. Many need to be short and simple. Rather, these exercises will help you find ways to save words by shortening two sentences into one. You will learn to fold your meanings into neater, more efficient packages.

Most of the exercises consist of three steps: COPY, COMBINE, and COMPOSE. First you neatly and accurately COPY a model or pattern sentence. *(Don't skip this step: it will help you get the feel of the structure.)* Next you COMBINE other pairs of sentences into single sentences. Then you COMPOSE new sentences of your own modelled on the pattern.

Practise these patterns. Make up as many sentences as you like for each one. Experiment with variations, and play around with other patterns you think of or come across in your reading. The final exercises are less controlled, giving you a chance to explore a wider variety of forms.

Note: We include minimal grammatical information in parentheses following each pattern number; you may ignore this, but you may wish to refer to relevant parts of the Glossary of Terms for further explanations.

Sentence-Combining 1: Coordination

PATTERN 1A (compound sentence, clauses joined by comma and *and*)

Base sentence *a*: The train pulled into the station.

Base sentence *b*: We were there to meet it.

RESULT of combining *a* and *b*:

> **The train pulled into the station, and we were there to meet it.**

First, COPY the pattern sentence carefully. (1) Join the two sentences with *and*; (2) be sure to put a comma in front of it.

Second, COMBINE each of the following pairs into a sentence modelled on the pattern sentence:

> *a.* I was delighted to receive your invitation.
> *b.* I'm sure the reception will be a great success.

> *a.* The main switch must be in the "off" position.
> *b.* The back-up generator must be on "standby."

Third, COMPOSE two or more sentences modelled on Pattern 1A.

PATTERN 1B (compound sentence, clauses joined by semicolon)

a. Gloria Diaz volunteered to finish the report.

b. She doesn't mind working late.

> **Gloria Diaz volunteered to finish the report; she doesn't mind working late.**

COPY the pattern sentence. Join *a* and *b* with a semicolon.

COMBINE: *a.* The clouds in the west are low and dark.
             b. It will probably rain by morning.

COMBINE: *a.* Colleen O'Brien will be promoted to manager.
             b. Paul Stansky will assume her present job.

COMPOSE sentences modelled on Pattern 1B.

PATTERN 1C (compound sentence, clauses joined by comma and *but*)

a. I applied for the position immediately.

b. It was three weeks before I received a reply.

> **I applied for the position immediately, but it was three weeks before I received a reply.**

COPY the pattern sentence. (1) Join the two sentences with *but*, and (2) put a comma before *but*.

COMBINE: *a.* We expected her to return on Thursday.
            b. She was apparently delayed by the storm.

COMBINE: *a.* Most of the players are in good shape.
            b. They are having trouble with the new tactics.

COMPOSE sentences modelled on Pattern 1C.

PATTERN 1D (compound sentence, clauses joined by comma and *for*)

a. I intend to buy a microcomputer.
b. It will help me in school and in business.

> **I intend to buy a microcomputer, for it will help me in school and in business.**

COPY the pattern sentence. (1) Insert *for*, and (2) put a comma before *for*.

COMBINE: *a.* Gloria Diaz volunteered to finish the report.
            b. She doesn't mind working late.

COMBINE: *a.* I was delighted to receive your invitation.
            b. I'm sure the reception will be a great success.

COMPOSE sentences modelled on Pattern 1D.

PATTERN 1E (clauses joined with correlative conjunctions)

a. Marie's parents ignored my letter.
b. They refused to return my telephone calls.

> **Marie's parents not only ignored my letter, but they also refused to return my telephone calls.**

COPY the pattern sentence. (1) Insert *not only* and *but also*; note that in *b* the word *they* interrupts *but also*. (2) Be sure to put a comma before *but*.

COMBINE: *a.* Acid rain kills lakes.
            b. It rots away statues and other stonework.

COMBINE: *a.* The economy continued to fluctuate wildly.
            b. It showed no signs of settling down.

COMPOSE sentences modelled on Pattern 1E.

PATTERN 1F (compound predicate, parts joined by *and*)

a. The popularity of the Beatles was highest in the sixties.
b. It lasted well into the seventies.

> **The popularity of the Beatles was highest in the sixties and lasted well into the seventies.**

COPY the pattern sentence. Note that (1) you delete the *it* of sentence *b* and that (2) no comma precedes the inserted *and.*

COMBINE: *a.* The president of the sailing club wants new members.
            b. She has asked us to drum up interest among our friends.

COMBINE: *a.* The computer revolution is changing the lives of ordinary people.
            b. It is also making a lot of money for software firms.

COMPOSE sentences modelled on Pattern 1F.

PATTERN 1G (compound predicate, parts joined by *but*)

a. Marilyn is showing some signs of improvement.
b. She is still being kept in the intensive-care unit.

> **Marilyn is showing some signs of improvement but is still being kept in the intensive-care unit.**

COPY the pattern sentence. Note that you (1) delete *she* and (2) DO NOT separate the two parts with a comma.

COMBINE: *a.* The Zipzap 640 computer has a relatively small random-access memory.
            b. It consistently outperforms its closest competitors.

COMBINE: *a.* Bruce always writes slowly.
            b. He always gets his work in on time.

COMPOSE sentences modelled on Pattern 1G.

PATTERN 1H (compound complement: predicate noun)

a. Sam is a good sport.
b. He is a pleasant companion.

> **Sam is a good sport and a pleasant companion.**

COPY the pattern sentence. Note that you (1) delete both *He* and *is* from sentence *b* and (2) DO NOT put a comma between the two.

COMBINE: *a.* Ottawa is the national capital.
            b. It is a fascinating place to visit.

COMBINE: *a.* China is a huge country.
            b. It is increasingly a force to be reckoned with.

COMPOSE sentences modelled on Pattern 1H.

Sentence-Combining 2: Subordination

PATTERN 2A (complex sentence, first clause subordinated)

a. Seamen did not have an accurate chronometer.
b. Therefore they could not plot a ship's position accurately.

> **Because seamen did not have an accurate chronometer, they could not plot a ship's position accurately.**

COPY the pattern sentence. (1) Put *Because* before sentence *a*, (2) delete *Therefore* from *b*, and (3) put a comma between *a* and *b*.

COMBINE: *a.* The committee did not have a clear precedent.
            b. Therefore they could make only tentative recommendations.

COMBINE: *a.* The biologist was frustrated by repeated failures.
            b. Therefore he considered abandoning the experiment.

COMPOSE sentences modelled on Pattern 2A.

PATTERN 2B (complex sentence, first clause subordinated)

a. The popularity of the Beatles was highest in the sixties.
b. It lasted well into the seventies.

> **Although the popularity of the Beatles was highest in the sixties, it lasted well into the seventies.**

COPY the pattern sentence. (1) Put *although* before sentence *a* and (2) separate the two parts with a comma.

COMBINE: *a.* Bruce writes slowly.
            b. He always gets his work done on time.

COMBINE: *a.* The quality of most television programs is poor.
            b. Many of them are highly popular.

COMPOSE sentences modelled on Pattern 2B, but in addition to *although*, begin some sentences with these subordinators: *if, unless, when, since, until, before, after, as long as.*

PATTERN 2C (complex sentence, second clause subordinated)

a. The popularity of the Beatles was highest in the sixties.
b. It lasted well into the seventies.

> **The popularity of the Beatles was highest in the sixties, although it lasted well into the seventies.**

COPY the pattern sentence. (1) Begin *b* with *even though, although,* or *though*, and (2) separate *a* and *b* with a comma.

COMBINE: *a.* Bruce writes slowly.
            b. He always gets his work done on time.

COMBINE: *a.* The quality of most television programs is poor.
            b. Many of them are highly popular.

COMPOSE sentences modelled on Pattern 2C. You may use *though, although,* or *even though* as the subordinator.

Sentence-Combining 3: Prepositional Phrases (*with* and *without*)

PATTERN 3A (second sentence reduced to prepositional phrase)

a. Some people can count themselves fortunate.
b. They have loyal friends.

People with loyal friends can count themselves fortunate.

COPY the pattern sentence. Note that you (1) delete *Some*, (2) move *people* to the beginning of *b*, (3) replace *they have* with the preposition *with*, and (4) reverse the order of *a* and *b*.

COMBINE: *a.* Some cars are known as gas-guzzlers.
     b. They have big and powerful engines.

COMBINE: *a.* Many countries are desperately poor.
     b. They have high birth rates.

COMPOSE sentences modelled on Pattern 3A.

PATTERN 3B (second sentence reduced to prepositional phrase)

a. McLeod's sells a hay-baler.
b. It has a three-point hitch.

 McLeod's sells a hay-baler with a three-point hitch.

COPY the pattern sentence. Note that you (1) replace *It has* of *b* with the preposition *with* and (2) add the resulting phrase to *a*.

COMBINE: *a.* Turn right at the yellow barn.
     b. It has a red cupola.

COMBINE: *a.* The engine has an oil filter.
     b. It has a replaceable gasket.

COMPOSE sentences modelled on Pattern 3B.

PATTERN 3C (first sentence reduced to prepositional phrase)

a. The students had a good outline to guide them.
b. They then found that they could continue easily.

 With a good outline to guide them, the students found that they could continue easily.

COPY the pattern sentence. Note that you (1) replace *They then* of *b* with *The students* from *a*, (2) replace *had* with the word *with*, and (3) put a comma after the opening *with*-phrase.

COMBINE: *a.* Janice had the evidence in her hand.
     b. She then went straight to see her lawyer.

COMBINE: *a.* The team has two new players on defence.
     b. The team now expects to make the playoffs.

COMPOSE sentences modelled on Pattern 3C.

PATTERN 3D (second sentence reduced to prepositional phrase)

a. Kim is ordering a new CB radio.
b. It does not have a side-band converter.

 Kim is ordering a new CB radio without a side-band converter.

COPY the pattern sentence. Note that you replace *It does not have* of *b* with the preposition *without*.

COMBINE: *a.* Abe Harrison has developed a new kind of holly tree.
          b. It does not have prickly leaves.

COMBINE: *a.* The Mandrells are going to record that song.
          b. It will not have the second chorus.

COMPOSE sentences modelled on Pattern 3D

PATTERN 3E (first sentence reduced to prepositional phrase)

a. The committee did not have a clear precedent.
b. Therefore they could make only tentative recommendations.

> **Without a clear precedent, the committee could make only tentative recommendations.**

COPY the pattern sentence. Note that you (1) move *the committee* to the beginning of *b*, replacing *Therefore they*, and (2) replace *did not have* with the word *without*.

COMBINE: *a.* The seamen did not have a reliable chronometer.
          b. Therefore they could not plot the ship's position accurately.

COMBINE: *a.* We do not have enough volunteers.
          b. Therefore we cannot complete the project.

COMPOSE sentences modelled on Pattern 3E.

Sentence-Combining 4: Relative Clauses

PATTERN 4A (restrictive clause with relative pronoun *who*)

a. A man telephoned me late last night.
b. He turned out to be a distant cousin.

> **The man who telephoned me late last night turned out to be a distant cousin.**

COPY the pattern sentence. Note that you (1) change the word *A* to *The*, (2) insert *who* between *man* and *telephoned*, and (3) delete *He*. You DO NOT add any commas.

COMBINE: *a.* A student interrupted the lecture.
          b. She had missed a page-reference.

COMBINE: *a.* One Canadian athlete greatly impresses me.
          b. He is Rick Hansen.

COMPOSE sentences modelled on Pattern 4A.

PATTERN 4B (restrictive clause with relative pronoun *who*)

a. Some people can count themselves fortunate.
b. They have loyal friends.

> **People who have loyal friends can count themselves fortunate.**

COPY the pattern sentence. Note that you (1) drop *Some*, (2) replace *they* with *who*, and (3) insert *b* after *people* in *a*. DO NOT add any commas.

COMBINE: *a.* Certain people are risking poor health and early death.
            b. They still smoke cigarettes.

COMBINE: *a.* Some drivers deserve to lose their licences.
            b. They persist in drinking and driving.

COMPOSE sentences modelled on pattern 4B.

PATTERN 4C (restrictive clause with relative pronoun *whose*)

a. Some people can count themselves fortunate.
b. Their friends are loyal.

> **People whose friends are loyal can count themselves fortunate.**

COPY the pattern sentence. Note that you (1) remove *Some* from *a*, (2) replace the possessive *their* with *whose*, and (3) insert *b* after *people* in *a*. DO NOT add any commas.

COMBINE: *a.* Some cars are known as gas-guzzlers.
            b. Their engines have to be big and powerful.

COMBINE: *a.* Certain countries are usually the poorest countries.
            b. Their birth rates are high.

COMPOSE sentences modelled on Pattern 4C.

PATTERN 4D (restrictive clause with relative pronoun *whom*)

a. The students have all won scholarships.
b. Professor Brown coached them.

> **The students whom Professor Brown coached have all won scholarships.**

COPY the pattern sentence. Note that you (1) replace *them* with *whom* and (2) move it to the beginning of *b*, and then (3) insert *b* after *students* in *a*.

COMBINE: *a.* The postman had taken over the route again.
            b. Everyone had come to like him.

COMBINE: *a.* Maybelle has made the person a partner in her law firm.
            b. She trusts him the most.

COMPOSE sentences modelled on Pattern 4D.

PATTERN 4E (restrictive clause with relative pronoun *that*)

a. I intend to buy a microcomputer.

b. It will help me manage my everyday finances.

> **I intend to buy a microcomputer that will help me manage my everyday finances.**

COPY the pattern sentence. Replace the subject pronoun (*it*) of *b* with *that*.

COMBINE: *a.* Francis misfiled the student activity reports.
                  b. They will be needed for Tuesday's meeting.

COMBINE: *a.* After the lecture we went to the reception.
                  b. It was sponsored by the Gorman Company.

COMPOSE sentences modelled on Pattern 4E.

PATTERN 4F (restrictive clause; pronoun *that* optional)

a. We are entirely out of copies of the report.

b. The investigators requested it.

> **We are entirely out of copies of the report [that] the investigators requested.**

COPY the pattern sentence. (1) Replace *it* with *that*, as in Pattern 4E, but here (2) it must be moved to the beginning of *b* before (3) *b* is added to *a*. Since in this pattern the relative pronoun *that* replaces an **object**, it may be omitted.

COMBINE: *a.* Genevieve has gone to the library for a book on beekeeping.
                  b. She needs it for her biology experiments.

COMBINE: *a.* Many people dream about owning expensive things.
                  b. They will probably never be able to afford them.

COMPOSE sentences modelled on Pattern 4F.

PATTERN 4G (nonrestrictive clause with relative pronoun *who*)

a. Gloria Diaz volunteered to finish the report.

b. She doesn't mind working late.

> **Gloria Diaz, who doesn't mind working late, volunteered to finish the report.**

COPY the pattern sentence. Note that you (1) replace *she* with *who*, (2) insert the resulting clause into sentence *a*, and (3) put a pair of commas around the inserted clause.

COMBINE: *a.* The early existentialists were a gloomy lot.
                  b. They believed life to be meaningless.

COMBINE: *a.* The minister took full responsibility for the program's failure.
                  b. He is nothing if not honest.

COMPOSE sentences modelled on Pattern 4G.

PATTERN 4H (nonrestrictive clause with relative pronoun *which*)

a. The popularity of the Beatles lasted well into the seventies.

b. It was highest in the sixties.

> **The popularity of the Beatles, which was highest in the sixties, lasted well into the seventies.**

COPY the pattern sentence. Note that you (1) replace *It* with *which*, (2) insert the resulting clause into *a*, and (3) put a pair of commas around the clause.

COMBINE: *a.* The Zipzap 640 computer consistently outperforms its closest competitors.
  b. It has a relatively small random-access memory.

COMBINE: *a.* Large cars are known as gas-guzzlers.
  b. They need big and powerful engines.

COMPOSE sentences modelled on Pattern 4H.

Sentence-Combining 5: Appositives

PATTERN 5A (second sentence reduced to inserted noun phrase)

a. One of the smallest animals has come to be seen as one of the fiercest.

b. That animal is the shrew.

> **One of the smallest animals, the shrew, has come to be seen as one of the fiercest.**

COPY the pattern sentence. Note that you (1) keep only the final noun phrase of *b*, inserting it after *animals* in *a*, and (2) enclose it in a pair of parenthetical commas.

COMBINE: *a.* One of my favourite foods is high in both protein and cholesterol.
  b. That food is cheese.

COMBINE: *a.* One of the best-known Greek philosophers left no writings.
  b. That philosopher was Socrates.

COMPOSE sentences modelled on Pattern 5A.

PATTERN 5B (second sentence reduced to inserted noun phrase)

a. Ottawa prides itself on being the nation's capital.

b. It is a pleasant place to visit.

> **Ottawa, a pleasant place to visit, prides itself on being the nation's capital.**

COPY the pattern sentence. Note that you (1) delete *It is* from *b*, (2) insert the remaining noun phrase into *a*, and (3) enclose the phrase in a pair of commas.

COMBINE: *a.* Ottawa is a pleasant place to visit.
             b. It is the nation's capital.

COMBINE: *a.* Sir John A. Macdonald was born in Glasgow, Scotland.
             b. He was Canada's first prime minister.

COMPOSE sentences modelled on Pattern 5B.

PATTERN 5C (second sentence reduced to opening noun phrase)

a. He was born in Glasgow, Scotland.
b. He was Canada's first prime minister.

Canada's first prime minister, he was born in Glasgow, Scotland.

COPY the pattern sentence. Note that you (1) delete *He was* from *b,* (2) put the remainder at the beginning of *a,* and (3) set it off with a comma.

COMBINE: *a.* She received the offer on Tuesday.
             b. She was the top candidate on the list.

COMBINE: *a.* He spoke movingly to the rally.
             b. He is a refugee from El Salvador.

COMPOSE sentences modelled on Pattern 5C.

PATTERN 5D (second sentence reduced to noun and relative clause)

a. "The Hammer" was the name they gave him as a young man.
b. It was a name that came to be feared throughout the West.

"The Hammer" was the name they gave him as a young man, a name that came to be feared throughout the West.

COPY the pattern sentence. Note that you (1) delete *It was* from *b,* (2) put the rest at the end of *a,* and (3) set it off with a comma.

COMBINE: *a.* The board announced the new regulations.
             b. They were regulations that ignored all our objections.

COMBINE: *a.* Francis misfiled the student activity report.
             b. It is a report that will be needed for next Tuesday's meeting.

COMPOSE sentences modelled on Pattern 5D.

Sentence-Combining 6: Noun Clauses

PATTERN 6A (*that*-clause used as direct object)

a. Supply-side economists believe one thing.
b. Limiting the money supply slows inflation.

Supply-side economists believe that limiting the money supply slows inflation.

COPY the pattern sentence. Replace *one thing* in *a* with the word *that* and all of *b.*

COMBINE: *a.* Most of the employers realized one thing.
           b. Workers weren't interested only in higher wages.

COMBINE: *a.* The director suggested only one thing.
           b. She should learn her lines well before the next rehearsal.

COMPOSE sentences modelled on Pattern 6A.

PATTERN 6B (*what*-clause used as object of preposition)

a. The auditors have told us something.
b. This means that the company is in bad shape.

   From what the auditors have told us, the company is in bad shape.

COPY the pattern sentence. Note that you (1) replace *something* in *a* with *From what,* (2) move it to the beginning of the sentence, (3) delete *this means that* from *b* and put it at the end of *a,* and (4) put a comma between the two parts.

COMBINE: *a.* I have discovered something about cameras.
           b. This shows that you get what you pay for.

COMBINE: a. I know something about gardening.
           b. It suggests that it involves more destruction than creation.

COMPOSE sentences modelled on Pattern 6B.

PATTERN 6C (*that*-clause used as appositive)

a. Ottawa's principal claim to fame is not the only reason to visit it.
b. It is the nation's capital.

   Ottawa's principal claim to fame, that it is the nation's capital, is not the only reason to visit it.

COPY the pattern sentence. (1) Add *that* to *b* and insert all of it into *a.* (2) Be sure to enclose the inserted clause in a pair of commas.

COMBINE: *a.* The employers' main belief turned out to be correct.
           b. Workers weren't interested only in wages.

COMBINE: *a.* Newton's third law of motion is the basis of rocket propulsion.
           b. For every action there is an equal and opposite reaction.

COMPOSE sentences modelled on Pattern 6C.

PATTERN 6D (*that*-clause used as subject of sentence)

a. Ottawa is the nation's capital.
b. This cannot be disputed.

   That Ottawa is the nation's capital cannot be disputed.

COPY the pattern sentence. (1) Put the word *That* at the beginning of *a*, (2) delete the word *This* from *b*, and (3) put *b* at the end of *a*.

COMBINE: *a.* Mr. Ricci was late.
              b. This surprised Hilda.

COMBINE: *a.* The university raised tuition fees again.
              b. This has infuriated many students.

COMPOSE sentences modelled on Pattern 6D.

PATTERN 6E (*that*-clause as delayed subject after anticipatory *It*)

a. One thing seems likely.
b. Many older people will postpone their retirement.

    It seems likely that many older people will postpone their retirement.

COPY the pattern sentence. Note that you (1) replace *one thing* with the word *It*, (2) put the word *that* at the beginning of *b*, and (3) put *b* at the end of *a*. DO NOT insert any commas.

COMBINE: *a.* One thing cannot be disputed.
              b. Ottawa is the nation's capital.

COMBINE: *a.* Two things are certain.
              b. The brakes were unreliable and the driver had been drinking.

COMPOSE sentences modelled on Pattern 6E.

PATTERN 6F (*whoever*-clause used as subject of sentence)

a. Someone gets to the cabin first.
b. He or she usually gets the fire going.

    Whoever gets to the cabin first usually gets the fire going.

COPY the pattern sentence. (1) Change *Someone* to *Whoever*, (2) delete *he or she*, and (3) put *b* after *a*. DO NOT put a comma between the two parts.

COMBINE: *a.* Someone interrupted the lecturer.
              b. He or she had missed a page reference.

COMBINE: *a.* Someone stole my purse.
              b. He or she has acquired little of value.

COMPOSE sentences modelled on Pattern 6F.

PATTERN 6G (*What*-clause used as subject of sentence)

a. Isabel learned something about other countries.
b. This made her content to stay home.

    What Isabel learned about other countries made her content to stay home.

COPY the pattern sentence. (1) Replace *something* with *What*, (2) move it to the beginning of *a*, (3) delete the word *this* from *b*, and (4) put *b* after *a*. DO NOT put a comma between the two parts.

COMBINE: *a.* Tom experienced something in Montreal.
          b. It made him want to go back as soon as possible.

COMBINE: *a.* These exercises teach you something about combining
             sentences.
          b. This will enable you to exercise greater control over your style.

COMPOSE sentences modelled on Pattern 6G.

Sentence-Combining 7: Participial Phrases

PATTERN 7A (phrase at end, modifying subject; comma required)

a. The prisoner stood on his chair.
b. He was shouting angrily.

> **The prisoner stood on his chair, shouting angrily.**

COPY the pattern sentence. Note that you (1) delete *He was* from *b*, (2) attach what's left to the end of *a*, and (3) set it off with a comma.

COMBINE: *a.* The children went on with their game.
          b. They were pretending not to notice us.

COMBINE: *a.* The economy continued to fluctuate wildly.
          b. It was showing no signs of slowing down.

COMPOSE sentences modelled on Pattern 7A.

PATTERN 7B (phrase at end modifying whole clause; comma required)

a. The wiring of the house was defective.
b. This posed a fire hazard.

> **The wiring of the house was defective, posing a fire hazard.**

COPY the pattern sentence. Note that you (1) delete *This* from *b*, (2) add *ing* to the basic form of the verb in *b* (*pose*), (3) put the new structure after *a*, and (4) insert a comma between the two parts.

COMBINE: *a.* The vacuum cleaner's bag burst.
          b. It spewed dust all over the room.

COMBINE: *a.* In this play the winger takes the puck and drives to the corner.
          b. This leaves the centre open behind him.

COMPOSE sentences modelled on Pattern 7B.

PATTERN 7C (opening phrase modifying subject; comma required)

a. The committee lacked a clear precedent.
b. They could make only tentative recommendations.

> **Lacking a clear precedent, the committee could make only tentative recommendations.**

COPY the pattern sentence. Note that you (1) replace *They* in *b* with *the committee* from *a*, (2) add *ing* to the basic form of the verb in *a* (*lack*), (3) put *b* after *a*, and (4) insert a comma between the two new parts.

COMBINE: *a.* Andrea moved quickly and easily up the corporate ladder.
           b. She made it to vice-president in just three years.

COMBINE: *a.* Some employers thought workers were interested in nothing else.
           b. They focussed entirely on wages.

COMPOSE sentences modelled on Pattern 7C.

PATTERN 7D (past-participial phrase modifying object; no comma)

a. After the meeting we went to the reception.
b. It was sponsored by the Gorman Company.

> **After the meeting we went to the reception sponsored by the Gorman Company.**

COPY the pattern sentence. Note that you (1) delete *It was* and (2) put the rest of *b* after *a*. DO NOT put a comma between them.

COMBINE: *a.* Mrs. Nordstrom demonstrated the new intercom system.
           b. It was designed by a student architect.

COMBINE: *a.* Francis misfiled the student activity records.
           b. They will be needed for Tuesday's meeting.

COMPOSE sentences modelled on Pattern 7D.

PATTERN 7E (opening phrase modifying subject; comma required)

a. Sarah was experienced at gardening.
b. She knew it involved more destruction than creation.

> **Experienced at gardening, Sarah knew that it involved more destruction than creation.**

COPY the pattern sentence. Note that you (1) replace *She* with *Sarah*, (2) delete *was*, and (3) put a comma between the two parts.

COMBINE: *a.* The biologist was frustrated by repeated failures.
           b. He considered abandoning the experiment.

COMBINE: *a.* The Porsche was washed and polished.
           b. It looked almost new again.

COMPOSE sentences modelled on Pattern 7E.

PATTERN 7F (opening phrase modifying subject; comma required)

a. The repair crew finished sooner than we expected.
b. They had often dealt with such problems.

> **Having often dealt with such problems, the repair crew finished sooner than we expected.**

COPY the pattern sentence. Note that you (1) delete *They*, (2) change *had* in b to *having*, (3) put the resulting phrase in front of *a*, and (4) set off the phrase with a comma.

COMBINE: *a.* You'll be able to write leaner and cleaner prose.
              b. You have learned to combine sentences.

COMBINE: *a.* Carlos was fluent in English, French, and Spanish.
              b. He had been born in Venezuela and had grown up in Montreal.

COMPOSE sentences modelled on Pattern 7F.

Sentence-Combining 8: Infinitive Phrases

PATTERN 8A (infinitive phrase as direct object)

a. Ms. Narayan will conduct the seminar.
b. She promised this.

   Ms. Narayan promised to conduct the seminar.

COPY the pattern sentence. Note that you (1) delete *She* and *this* from *b*, (2) insert the remaining word, the verb *promised*, after *Ms. Narayan* in *a*, and (3) change *will conduct* to *to conduct*.

COMBINE: *a.* Stanley met with the volunteers.
              b. He had previously arranged this.

COMBINE: *a.* Rose operates both machines quickly and efficiently.
              b. She learned it in less than three hours.

COMPOSE sentences modelled on Pattern 8A.

PATTERN 8B (phrase and its subject act as direct object)

a. The storm should arrive just in time for the weekend.
b. Mr. Reimer fully expects it.

   Mr. Reimer fully expects the storm to arrive just in time for the weekend.

COPY the pattern sentence. Note that you (1) replace *it* in sentence *b* with all of sentence *a*, and (2) change *should arrive* to *to arrive*.

COMBINE: *a.* Ms. Mueller reported her travelling expenses.
              b. Her financial counsellor advised it.

COMBINE: *a.* You may attend the banquet as well.
              b. Your registration receipt will permit it.

COMPOSE sentences modelled on Pattern 8B.

PATTERN 8C (infinitive phrase used as subject of sentence)

a. The professor was seen by the two students.
b. This embarrassed him.

   To be seen by the two students embarrassed the professor.

COPY the pattern sentence. Note that you (1) replace *him* with *the professor* from *a*, (2) change *was* to *to be*, and (3) replace *This* with the new form of *a*.

COMBINE: *a.* Annette won the scholarship.
　　　　　　b. This was a great satisfaction to her.

COMBINE: *a.* Sharon visited the Pyramids and the Parthenon.
　　　　　　b. This made her Mediterranean tour complete.

COMPOSE sentences modelled on Pattern 8C.

PATTERN 8D (infinitive phrase modifying subject)

a. Ottawa's claim cannot be disputed.
b. It is the nation's capital.

Ottawa's claim to be the nation's capital cannot be disputed.

COPY the pattern sentence. Note that you (1) insert *b* after the subject (*claim*) of *a*, (2) drop *it*, and (3) change *is* to *to be*.

COMBINE: *a.* Your ability will be improved with practice.
　　　　　　b. You write good sentences.

COMBINE: *a.* Allen's hope was realized that year.
　　　　　　b. He travelled all the way up the Amazon.

COMPOSE sentences modelled on Pattern 8D.

PATTERN 8E (infinitive phrase expressing purpose)

a. I bought a smaller car.
b. I save money on fuel.

I bought a smaller car to save money on fuel.

COPY the pattern sentence. Note that you (1) put *b* after *a*, (2) delete the repeated *I* , and (3) insert *to* before *save*.

COMBINE: *a.* I skipped most of the season but watched the World Series.
　　　　　　b. I saw how it all came out.

COMBINE: *a.* Many people are eating less and exercising more.
　　　　　　b. They keep their weight down and stay in better shape.

COMPOSE sentences modelled on Pattern 8E.

PATTERN 8F (infinitive noun phrase as delayed subject)

a. Mr. O'Malley had been quickly promoted.
b. This delighted him.

It delighted Mr. O'Malley to have been quickly promoted.

COPY the pattern sentence. Note that you (1) change *This* in *b* to *It*, (2) replace *him* with sentence *a*, and (3) change *had been* to *to have been*.

COMBINE: *a.* Sally had broken her promise.
                   b. This distressed her a great deal.

COMBINE: *a.* The professor had been seen by two students.
                   b. This embarrassed him.

COMPOSE sentences modelled on Pattern 8F.

Sentence-Combining 9: Gerund Phrases

PATTERN 9A (gerund phrase used as direct object)

a. The treasurer forgot to deposit the cheques.
b. She admitted this.

> **The treasurer admitted forgetting to deposit the cheques.**

COPY the pattern sentence. Note that you (1) replace *She* in *b* with *The treasurer* from *a*, (2) change *forgot* in *a* to the basic form *forget* and add *ing* to it, and (3) replace *this* in *b* with the changed form of *a*.

COMBINE: *a.* Alan works the late shift.
                   b. He enjoys it.

COMBINE: *a.* The coach met strong opposition.
                   b. He didn't anticipate this.

COMPOSE sentences modelled on Pattern 9A.

PATTERN 9B (gerund phrase used as subject of sentence)

a. Timothy is learning to use a microcomputer.
b. This will help his job prospects.

> **Learning to use a microcomputer will help Timothy's job prospects.**

COPY the pattern sentence. Note that you (1) shorten *Timothy is learning* to simply *Learning,* (2) replace *This* in *b* with the shortened form of *a*, and (3) change *his* to *Timothy's*.

COMBINE: *a.* The Smiths are eating less and exercising more.
                   b. This helps them keep their weight down and stay in shape.

COMBINE: *a.* Annette won the scholarship.
                   b. This was a great satisfaction to her.

COMPOSE sentences modelled on Pattern 9B.

PATTERN 9C (gerund phrase with possessive noun, used as subject)

a. Mark smoked continually.
b. This annoyed the others at the meeting.

> **Mark's continual smoking annoyed the others at the meeting.**

COPY the pattern sentence. Note that you (1) replace *This* with sentence *a*, (2) add *'s* to *Mark*, (3) change *smoked* to *smoking,* and (4) change *continually* to *continual* and put it in front of *smoking*.

COMBINE: *a.* He flirts occasionally.
              b. This amuses the whole class.

COMBINE: *a.* Shelly drove carefully and confidently.
              b. This reassured Mary Jane.

COMPOSE sentences modelled on Pattern 9C.

PATTERN 9D (phrase with possessive pronoun, used as appositive)

a. Ottawa's main attraction is only one reason to visit it.
b. It is the nation's capital.

> **Ottawa's main attraction — its being the nation's capital — is only one reason to visit it.**

COPY the pattern sentence. Note that you (1) change *It is* in *b* to *its being*, (2) insert *b* after the subject of *a*, and (3) enclose it in a pair of dashes.

COMBINE: *a.* Annette's achievement was a great satisfaction to her.
              b. She won the scholarship.

COMBINE: *a.* One of Bill's habits amuses the class.
              b. He flirts.

COMPOSE sentences modelled on Pattern 9D.

Sentence-Combining 10: Absolute Phrases

PATTERN 10A (absolute phrase at beginning)

a. The minister was unusually efficient.
b. Her report was ready in two days.

> **The minister being unusually efficient, her report was ready in two days.**

COPY the pattern sentence. Note that you (1) change *was* to *being*, (2) put the new form of *a* in front of *b*, and (3) insert a comma between the two parts.

COMBINE: *a.* No precedent was established.
              b. The committee could make only tentative recommendations.

COMBINE: *a.* The program for the festival had been decided upon.
              b. The committee could return to its usual business.

COMPOSE sentences modelled on Pattern 10A.

PATTERN 10B (absolute phrase at beginning)

a. The committee could return to its usual business.
b. The program for the festival was decided upon.

The program for the festival decided upon, the committee could return to its usual business.

COPY the pattern sentence. Note that you (1) delete the word *was*, (2) put *b* in front of *a*, and (3) put a comma between them.

COMBINE: *a.* Henri Lebrun sat at his desk.
b. His arms were folded stiffly across his chest.

COMBINE: *a.* The president of the student body stood up to speak.
b. An expression of controlled rage was on her face.

COMPOSE sentences modelled on Pattern 10B.

PATTERN 10C (absolute phrase at end)

a. Annabelle submitted her report to the committee.
b. The bad news was neatly underlined in red.

Annabelle submitted her report to the committee, the bad news neatly underlined in red.

COPY the pattern sentence. Note that you (1) delete the word *was*, (2) put the new form of *b* after *a*, and (3) put a comma between the two parts.

COMBINE: *a.* The petition will be circulated next week.
b. The letter from the prisoner will be printed in full.

COMBINE: *a.* The results of the election were finally coming through.
b. My choices, as usual, were not winning.

COMPOSE sentences modelled on Pattern 10C.

PATTERN 10D (compound absolute phrase at beginning)

a. The Ferrari took the turn at over 150 km/h.
b. Its engine was roaring and its tires were screaming.

Its engine roaring and its tires screaming, the Ferrari took the turn at over 150 km/h.

COPY the pattern sentence. Note that you (1) drop *was* and *were* from *b*, (2) put the new form of *b* in front of *a*, and (3) insert a comma between the two parts. (Note that the possessives — *Its* and *its* — also could be dropped, heightening the style even more.)

COMBINE: *a.* Julie skated and whirled gracefully around the pond.
b. Her eyes were aglow, and her cheeks were red from the cold.

COMBINE: *a.* The sentry spoke into the darkness.
b. His face was drawn and white, his hands were trembling, and his voice was a mere whisper.

COMPOSE sentences modelled on Pattern 10D.

Sentence-Combining 11: Colons And Dashes

PATTERN 11A (colon introducing defining infinitive phrase)

a. Bill Andreychuk had only one goal that year.

b. He wanted to win the men's downhill championship.

> **Bill Andreychuk had only one goal that year: to win the men's downhill championship.**

COPY the pattern sentence. Note that you (1) remove the subject and verb *He wanted* from *b*, (2) put the resultant phrase at the end of *a*, and (3) insert a colon to introduce it.

COMBINE: *a.* The government expects only one thing.
              b. It wants to reduce the deficit.

COMBINE: *a.* These exercises have one purpose.
              b. They are meant to help you write better sentences.

COMPOSE sentences modelled on Pattern 11A.

PATTERN 11B (colon introducing explanatory clause)

a. Money is important to all of us.

b. We need it to get along from day to day.

> **Money is important to all of us: we need it to get along from day to day.**

COPY the pattern sentence. (1) Put *b* after *a* and (2) use a colon to look forward to it.

COMBINE: *a.* Science-fiction movies are getting boring.
              b. They use the same tricks over and over again.

COMBINE: *a.* The holiday meal was finally made complete.
              b. My uncle made his customary after-dinner speech.

COMBINE: *a.* Two things are certain.
              b. The brakes were unreliable, and the driver had been drinking.

COMPOSE sentences modelled on Pattern 11B.

PATTERN 11C (dash setting off phrase for tonal effect)

a. The trumpeter swan is a magnificent bird.

b. It is also a rare one.

> **The trumpeter swan is a magnificent bird—and also a rare one.**

COPY the pattern sentence. Note that you (1) replace *It is* with *and*, (2) put *b* after *a*, and (3) introduce it with a dash. (You may want to leave out the word *also*, as well.)

COMBINE: *a.* Television is a prime source of home entertainment.
              b. It is also a cheap babysitter.

COMBINE: *a.* Home-made wine is sometimes as good as commercially produced wine.
              b. It is also much less expensive.

COMBINE: *a.* Stars of stage and screen sometimes lead a romantic kind of life.
          b. It is also a hectic one.

COMPOSE sentences modelled on Pattern 11C.

Sentence-Combining 12: Variety And Experiment

In the preceding exercises we often use the same or similar sentences in order to demonstrate that you can express the same basic idea in a variety of ways. You usually have several choices of how to write something. Nor do the patterns in these exercises exhaust the possibilities. They show some of the basic forms and variations, but your own experience and experimenting will give you many more. The way you compose any given sentence will depend on such variables as your thesis, your readers, your purpose, and the tone you've chosen — in other words, on the elements of the writing context for a particular occasion.

EXERCISE 12A

Below are several sets of sentences to combine. You will find that some of them seem to invite a particular kind of combining. Nevertheless, try to come up with at least two potentially useful versions for each set. For some, you may want to try several combinations. Further, this exercise is intended to be less structured: don't feel so bound to certain mechanical patterns as you were in the earlier exercises. Feel free to move elements around, to add or change words, to delete words that seem unnecessary. But try to retain the sense of the base sentences.

1.*a.* The truck rattled to a stop.
  b. Its grill and right fender were hopelessly crumpled.

2.*a.* Joe Fitzgerald is our most effective union organizer.
  b. He organized the plant in Winnipeg.
  c. He arrived here on the morning plane.

3.*a.* There is nothing inherently funny about locker rooms.
  b. Locker rooms have a reputation for producing a certain kind of humour.

4.*a.* Wolverines are seldom encountered by tourists.
  b. A wolverine is an animal rightly respected for its ferocity.

5.*a.* Some children are disabled.
  b. Disabled children deserve special attention.
  c. School systems have room for disabled children.
  d. Disabled children benefit from their peers' attention.
  e. Regular teachers can be trained to work with disabled children.

6.*a.* George Bernard Shaw had a low opinion of politicians.
 b. He called Parliament a talking-shop.

7.*a.* Many people may not like the metric system.
 b. Younger people are more likely to favour it.
 c. It seems to be here to stay.

8.*a.* Conventional broadcasting is becoming less profitable.
 b. It may have to change its strategies.
 c. Competition from cable operators is increasing.

9.*a.* The Day Care Centre is understaffed.
 b. Two of the children have suffered minor accidents.

10.*a.* Junk food is usually low in nutritional value.
 b. It is often expensive.
 c. People buy a lot of it anyway.

11.*a.* The library shelves are overcrowded.
 b. The new wing won't be ready for another six months.
 c. The head librarian is accustomed to crises.

12.*a.* Many recent graduates have trouble finding employment.
 b. Some are willing to accept work outside their major fields.

13.*a.* People sometimes smoke from nervousness.
 b. They need something to occupy their hands.
 c. I intend to learn how to knit.

14.*a.* The bricklayers came early in the morning.
 b. They are fast workers.
 c. By mid-afternoon they had finished the fireplace.

15.*a.* Provincial politics don't interest me very much.
 b. I do not subscribe to a local newspaper.

16.*a.* Jack Sprat can eat no fat.
 b. His wife can eat no lean.
 c. Dietary problems can plague the ordinary household.
 d. Marketing is a problem.
 e. Meal-planning is a problem.
 f. Cooking is a problem.

17.*a.* Alicia needs a holiday.
 b. She usually enjoys her job.
 c. She's bored with her job, now.

18.*a.* Over a hundred people waited in line all night.
 b. They wanted to get tickets to the concert.
 c. The concert will be by the Mental Defectives.

19. *a.* Peanut butter is a nourishing food.
    b. Parents sometimes hurriedly slap together a peanut-butter sandwich.
    c. They feel guilty when they do so.
    d. Kids love peanut butter.

20. *a.* One thing is clear.
    b. Everyone has an off-day now and then.
    c. Even the best athletes can't be entirely consistent.

21. *a.* Bill Andreychuk has gone to Chile.
    b. He wants to train in the Andes.
    c. He is probably the strongest skier on the team.

22. *a.* Some people think one thing is more important than anything else.
    b. That thing is money.
    c. That thing is love.

23. *a.* The Board of Governors announced the new tuition.
    b. It acted as though there had been no protests.

24. *a.* Ordinary teas and coffees can be boring.
    b. Herbal teas can provide a pleasant change.
    c. They include a wide range of flavours.
    d. Some offer a single flavour.
    e. Others offer a blend of flavours.

25. *a.* The history assignment was longer than usual.
    b. The instructor had threatened to give a quiz.
    c. I missed the TV program everyone was talking about the next day.

EXERCISE 12B

Here is another way to practise combining sentences. Write at least five short sentences (no more than five words each) about each of the subjects in the list below. Then combine each group into a single sentence with only one independent clause; subordinate everything else. Try at least two combinations for each set. Again, try to retain the sense of the base sentences.

1. parents	4. my favourite game	7. what I eat
2. pets	5. music in my life	8. my hair
3. books	6. part-time jobs	9. Canada

Here is an example with the topic "my car":

My car is green.
It was orange.
It is ten years old.

1. My rusting, ten-year-old orange car looks like new now that I've had it fixed and painted green.

It was rusting.
I got it fixed.
I got it repainted.
It looks like new.

2. De-rusted, green, and looking like new, my formerly orange heap hides its ten years well.

Sentence-Combining 13: Revising

Here, from students' drafts, are a number of passages that you can improve by using some of the sentence-combining skills from earlier parts of this chapter. Change whatever you think needs changing, as if you were revising your own draft. You may not want to combine all of a passage's sentences into one.

1. I had only one reason for keeping on digging trail. I did not quit this hard work. I was helping to protect my fellow firefighters. If the fire was to jump the trail, we all would have been in the path of the oncoming inferno.

2. Many people think inflation is caused by higher wages. This is erroneous. Inflation is not primarily caused by higher wages.

3. I would very much like to avoid sexually specific language. Avoiding sexually specific language can create problems. I never saw a *chair* — straight, rocking, or easy — conduct a meeting.

4. There are a number of options. The president can choose one of those options.

5. A good ventilation system in the tent is also necessary. The average camper will produce much moisture from breathing and perspiring. This will happen even in winter.

6. Some countries have little or no choice about what energy source they can use. In Canada we are fortunate to possess many energy options. All have advantages and disadvantages unique to each.

7. My lab partner ruined our experiment. Both homicide and suicide crossed my mind.

8. Along the west coast there is a very great tendency for large numbers of storms. These storms produce rough seas, poor visibility, and generally poor boating conditions. The chance of an oil spill is immeasurably increased by this fact.

9. Pitt was sent by King George III to form a cabinet in 1766. This was when he took the title of the Earl of Chatham and the post of Lord Privy Seal. The Lord Privy Seal is a post where no active duties were attached.

Glossary of Terms

GLOSSARY OF TERMS
A Selected Vocabulary of Writing

Here are definitions of some useful terms referring to syntax and style. For further information, check the cross-references provided. (Some terms discussed and defined elsewhere are here cross-referenced only; you may also consult the index. For punctuation marks, see Ch. 9.)

absolute term An **adjective** or **adverb** that cannot logically be used in a **comparison**. See **unique** in the Checklist of Usage, Ch. 8.

absolute phrase A phrase that modifies the rest of the sentence rather than some element in it: *Tail between its legs*, the dog slunk away. *It being Sunday*, they all slept in. *All things considered*, his health isn't bad. See also **sentence modifier** and Ch. 15, #10.

abstract, concrete See pp. 147-48.

active voice See **voice** and pp. 139-42.

adjective A **part of speech**. Adjectives modify **nouns** and **pronouns**, usually answering the questions What? What kind of? How many? (*that* man; *large* meal; *abstract* noun; *three blind* mice; *fast* car; He was *ill*). Another **noun** or a **phrase** or a **clause** can also function adjectivally (*patrol* car). See also **participle**.

adverb A **part of speech**. Adverbs modify **verbs**, **adjectives**, other **adverbs**, and even all the rest of a sentence. They usually answer the questions How? When? Where? Why? To what degree? (drive *slowly*; *stubbornly* persist; live *well*; go *now*; *mortally* ill; *very* quickly; *Unfortunately*, I was ill that day and couldn't attend). A **phrase** or a **clause** can also function adverbially.

agreement Grammatical correspondence in **person** and **number** between **verbs** and their **subjects**, or in **person**, **number**, and **gender** between **pronouns** and their **antecedents**. See pp. 125-27; see also **collective noun**.

alliteration The same beginning sound for nearby words: **a**n **a**mbitious **a**ctor; a **p**leasing but **p**roblematic **p**roposal; a **f**ine **ph**ysique. Compare **assonance** and **consonance**.

allusion A brief or indirect reference to a person, event, or other phenomenon, often from history, literature, or mythology, sometimes for purposes of comparison but also as a way of enriching content. For example you could say someone is *as rich as Croesus* or *as strong as Atlas* or *a regular Superman*. A messy room might be referred to as another *Augean Stables*. (You can check many such terms in a standard college or desk dictionary.) A woman supposedly about half as beautiful as Helen of Troy might be said to have "a face capable of launching five hundred ships." But some popular allusions are already **clichés**, for example a reference to someone having *met his Waterloo* or being *as rich as Croesus*. Use allusions, but try to avoid the more trite ones.

analogy See pp. 76 and 209.

antecedent From Latin for "coming before": the word or words a **pronoun** refers (usually back) to. See pp. 123-24 and 126-27.

apostrophe See pp. 196-97.

appositive Usually, a noun or noun phrase that further identifies another noun by identifying it in different words: Anna, *the lawyer*; the watchman, *George Smith*; the salmon I caught yesterday, *a twenty-pounder*. See p. 180 and Ch. 15, #5.

article The definite article *the* and the indefinite article *a* or *an* are "determiners" always followed soon by nouns: *a* champion *athlete*; *an apple*; *the idea*; *the* present *government*. Articles are often classed as **adjectives**.

assonance The same or similar **vowel** sounds in nearby words: a b**u**nch **o**f tr**u**mped-**u**p charges. Compare **consonance** and **alliteration**.

auxiliary A "helping" **verb**. The principal auxiliaries are *do, be, have, shall, will, can, could, may, might, must, should,* and *would*.

Auxiliaries are used with other verbs to form different **tenses**; for example: *is* going, *will* go, *will be* going, *can* go, *should* go, *has* gone, *did* go, *must have* gone.

case Designating the forms of pronouns or nouns according to their function: **subjective** (or nominative) *he, they*; **objective** *him, them*; **possessive** *his, their, Susan's*. See pp. 128-29.

clause A group of words including a **subject** and a **finite verb**. A clause may be **independent (main)**, capable of standing by itself as a simple sentence (*Dogs have fleas*), or **subordinate (dependent)** (*Since dogs have fleas,*). Subordinate clauses function as elements in **complex** and **compound-complex** sentences. See pp. 116-17, 171-82, and Ch. 15, #1, #2, #4, and #6.

cliché A trite phrase. See pp. 152-53.

coherence The logical or mechanical connection (or both) between the parts of a piece of writing, whether words, sentences, paragraphs, or sections. See pp. 107-11.

collective noun A **noun** that names a group, for example *committee, army, family, flock*. Collective nouns are **singular** when the group is considered as a unit, **plural** when the focus is on its individual members: The *jury is* unanimous in *its* decision. The *jury are* still divided in *their* opinions. See **agreement**.

comma splice Joining two independent clauses with only a comma — a serious error. See pp. 172-75. Also called **comma fault**.

common noun See **noun**.

comparison Changing the forms of **adjectives** and **adverbs** in order to express degree: the basic form or **positive degree** (*beautiful, low, slowly*); **comparative degree** (*more beautiful, less beautiful, lower, more slowly*); and **superlative degree** (*most beautiful, lowest, most slowly*). But see **absolute term**.

complement Something that completes the meaning of a verb. Strictly, a complement, or **subjective complement**, is a noun, pronoun, or adjective that follows a **linking verb**: Sandra is a *consultant* (**predicate noun**); Jasper's report is *excellent* (**predicate adjective**). More broadly, complements also include objects that complete the meanings of verbs: We sent *him* (**indirect object**) a *copy* (**direct object**) of the book. She appointed Ambrose *secretary* (**objective complement**) of the subcommittee.

complex sentence A sentence consisting of one **independent clause** and one or more **subordinate clauses**: *I know that she knows.*

When I arrived, the owner, who was badly shaken, explained what had happened. See Ch. 15, #2.

compound Two or more like elements (words, phrases, clauses) joined so that they function as a unit: *Apollo* and *Hermes* were Greek gods (compound **subject**); people *feared* and *worshipped* them (compound **predicate**); they brought both *fortune* and *misfortune* (compound **object**). Single words combined into one are also called compounds: *well-being, textbook, bathtub* (compound **nouns**); *cherry-red, overdone, drip-dry* (compound **adjectives**); *baby-sit* (compound **verb**). See also the next two entries.

compound sentence A sentence consisting of two or more **independent clauses**: *He commanded, and they obeyed. He came, he saw, he conquered.* See Ch. 15, #1.

compound-complex sentence A sentence consisting of two or more **independent clauses** and one or more **subordinate clauses**: *He felt terrible, but the doctor assured him that he would soon be well.*

concrete, abstract See pp. 147-48.

conjunction A **part of speech**. A **coordinating conjunction** (*and, but, or, nor, for, yet, so*) joins equal elements. A **subordinating conjunction** (for example *because, when, though, since*) joins subordinate (dependent) clauses to independent (main) clauses. **Correlative** conjunctions are coordinating conjunctions that come in pairs (for example *not only . . . but also, both . . . and, neither.. . nor*); they link **parallel** pairs of sentence elements. See Ch. 15, #1 and #2, and pp. 138, 171-74.

conjunctive adverb An adverb (for example *therefore, however, nevertheless*) used to connect **independent clauses**, but not equivalent to a **coordinating conjunction**. See pp. 173-76.

connotation The suggested or associative meaning of a word. Compare **denotation**, and see pp. 144-45.

consonance The same or similar **consonant** sounds within nearby words: In*tr*epid had mas*t*er*l*y con*tr*ol; what e*st*ablishments in the pa*st* insisted on; fu*ss*ing over *s*illy que*st*ions. (When the repeated sound is that of *s, z,* or *sh,* the result is called *sibilance.*) Compare **assonance** and **alliteration**.

contraction An informal or colloquial combining of two words, spelled with an **apostrophe** to mark the omitted letter or letters: *there's* (there is), *isn't* (is not), *they're* (they are), *she'd* (she had, she would), *could've* (could have).

coordination Combining elements of equal weight or importance into a **compound** construction. See **compound**, **conjunction**, and Ch. 15, #1.

correlative See **conjunction**.

dangling modifier See pp. 122-23.

declarative sentence See **sentence**.

degree See **comparison**.

demonstrative (*this, that, these, those*) A word that in effect points: *That* is the man I saw; *this* is my car; *these* are my books (**demonstrative pronouns**). *That* man is the one I saw; *this* car is mine; *these* books are mine (**demonstrative adjectives**). See also **pronoun** and pp. 109, 123-24.

denotation The specific, direct meaning of a word. Compare **connotation**, and see pp. 144-45.

dependent clause See **clause**.

diction Choice and use of words. See Ch. 8.

direct object See **object**.

ellipsis The three spaced periods (. . .) replacing material omitted from a quotation. See pp. 230-31.

etymology The origin and history of a word's form and meaning. The word *helicopter*, for example, was formed from the Greek roots *helix, helicos* (spiral) and *pteron* (wing). See pp. 32-34.

euphemism From the Greek *eu* (well) and *phemizein, phanai* (to speak): the use of a mild or roundabout expression to avoid another that is felt to be too harsh or unpleasant. Some **jargon** is notoriously euphemistic and misleading, for example the used-car salesman's reference to his merchandise as "pre-owned units."

exclamatory sentence See **sentence**.

figurative language Language used non-literally, usually **metaphors** and **similes**: Sally *cruised* down the street *like a yacht under full sail.* See pp. 35-36, 75-76.

finite verb A verb form that functions as the main verb in a clause. You can distinguish a finite verb from a **nonfinite** form (the **verbals**: **gerunds**, **infinitives**, and **participles**) by seeing if you can add an *s* to make the third-person-singular present-tense form: I *make*, he *makes*. See pp. 116-17.

fragment A non-sentence written (with an opening capital letter and a closing period) as if it were a sentence — a serious error. See pp. 116-17.

fused sentence See **run-on**.

future tense See **tense**.

general, specific See p. 148.

gender Designating whether nouns and pronouns are **masculine** (*men, boys, John, bull, he, his*), **feminine** (*woman, girl, Mary, mare, she, her*), or **neuter** (*machine, it*). See also pp. 127-28, on avoiding sexist language.

gerund A **verbal** (see also **infinitive** and **participle**); an *ing* form of a verb. Gerunds and gerund phrases function as **nouns**: *Hiking* is good exercise; His Saturday chore was *washing the car*. A gerund does not function as a **finite verb**. See also **subject** and Ch. 15, #9.

grammar The systematic study and description of how the elements of a language operate in themselves and in relation to one another. See **syntax**.

helping verb See **auxiliary**.

idiom See Ch. 14.

imperative See **mood** and **sentence**.

indefinite pronoun See **pronoun**.

dependent clause See **clause**.

indicative See **mood**.

indirect object See **object**.

infinitive A **verbal** (see also **participle** and **gerund**); a verb form usually consisting of *to* and the basic form of the verb: *to go, to listen, to run*. Infinitives and infinitive phrases function as **nouns**, **adjectives**, or **adverbs**, but not as **finite verbs**. See Ch. 15, #8, and "split infinitive," pp. 121-22.

intensive pronoun See **pronoun**.

interjection A **part of speech** having no syntactical properties, but merely interjected into a sentence (It was, *well*, not so easy after all) or used by itself, often with an exclamation point (*Heavens! Ouch!*).

interrogative pronoun See **pronoun**.

interrogative sentence See **sentence**.

intransitive verb See **verb**.

irony A way of saying one thing while meaning something else, often just the opposite. For example a speaker might begin, "I don't wish to alarm anyone, but . . . ," and then proceed to divulge some alarming statistics. Or consider the famous opening sentence of Jane Austen's *Pride and Prejudice*: "It is a truth universally acknowledged, that a single man in possession of a good fortune, must be in want of a wife." That is **verbal irony**. There can also be **situational irony**, as when expectations are aroused but unfulfilled, or when something happens at precisely the wrong moment. Also see **sarcasm**.

irregular verb A verb that doesn't form its **past tense** and **past participle** by adding *d* or *ed* but in some other way; for example, *swim, swam, swum; give, gave, given; send, sent, sent.* Dictionaries list the **principal parts** of such verbs.

jargon Strictly, the specialized technical vocabulary of a particular profession; broadly, unintelligible or confusing language, often familiarly referred to as gobbledygook, bafflegab, or — more specifically — psychobabble, computerese, bureaucratese, sociologese, educationese, and so on. See pp. 154-55.

linking verb A verb that links subject to complement. See **verb**.

major sentence See **sentence**.

metaphor A kind of **figurative language** which implicitly likens two apparently unlike things. See pp. 35-36 and 75-76.

minor sentence See **sentence**.

misplaced modifier See pp. 121-22.

mixed construction See p. 130.

modifier A word, phrase, or subordinate clause that in some way describes, qualifies, or restricts another word or group of words. **Adjectives** and adjectival phrases and clauses modify nouns; **adverbs** and adverbial phrases and clauses modify verbs, adjectives, and other adverbs. An **absolute phrase** can be thought of as modifying the rest of the sentence (a **sentence modifier**), as can an adverbial phrase or even a single adverb: *Ironically*, the equipment arrived just as we finished doing the job by hand.

mood The attitude of a writer or speaker as expressed by the form of the verb. The most common mood is the **indicative**, used to state facts or opinions and to ask questions (The weather *was* odd last summer. The popularity of video games *is declining*. What *will* the government *do* next?) The **imperative** mood is used for commands and instructions (*Stir* the sauce continuously. *Bring* your own paper for the examination.) English uses **subjunctive** mood in some standard expressions (for example "Long *live* the Queen!" "as it *were*," and "*Be* that as it may"), in *that*-clauses to express wishes or demands (It is essential that we *be* on time; I wish [that] I *were* five years younger), and for impossible or contrary-to-fact conditions (If I *were* you; *Had* I *known*) and other conditional clauses (*Should* the pressure-relief valve *malfunction* . . .).

nominative case See **case**.

nonfinite verb See **verbal**.

nonrestrictive modifier A word, phrase, or clause that does not restrict or limit the meaning of what it modifies. Such a modifier is **parenthetical**, not essential to the meaning of the sentence, and is therefore set off by punctuation. Compare **restrictive modifier**, and see pp. 179-84 and Ch. 15, #4 and #5.

noun A **part of speech**. A noun names a person, place, thing, idea, quality, action, event, or the like. **Proper nouns** refer to particular persons, places, or things and are capitalized: *Ingrid, Halifax*, the *Panama Canal*, the *Bounty, World War I*. **Common nouns** refer to one or more members of a class of things, ideas, or qualities: *women, city, canal, ship, wars, integrity, harshness, isolation*. See also **collective noun** and pp. 147-48 (**concrete, abstract; general, specific**).

noun clause A subordinate clause functioning as a noun: *That the ship is unseaworthy* is beyond question. I'll accept *whatever answer you give me*. See Ch. 15, #6.

number Refers to either **singular** or **plural** as the form of a noun, pronoun, or verb.

object A **noun** (whether word, phrase, or clause) or **pronoun** that receives the action of a **transitive** verb or completes a **prepositional phrase**. Objects of transitive verbs can be **direct** (Samantha snubbed *Roger*) or **indirect** (She gave *him* the air). The **object of a preposition** usually follows it (*on* the *table, under* a *cloud*), except sometimes in direct questions or similar constructions (*What* are they talking *about*? I didn't know *what* they were talking *about*).

objective case See **case**.

parallelism Using the same structure for two or more parts of a sentence or paragraph, or even of a larger part. See pp. 137-39.

parenthetical element An inserted word, phrase, or clause that interrupts the flow of a sentence and that *could* be enclosed in parentheses, but is more often set off with commas or dashes. See pp. 165, 166, 170, 180.

participle A **verbal** (see also **gerund** and **infinitive**); a verb form ending in *ing* (**present participle**) or, for regular verbs, in *ed* (**past participle**), used either as part of a **finite verb** with an auxiliary (*was running*, *have been instructed*) or, without an auxiliary, as an **adjective** (the *alarming* news, the *engraved* invitation). See Ch. 15, #7.

parts of speech The eight categories into which traditional grammar divides words according to their function: **noun**, **pronoun**, **verb**, **adjective**, **adverb**, **conjunction**, **preposition**, **interjection**. **Articles** are sometimes added to this list.

passive voice See **voice** and pp. 140-42.

past tense See **tense**.

perfect tense See **tense**.

person A feature of **pronouns** and **verbs** that shows whether they refer to someone speaking (first person: *I write*; *we write*), to someone spoken to (second person: *you write*), or to someone or something spoken about (third person: *she writes*, *he writes*, *they write*, *it writes*).

personal pronoun See **pronoun**.

phrase A group of words lacking a subject-finite verb combination; compare **clause**. Any group of words can loosely be called a phrase, but in discussions of writing the term usually refers to any group of words that functions as a syntactical unit, as a particular **part of speech**: a **noun** phrase, a **verb** phrase, an **adjective** phrase, an **adverbial** phrase, an **infinitive** phrase, a **participial** phrase, a **gerund** phrase, a **prepositional** phrase, an **absolute** phrase.

positive degree See **comparison**.

possessive See **case**.

predicate The part of a sentence or clause that asserts something about the subject. The complete predicate consists of the **finite verb** and any **complements**, along with any **modifiers** of either.

predicate adjective; predicate noun See **complement**.

prefix One or more letters that can be added to the beginning of a word or root to make a new word; for example *mis*spell, *proto*type, *self*-awareness, *un*known, *pre*-war, *dis*approve. Compare **suffix**.

preposition A **part of speech**. Prepositions are words like *into, of, on, among, about, under*. A preposition links a **noun** or **pronoun** (its **object**) to some other word in the sentence: *He* went *into* the *house*; The *book* is *on* the *table*. They are usually "pre-positioned," put before the nouns or pronouns which are their objects.

prepositional phrase A group of words consisting of a **preposition** and its **object** or objects, along with any modifiers. A prepositional phrase usually functions as either an **adjective** (The pen *on the desk* is mine) or an **adverb** (Algy was sent *to the big house. In my opinion*, he got what he deserved.). See Ch. 15, #3.

present tense See **tense**.

principal parts The forms of a **verb** from which all its tenses are made, either by themselves or with the addition of an **auxiliary**: its **base** form (*write, call, set*), its **past tense** form (*wrote, called, set*), and its **past participle** form (*written, called, set*). Also usually included is the **present participle** form (*writing, calling, setting*). Dictionaries list the principal parts of **irregular** verbs.

progressive tense See **tense**.

pronoun A **part of speech**. A pronoun stands for or refers to a **noun** or another pronoun, its **antecedent**. Pronouns are **personal** (*I, me, my, you, she, her, his, they,* etc.), **interrogative** (*who, whom, which, what, whose*), **relative** (*who, whom, which, that, whose*), **demonstrative** (*this, these, that, those*), **indefinite** (*any, some, all, one,* etc.), **reflexive** or **intensive** (*myself, himself, themselves,* etc.), or **reciprocal** (*each other, one another*). See **agreement**, **antecedent**, **case**, **number**, and **person**.

proper noun See **noun**.

reciprocal pronoun See **pronoun**.

reflexive pronoun See **pronoun**.

relative clause An adjective clause usually introduced by a **relative pronoun**. See Ch. 15, #4, and pp. 179-80.

relative pronoun See **pronoun**.

restrictive modifier A word, phrase, or clause that, because it limits or identifies the meaning of what it modifies, is essential to the meaning of the sentence and is therefore not set off with punctuation. Compare **nonrestrictive modifier**, and see pp. 179-84 and Ch. 15, #4 and #5.

run-on Two **independent clauses** or sentences run together without punctuation between them — a serious error. See p. 176. Also called **fused sentence**.

sarcasm From the Greek *sarkazein* (to tear flesh): a cutting and obvious kind of **irony** whose purpose is to hurt, or at least cause discomfort; for example, you might say to someone who has just spilled hot coffee in your lap, "My, you do have elegant serving techniques!"

sentence A group of words constituting a satisfactorily complete utterance, opening with a capital letter and ending with a period, question mark, or exclamation point. Most sentences are **major**, containing at least one **subject** and **finite verb**; a **minor sentence** lacks one or both of these. See pp. 115-19. Sentences are also classified as **declarative** (stating a fact or opinion), **interrogative** (asking a question), **imperative** (giving a command or making a request), and **exclamatory** (expressing strong feeling or emphasis). See also **simple sentence**, **compound sentence**, **complex sentence**, and **compound-complex sentence**.

sentence modifier A word or group of words that modifies the rest of a sentence rather than a particular element in it. See **absolute phrase**, **adverb**, and **modifier**.

simile A common form of **figurative language** which explicitly compares one thing to another: He's *like a clinging vine*. See pp. 35-36 and 75-76.

simple sentence A group of words consisting of a single **independent clause** — that is, containing only one subject-verb combination: *Pollution kills*. But a simple sentence doesn't have to be simple in its thought or its diction. Here for example is another: *Much radio and television advertising, by trying to make us want something unnecessary, or make us envious of our neighbours, or make us desire our neighbours to be envious of us, not only treats us as unintelligent bumpkins but also appeals to some of our basest instincts.* Long and complicated, but no subordinate clauses, therefore technically only a simple sentence.

slang See pp. 153-54.

specific, general See p. 148.

split infinitive See pp. 121-22.

subject The **noun** or **pronoun** (along with modifiers) about which the **finite verb** and the rest of the **predicate** makes a statement or asks a question. A **noun clause** can function as a subject (see Ch. 15, #6D-6G). An **infinitive** can also have a subject — always in the **objective case**: The committee urged *her to accept* the nomination (see Ch. 15, #8B). So can a **gerund** have a subject — usually in the possessive case: *His embarking* on the cross-country trip was an inspiration to thousands (see Ch. 15, #9C and #9D).

subjective case See **case**.

subjunctive See **mood**.

subordinate clause See **clause**.

subordination Combining elements of unequal weight in a sentence — usually, making one clause subordinate to or dependent on another, thereby forming a **complex** sentence. See **conjunction** and Ch. 15, #2.

suffix One or more letters added to the end of a word, for example to change its **number** (boy, boy*s*) or **tense** (walk, walk*ed*) or **degree** (warm, warm*er*), or to change its part of speech (hope*less*, standard*ize*, fool*ish*, happi*ly*). Compare **prefix**.

superlative degree See **comparison**.

syntax The arrangement of words in sentences and the grammatical and semantic relations among them.

tense The quality of a **verb** that indicates time: Yesterday I *misunderstood* (past tense); today I *understand* (present tense); tomorrow I *will understand* even better (future tense). Here is a table showing the standard tenses, using the first person singular:

present	I look
past	I looked
future	I will look
present perfect	I have looked
past perfect	I had looked
future perfect	I will have looked
present progressive	I am looking
past progressive	I was looking
future progressive	I will be looking
present perfect progressive	I have been looking
past perfect progressive	I had been looking
future perfect progressive	I will have been looking

thesis See pp. 38-39, 55-57, 101.

tone The attitude toward subject matter and audience that a writer's style and ideas reveal. See pp. 86-90.

transitive verb See **verb**.

unity The desired quality of oneness of a piece of writing or of a paragraph (see pp. 106-07, 110) that is about a single topic or **thesis**, with everything directed toward that topic, and without digressions.

usage The customary way of using words and combinations of words in a given language; the conventions. See the Checklist in Ch. 8; see also Ch. 14, on idioms.

verb A **part of speech**. Verbs indicate action or assert existence or condition. Verbs may be **transitive**, taking a direct **object** (Richard *hates* mathematics; Melanie *lifts* weights); **intransitive**, requiring no object (Mark *relaxed* in the sun; Annette *snores*); or **linking**, requiring either a predicate noun or a predicate adjective as a **complement** (René *was* a journalist; Sally *is* ambidextrous; the building *looks* solid; the sauce *smells* delicious). By far the most common linking verb is *be*. See also **irregular verb**.

verbal A word formed from a verb but acting as another part of speech; also called a **nonfinite** verb. Compare **finite verb**, and see **gerund**, **infinitive**, and **participle**.

voice A term designating whether a verb is **active** or **passive** in form. With a verb in the active voice, the subject of the sentence is performing the action (I *wrote* this sentence); with a verb in the passive voice, the subject of the sentence is being acted upon (This sentence *was written* by me). Active voice is almost always preferable to passive voice. See pp. 139-42.

Index

facts *continued*
    true facts, 145
fallacy, *post hoc*, 54
faulty comparisons, 131
faulty coordination, 131-32
faulty parallelism, 138-39
fewer, less, 158
field, 150-51
figurative language, 35-36, 300, 302, 306. *See also* metaphors, similes.
figures. *See* numerals.
final consonants, before suffixes, in spelling, 194
final draft, 13-14, 189-98
    of essay examinations, 260
    of research paper, 236-37
final *e* before suffixes, in spelling, 194
final *y* before suffixes, in spelling, 194
finding material for writing, 7-8, 28-40
    for argument, 203-08
    clichés for, 32
    for essay examinations, 257
    etymology for, 32, 33-34
    metaphors and similes for, 35-36
    proverbs for, 32
    quotations for, 32
    random association for, 36-37
    for research paper, 214-21
    shifting categories for, 34-35
    statistics for, 32
finding topics, 17-18
    for argument, 201-02
    for essay examinations, 256
    for research papers, 212-13
finite verbs, 300
    as part of predicates, 304
first draft, 9, 62-67
    of argument, 210
    of essay examinations, 260
    mechanics of, 66
    of research paper, 224-26

firstly, 157
first person, 304
footnotes, 234, 235-36, 241
for, 176
    punctuation with, 168, 171-72
foreign words
    italics for, 192
    plurals of, 195
formal style, 87
forms and formats, 189
forms, special
    argument, 200-11
    for different occasions, 189
    essay examinations and in-class essays, 255-61
    research paper, 212-54
fractions, hyphens with, 197
fragments, 116-19, 167, 301
    checking for, 116-17
free-writing, 64
fused sentences. *See* run-on sentences.
future perfect progressive tense, 307
future perfect tense, 307
future progressive tense, 307
future tense, 307

G

gazetteers, atlases, yearbooks, as research sources, 216
gender
    avoiding sexist language, 127
    of nouns and pronouns, 301
general and specific, 25, 71, 148
    in organization, 71, 106
general consensus, 146
generalizations
    in beginnings, 96
    in induction and deduction, 205-07
    supporting, with examples and illustrations, 47, 71
genus and differentiae, defining by, 72
gerund phrases, 301